W9-CEW-470

*f*P

Comes the Peace

My Journey to Forgiveness

Daja Wangchuk Meston
with Clare Ansberry

Free Press
New York   London   Toronto   Sydney

This book is a memoir. It reflects the author's present recollection of his experiences over a period of years. Certain events and dialogue have been re-created based on the author's memory, correspondence, and conversations with friends and relatives and are not intended to be an exact representation of past events.

*f*P

FREE PRESS
A Division of Simon & Schuster, Inc.
1230 Avenue of the Americas
New York, NY 10020

Copyright © 2007 by Daja Wangchuk Meston and Clare Ansberry
All rights reserved, including the right of reproduction in whole or in part in any form.

FREE PRESS and colophon are trademarks of Simon & Schuster, Inc.

For information about special discounts for bulk purchases,
please contact Simon & Schuster Special Sales:
1-800-456-6798 or business@simonandschuster.com

Designed by Davina Mock-Maniscalco

Manufactured in the United States of America

1   3   5   7   9   10   8   6   4   2

Library of Congress Cataloging-in-Publication Data
Meston, Daja Wangchuk.
Comes the peace: my journey to forgiveness / Daja Wangchuk Meston with Clare Ansberry.
p. cm.
1. Meston, Daja Wangchuk, 1970–. 2. Tibet (China)—Biography.
I. Ansberry, Clare. II. Title.
DS786 .M475   2007
951'5095092 [B]—dc22   2006041282

ISBN-13 978-0-7432-8747-0
ISBN-10   0-7432-8747-9

To my beautiful wife, Phuni, for teaching me about love and family

In loving memory of Charlotte Greenberg and Apa Sonam

And finally, I thank my parents, Lawrence Greenberg and
Feather Wongmo Meston, for giving me this precious human life.

We do not come upon only flowers, stars, mountains, rivers. Over and above all things there is a sublime expectation, a waiting-for. With every child born, a new expectation enters the world.

Abraham Joshua Heschel, *A Passion for Truth*

Contents

Comes the Peace

Chapter One
Room 301

Istood on the third-story windowsill of a hotel in a remote part of Tibet, said, "Here I go," and jumped.

Within seconds, my body landed fifty feet below in a dusty street. My heels shattered on impact. I crumbled on the ground. Peasants and pedestrians in gray-and-blue Mao jackets and caps likely gathered around me, wondering who I was, a white-skinned foreigner, my face unshaven, my hiking boots caked in red mud, my wire-rimmed glasses unbroken but askew. Thick-tired bicycles, their wire baskets heavy with fruits and vegetables, veered wobbly around me. Vendors in the street's open-air stalls abandoned their row of shiny apples and plums and rushed over. A handful of Tibetan monks in maroon robes, dotting the nearby green hillside like fallen rose petals, glanced up, their meditation broken. They wouldn't have known how alike we were, that their robes and prayers were mine as a child.

It was a dry, hot August afternoon in 1999. The sun seemed unusually bright. I had been sitting on the windowsill of my corner hotel room for more than an hour, staring at the marketplace below. When I jumped I had no intention of living. I was in a terrible situation and felt like death was the only way out.

I was in the custody of Chinese authorities, unable to leave my room or make phone calls. A stocky, clean-cut security guard was stationed in the hallway. When I opened the door earlier, he put his hands against my chest and gently pushed me back inside my room. He didn't speak English. I didn't speak Chinese. He pointed to the bed, directing me to sit. The room was more sanitized box than comfortable hotel room. The concrete walls, floor, and starchy sheets were white. A single fluorescent tube dangled overhead. There was no phone. I turned on the television set and flipped through the four channels. All carried the same government-controlled programs denouncing a popular religious group as a cult.

I was twenty-nine years old, without any real direction in my life, and had been living in Boston. I had traveled to a remote province in China on a humanitarian mission that had gone horribly awry three days earlier, when a squad of security officers from the Chinese foreign ministry had taken me and two companions into custody. I hadn't wanted to make the trip in the first place, because it seemed dangerous. The officers confiscated my Minolta camera, seven rolls of film, and notes.

We had come to look at the site of a proposed project, to be funded by the World Bank, that would involve bringing fifty-eight thousand mostly Chinese farmers into Tibetan areas. Our aim was to gauge local Tibetan sentiment. Since the Chinese government had promised unfettered access, I thought we would just explain to the officers what we were doing and be released.

Instead, we were loaded in separate jeeps and taken on a thirty-hour drive to Xining, a city on the northeastern border of China and Tibet. Along the way, I tried to explain that we had done nothing wrong, that we were simply interested in the project. The guards listened in stony silence. At 2 A.M., we pulled up in front of a dimly lit vacant hotel. We got out and were escorted to different rooms.

A series of interrogations followed. I felt I was being ordered to confess to crimes I didn't know I had committed.

I was led down a tiled corridor to room 301. Inside, the curtains were closed. Against the far wall, a thin, light-skinned man in a dark green military uniform eyed me from behind a desk, where his folded hands rested. The medals pinned to his uniform glistened. Around him, a handful of men stood on chairs and tables, their faces hidden behind cameras with bright lights beaming at me. The one with the still camera moved from one corner of the room to another, snapping photos of me from different angles. Two men huddled on a couch, smoking cigarettes. A cup of black tea cooled on the table in front of me. The window was open. A hot breeze blew in. The curtains puffed.

An empty chair directly across from the officer was waiting for me. An ugly woman with cream-colored pants and deep-set eyes, the interpreter, sat next to me. The corners of her thin mouth drooped in an angry frown. A tape recorder whirred quietly.

I stared at the uniformed man, waiting. He spoke deliberately and slowly in a low, gravelly voice. The translator waited until he was done, then relayed his message.

"What is your name?"

"Daja Meston."

"Spell it."

"*D-A-J-A M-E-S-T-O-N.*"

"When did you come to China?"

"In August."

"Why did you come to China?"

"I came to see the World Bank project site."

"What places have you been to?"

"My flight landed in Beijing. From there I went to Xian, Xining, and Dulan."

"What did you do in these places?"

"Not much. I went to visit the monasteries and to see the grasslands where the Tibetan nomads are."

He paused and leaned forward. "You have broken the laws of the People's Republic of China," he said.

My offense, he said, was taking photos of an abandoned prison labor camp in an area that was off-limits to foreigners without a permit.

I remembered a few days earlier. We wanted to see land connected with the World Bank project and hired a local man to drive us. On the way, he stopped on the road outside the prison to stretch his legs and get a drink of water. I took some pictures because we had stopped and I was taking pictures of every place we stopped. I had no idea it was off-limits. No signs were posted. Coming back on the same road later that day, I saw a sign nailed to a tree outside the prison grounds that had not been there earlier. "Restricted Area. Foreigners without a permit not allowed beyond this point." I wondered later whether the new sign was put up to trap us into breaking the law.

"I didn't ask to be taken there," I explained. Blaming the driver was a perfectly reasonable explanation and true. I was confident that this questioning was all just a formality that would end with me being scolded and sent back to the United States.

Instead, he pressed further, his tone growing angry and impatient. "Why are you really here? Who sent you?"

I lied. "No one sent me. I'm a student researcher. I came on my own." My heart pounded. I prayed they could not tell I was lying. The organization that paid for my trip was the leading opponent of the World Bank project and well known internationally for defending Tibetan rights and criticizing China. Any association with it would incriminate me and my two companions, including an innocent, soft-spoken Tibetan man who had agreed to be our translator. He was the one I was most concerned about. I remember the terrified look on his face, his eyes widening and the color draining, when the security guards took us into custody. I knew he had a family. At least I had an American passport and a plane ticket home. He could be thrown in jail for life. In theory, according to Chinese law he could even be executed. Anything I said could be used against him. I couldn't take any chances implicating him.

The questioning continued for six hours. A security man kept refilling my teacup to keep me awake. My muscles began tightening. Trying to be cooperative, I signed a half-dozen statements written in Chinese. My hand shook as I did so. I dipped my thumb in red ink and fingerprinted each page as they demanded. I gushed, "Thank you," in Chinese every time they offered some tea. The video cameraman got on top of the bed with his shoes still on and directed the flood of camera lights on me. I wanted to look away but everywhere I glanced, eyes glared at me.

I had had only a few hours of sleep in the last forty-eight hours and eaten nothing but a couple of stale crackers stuffed inside my waterproof jacket. My eyes burned from fatigue. I couldn't concentrate on my answers. In my mind, I replayed what I had said in the last three days so I didn't contradict myself. Did I say I was an undergraduate student or a graduate student, that I was studying international development? What if one of my companions mentioned that an organization sent us? I would be caught in a lie.

As the hours passed, any sense of privilege I had, of being an

American, having a passport, of being involved, albeit as a critic, with the prestigious World Bank, of being right and innocent, evaporated. My neck developed a nervous twitch, jerking sharply to the left, as if it were rebelling against my decisions. No one back home knew that I had been arrested and taken here. Everything I said or did haunted me. I began regretting the picture taken days earlier by a passing tourist: I was stupidly grinning and flashing a defiant peace sign in front of a mural of Chairman Mao at Tiananmen Square. I kicked myself for signing the papers because I had no idea what the statements really said. For all I knew, they had tricked me into admitting that I was a spy.

Scenes from the movie *Red Corner* played through my head. I became the character played by Richard Gere—an attorney captured in China, tortured, and thrown in a dark prison cell—with the Chinese authorities running after me. I get caught. They put me through the corrupt legal system without any legal representation. I am found guilty of espionage and spying. I imagined myself walking past the thick main gate of the prison. A guard in the prison tower above, looking down on me, watches every step I take. A metal door slams, leaving me alone in a dark, dirty cell, where I am tortured, spit upon, beaten, and forgotten. To me, it was a very real possibility. A friend of ours, a musicology student, had gone to Tibet to record folk songs three years earlier. He visited us a few months before he left. We had not heard from him since. He had been arrested on charges of espionage and was still serving an 18-year jail sentence, in spite of efforts by his family and the international community to get him out.

"Why are you treating me like a criminal?" I asked. "I am not a criminal."

When there was no response, I made the ultimate demand. "I am an American, and I have the right to representation from the U.S. consulate. I need to make a call to my embassy." I had scribbled the phone numbers of the U.S. consulate in

Guangzhou and the embassy in Beijing on a small piece of paper and tucked them in my wallet.

The chief interrogator responded, "This is not important now. You have not told us everything. You need to think carefully and tell us everything."

I stared at his uniform and began sweating. As a young boy, whenever a police officer walked by, I hid under benches and behind clusters of bamboo until they passed, afraid that they would arrest me. I'd forgotten how terrified I was of authority figures until that moment.

With that, the interrogation session ended and I was led back to my room. I turned off my lights and climbed into a starchy white bed, my eyes wide open staring at the dark above me.

✤

I had dreaded this trip. I had received a telephone call only two weeks before I left from the head of a human rights organization, asking if I was available to travel to Tibet to see whether Tibetans, as well as some Mongolians and other indigenous peoples from the area, were being pushed out of the lush, vast, flat grasslands where they fed their herds of yaks and sheep, to make room for the Chinese. By talking to Tibetans, I would find out whether they supported the World Bank project, as the Chinese claimed. I knew that having the World Bank fund a project that involved the transfer of populations from China proper into lands historically claimed by Tibet would legitimize Chinese occupation of Tibet and push Tibetans further into the margins. This wasn't just any piece of land either. It was not far from the birthplace of His Holiness the Dalai Lama, which made it more high-profile and controversial. Trying to salvage the project, the Chinese government had promised that outsiders, like me, would be welcome and be allowed to freely see for themselves that the Tibetans were happy. That's what I was going to do.

In the eyes of many, everything about me made me uniquely suited for the trip. I am an American who grew up among Tibetans and spoke Tibetan fluently. I had made three trips to Tibet in the last few years, acting as an interpreter for reporters and a congressman looking into human rights abuses of Tibetans. I had married a Tibetan woman, Phuntsok Dolma. Through her, I learned the hardships facing exiled Tibetans. She spent her childhood living in refugee camps in India after the Chinese made her nomadic family flee their Tibetan pasturelands. After leaving all of their animals behind in Tibet, her father rummaged through the garbage of local Indian armies to feed his family. Although she came to Boston when she was sixteen, most of her family still lived in the camps and relied on us for money and clothing. "You're the only one who could do this," she had said. A soft-spoken but relentlessly persuasive woman, she rattled off several reasons why I should go: You've been there before. You know the people, the history, and the language. People would open up to you. They would feel safe. No one else could do that. It would be too risky for a Tibetan to go. Plus you're American. The Chinese government wouldn't jeopardize the project by arresting an American for talking to people. This is a golden opportunity, a chance to affect a nation and a people.

Everything she said made sense. I seemed to be the only person who wasn't convinced that I could handle it. That had often been the case in my life. To others I seemed self-assured, calm, and capable. Little did they know that inside, I battled private demons of insecurity and fear. A friend had told me he thought those trips with the congressman landed me on a blacklist kept by the Chinese government. What made me even more edgy was that this time I was going on my own. I was not acting as someone else's interpreter. The significance of this trip had been so drilled into my head that I was terrified of not getting the information needed or, worse yet, getting arrested. I felt totally ill-equipped. I didn't know much of the history of this particular region of Tibet and had little time to study up or make contacts. What if I failed? If I missed a historic opportunity? I would be letting down my wife, her father, the organization, and, some people might say, the entire Tibetan nation. Yet if I backed out, who would go? It would seem to many people that China would score another victory against indigenous people because I was a coward. If nothing else, going would prove to me that I was capable of offering something worthy to the world, something I had been unable to accomplish so far.

I was almost thirty, sitting around doing nothing much except obsessing about doing nothing. I'd had a string of lousy jobs: mowing lawns, making salads, and packing and shipping boxes of fancy paper napkins. Since we couldn't afford a place of our own, my wife and I lived in a complex for students and missionaries. We shared a communal kitchen with twenty other people. My wife worked fifty hours a week at bagel shops and a jewelry store to support us and her family in India, as well as pay for my college tuition. I got the degree I wanted and had done nothing of substance with it. I seemed incapable of accomplishing anything, as if a critical part of my body, like its motor, was broken and made me completely inoperable. At times, my arms and legs seemed too leaden to move. My wife was a doer. Why couldn't I be like her? Get a job or even two? Work hard? I didn't have any idea what I was supposed to do or even where I belonged.

In the days before the trip, I hoped privately that my visa from the Chinese consulate in New York would not be granted. When it arrived in the mail, I considered tearing it up. The night before I left, my wife and I were driving home from the store and had an argument in the car. I wanted to back out at the last minute. She said I was being paranoid. I tried to reassure myself. My wife was right. People could get run over by a car on their way to the supermarket, but that didn't mean they didn't go. Other people who were more active in the Tibet movement had managed to get in and out without being arrested. Compared to them, I was small potatoes, hardly worth anybody's attention.

The morning I left, Phuni's father, a deeply religious man, rose at 4 A.M. and began burning juniper incense on the fire escape of our tiny one-bedroom apartment. He strung colorful prayer flags along the railings of the fire escape for good luck and my safety. I looked at him as I walked out the door and felt unsettled, as if he knew how dangerous this was.

❈

Just after midnight, a man dressed in a suit and tie came into my room and flicked on the lights. I was startled, and my heart started pounding. He told me to get up and be ready in one hour for more questioning. I fumbled for my clothes, putting on a khaki shirt and baggy blue pants. Sitting on the edge of my bed, I stared blankly at my watch, growing more paranoid. Their ominous warning rang in my ear: "You need to think carefully and tell us everything."

What would it take to satisfy them? I had already admitted I'd made a mistake, apologized, and signed confessions. Why was he all dressed up at midnight? Were they taking me somewhere? Why at one in the morning? I had no idea that interrupting sleep was a tactic in questioning. I read it as unsettling urgency.

I stared at my Casio, watching the minutes change. It was 1 A.M. I looked up at the doorknob, waiting for it to turn. No one came. Another hour passed. Still nothing. I took a small narrow spiral notebook out of my black backpack and ripped out a page. Sitting at the bottom of my bed, I wrote a letter stating I was innocent and that my captors were part of an oppressive state. Then fearing what further problems the letter might unleash, I chewed it up and swallowed it. I was too afraid to try to wash it down the sink or flush it down the toilet. When I ran water in the sink, I could hear it falling into a bucket on the floor below to collect whatever I might have tried to get rid of.

I walked around the room, trying to figure out what to do next. Inside my backpack was a Swiss army knife I had stolen from my mother when I was a boy. I picked it up and pulled the small, thin silver blade out. Sitting on the bed, I studied my wrists for the most visible vein. Clenching my teeth, I dug the blade slowly and firmly into my wrist until I bled. I did the same with the other wrist. Capturing the dripping blood on my fingertips, I smeared it on my shirt. My plan was for them to open the door, see the blood, stop everything, and take me to the hospital.

Exhausted, I lay back down in bed and waited for them to return. I kept repeating to myself: I am not a criminal. I have nothing to be afraid of. They are the ones who are wrong. Every once in a while I dozed off, only to awake in a cold sweat from nightmares of prison doors locking behind me, and of me staring through the bars of a tiny dark cell.

The next morning, a young security officer knocked on my door and handed me sticks of fried dough bought from the street vendors outside. The two small wounds on my wrist had already closed. He said nothing of the blood on my shirt and walked away.

I bit into the crunchy stick and tried to swallow but couldn't. It felt as if I had a stone stuck in my throat. A thermos, left from the day before, still had some warm water inside. I poured it into a cup and made some black tea. I took a few sips and decided to shave, wanting to continue my regular routine and show I wasn't so defeated that I didn't care how I looked. I turned the razor on. The batteries were dead.

Looking for any diversion, I flicked on the television set. Images of Chinese police arresting and beating members of Falun Gong flashed on the screen. I looked at the terrified faces and began feeling sick. I paced the room and caught a glimpse of my reflection in the large mirror. I saw my neck twitching. For the first time in years, I prayed for help, asking for the blessings of the Dalai Lama and reciting the mantra of the Green Tara, the goddess of compassion. "Guide me and remove all obstacles," I prayed.

I had recited those same prayers thousands of times when I was a young boy. My parents were quintessential hippies, living in communes in the 1960s before trekking across Europe in a green VW van. I was born along the way, and barely walking when my parents were swept up in a generational tide of young people seeking spiritual fulfillment and decided to head to India and Nepal to study Buddhism. My mother was so enraptured with the teachings that she took the full plunge and became a Buddhist nun. My father, who relied on my mother for everything, had a breakdown. I was two years old at the time and essentially parentless. My mother found a local Tibetan family with ten children, two mothers, and one father who agreed to take me in. Four years later, my mother decided I should follow in her footsteps and arranged to have me sent to the Buddhist monastery to spend the rest of my life as a monk, wearing a maroon robe and chanting mantras. From the start and throughout my childhood and teen years, I was an outsider. The little white boy in a Tibetan family. Then the white boy monk. My parents were distant figures. I really belonged to no one. After ten years in the monastery, feeling quite alone, I left and made my way to the United States to get an education. After standing out for most of my life, all I wanted was to live a quiet life.

Now I was at the center of a hostile investigation that I still didn't understand. Naively, I had thought they would realize I'm a nice person.

✤

From the moment we were arrested, I had been trying to figure out how to get out of this mess. Apologizing, signing confessions, cutting my wrists, demanding a phone call to the embassy. Nothing worked.

I paced the room, trying to divine what they were thinking and anticipate their next move. Could they really be preparing to pursue a full espionage case against me? Did they have enough evidence? If they didn't, did it matter?

The interrogations would only get worse. I knew that. They wouldn't let up until I told them who sent me and who I talked to. I wouldn't budge on that.

I had already failed by being arrested. I wouldn't fail further by putting other people in danger. Most were nomads, mountain people much like my father-in-law, who slept with newborn sheep next to his skin in his sheepskin chuba, keeping both him and the baby animals warm until the sun rose. The terrified face of our Tibetan translator kept flashing in front of me. I felt like I was going to throw up.

Since I was not going to cooperate and give them the answers they were looking for, the next logical step would be prison. They would torture me to try to get me to talk. They would win because they had me in prison, where I was terrified of being. I wanted to deny them any victory.

Shouting came from the television. I glanced up. People on the screen were cowering beneath the blows of the police. As disturbing as the scenes were, I couldn't stop watching. The government was demonizing these people just as it did the Dalai Lama and his Tibetan followers. I don't know what I was more afraid of—prison, or failing this mission and jeopardizing innocent people's lives.

If only I could pick up the phone and call someone. My heart ached for a friendly voice. I saw an image of Phuntsok sitting in our tiny living room, her long, dark hair and kind, heart-shaped face. I wanted her there with me. She was always stronger than I. She would move mountains for a cause. As she grew up, her father would advise her to "grow a bone in your heart"—be strong. I wanted to hear her gentle and assuring words. The more I thought of her, the more frustrated I was at my powerlessness.

I wondered if my mother knew that I was in Tibet. She was in India practicing and teaching Buddhism. We saw each other every few years and kept in touch through e-mail, letters, and phone calls. It was better that way. I had spent most of my childhood missing her, my teen years embarrassed by her robes, and my adult life angry at her for leaving me. I was in my mid-twenties the first time I remember her saying she loved me. Whether she said it before, I don't recall. I imagined her, with her head shorn, meditating and chanting, moving more slowly with age. Though we were never close, over the years I'd send her atomizers and warm slippers. I worried about her. I always have.

Same with my father, a big bear of a man. I knew he had no idea where I was or what I was doing. On medication for schizophrenia, he lived in a Los Angeles home with older people with dementia. Medication had dulled his emotions. Our conversations were short. He never asked questions and usually answered mine with yes or no. I have only one childhood memory of him. We are playing peekaboo, his bushy, bearded face close to mine. I used to fantasize about a perfect family, sitting together around a table, talking and laughing.

My thoughts returned to the present. I was desperate to get out of there. I had already tried to leave my room and was stopped by the security guard. I couldn't imagine myself wrestling with him, trying to take his gun or overpowering him. I'm not that strong. I'd likely get killed in the process. At one point during the thirty-hour jeep ride, I thought of jumping out the door and running like hell, but I was afraid I might get into more trouble or they might actually shoot me.

After about a half hour, I looked at the huge window. The

curtains were open and the sun was pouring in. The sounds of rattling bicycles, heated bartering, and chickens squawking melted together in an indiscernible din.

It was the only way out. No one would know whether I jumped or was pushed. I didn't expect to live. The American government would demand an investigation into why a U.S. citizen died while in Chinese custody. Tensions between the two governments would be further strained. The human rights group that sent me would protest and the World Bank would have to look more closely at the project. I had already failed by being arrested. Maybe this could make things right.

I was tired of thinking and trying to figure out what my captors would do or what I should be doing. I didn't dwell on my body landing. I didn't think of actually dying or of never being able to see Phuntsok again or having a family. I just thought of getting out of there.

I put on my Gore-Tex hiking boots. For some reason, it made sense. I was going out. My hands trembled as I tied the laces.

Up on the windowsill, I stared out. Blinded by the blistering sun, I took what I thought would be my final step.

Unbeknownst to me at the time, my jump that hot August afternoon marked the beginning of another journey.

Chapter Two

Roots

J took my first steps near a fishing village on the Greek island of Corfu, down a dirt path near the sea, holding the hand of a young blond village girl who told my mother it was time for me to learn to walk. The girl's parents had a vegetable garden next to our small house near the beach. It was the first house our family had together, and the last. My mother, her shoulder-length brown hair and long print skirts blowing in the sea breeze, cooked on a propane stove on the front porch and macraméd, me at her feet, a pacifier in my mouth. My father, a self-taught artist, set up his easels at the back of the house and painted. With his thick, bushy head of hair, a beard, and thick black plastic glasses, he looked like one of his favorite poets, Allen Ginsberg. The three of us bathed in the sea and relaxed on the patios of local restaurants, eating Greek curd topped with local honey. We were a hippie version of Norman Rockwell.

The town was quiet and domestic. The men ran small shops and fished, drank wine and played dominoes on the outside patio at the beachside restaurant. The women worked in the gardens, cooked, and raised the children. They adopted our young family, bringing us huge cabbages and freshly squeezed olive oil from the trees that lined the narrow roads. The women would sit outside in the sun, taking turns holding me and lifting me up in the air, my curly mop of dirty-blond hair falling into my eyes. They taught my mother how to speak Greek and advised her on such things as what to feed me.

I knew little of our short life together as a family until I was well into my twenties. Until then I didn't have a chance or a reason to learn more. Growing up, I didn't sit down to eat with my parents, so I missed the stories about them growing up in California and leaving the States that would have been recounted at the dinner table or over a late-night cup of coffee. I didn't have family pictures that could have provided three-by-five glimpses of our past. My parents and I didn't even share a common language. By the time I learned to talk I was living with a Tibetan family. More than likely, my first words were *Ama la,* for Mother, and *Pa la,* for Father. On my mother's occasional visits, she had to communicate with hand gestures. I had no idea where my father was and didn't even know I should care.

Besides not having an opportunity to ask questions, I didn't have a reason. As strange as it now sounds, I didn't know my parents were supposed to be a part of my life and that there must be a reason why they weren't. It was only after I left the secluded life of the monk and saw families on picnics, or a mother walking down the sidewalk holding a child's hand, or a car pulling up at a curb and a father dropping a child off at school, that I even thought to ask why.

How my parents met, whether they were rich growing up or poor, happy or sad, whether I had grandparents or aunts and uncles—all this was unknown to me. I had no hint as to why they had left their childhood homes and country or why they decided to leave me as a small boy in a foreign land, away from any family members. I was here and didn't know where I came from. My unconventional life was even more incongruous absent a prologue. I would have loved to hear the phrase "When I was your age" and the tales that typically follow. It would have helped. Woven into those stories are telling strands about the past that illuminate the present.

At some point in my twenties, hungry for explanations and insight, I began asking questions, reading forgotten letters, tracking down distant relatives, and reaching out to my mother and to my father. Bit by bit, I was able to reconstruct my past.

It was 1971 and I was about a year old when I took those steps in Greece. Before that, we lived in a green Volkswagen van and traveled across Europe, guided by a map in the *Whole Earth Catalog* and by whim. We came to Corfu, via Morocco and Tunisia, because a family in a restaurant said it was nice. A local man named Yani offered a house with a very small rent. Before that, we had lived in Spain, following the advice of an artist who made silver belt buckles and got high with my father. A bright parrot, Farly Zuba, traveled with us.

My actual birthplace was a stone house in a small Swiss town at the foot of the Alps. My parents had been sleeping in a car in a quiet neighborhood because the hotels in Geneva were too expensive. Early one morning, an older woman tapped on the car window and motioned for my parents to come into her home. Over breakfast, the woman, concerned about my pregnant mother, told them about a house near the French-Swiss border that had become a way station of sorts for a generation of flower children. My parents, Feather and Larry Greeneye, must have looked the part of wanderlust hippies. My father's name had been Greenberg, but they officially changed it when they got married, because Greeneye sounded more poetic and was unconventional, which is what the sixties were largely about.

The large stone house, flanked by daffodils, pink-blossomed trees, and the Alps, was owned by a couple that also came from California, Stan and Louise White. The Whites weren't exactly hippies as much as exiles, having been labeled Communists during the McCarthy Red Scare. They welcomed young travelers who likewise had left their homes, some just for a short-lived adventure, others, like my parents, for good. Louise smoked a pipe. Everyone ate at a big supper table. Couples were having babies. A sunny room upstairs with a mountain view evolved into the birthing room, reserved for women about to deliver.

My parents lived there for about a month. My mother, who all her life had told relatives and friends she never wanted to have children, crocheted a multicolored baby blanket.

❧

One September afternoon in 1970, my mother was sewing an olive green velvet dress. Standing in front of the mirror to see how it looked, she felt contractions and went into labor. The Swiss midwife arrived. I was born shortly thereafter and named Daja Mizu Greeneye. My mother picked Daja because she liked the sound of it. Mizu, which means "water" in Japanese, was my father's choice. My father took dozens of pictures. My mother, not prone to sentimentality, told me later that she was lying in bed and looked down at me resting peacefully in a woven straw baby basket. Tears streamed down her face. She remembers thinking, "At last, someone to love completely."

I had her dimples and long, narrow face, my father's eyes

and long lashes. In a photo of her carrying me like a papoose, her hands on her hips, half smiling, half squinting in the sun, she looks proud and defiant. My father handed out cigars and recited poems to me as I slept. A package of photos of me as a newborn arrived back in California to announce my birth. "I'm trying to hold my head up to SEE!" my mother wrote on the back of one, which showed her straining her head to catch a glimpse of my birth.

Over the years, distant relatives would clean out their drawers or attics and send me packets of random photos of various couples holding babies, group shots of older women squinting in the sunlight, and clusters of people hoisting champagne glasses at wedding receptions. They were meaningless. The people in them might as well have been staring out of a history textbook, their connections unknown to me.

Later, when I realized who these people were, I began looking at them more closely. I noticed that my father was sometimes cut out of a scene. So too was my grandmother Rosemary, who was my mother's mother. In one photo, her body was crudely lopped off a group shot on a grassy lawn. In another, a black marker has colored in where Rosemary's sculpted face should be; brown curls wreathed the black smudge. My faceless grandmother wore a striped summer dress and cradled my mother, then a chubby baby in diapers, in her arms.

Apparently, the faces were eliminated by Bernardine Szold Fritz. Bernardine, or Dena as she was often called, was my maternal great-grandmother and a bit of a snob. She didn't like my father, who came from a poor neighborhood and seemed to have no ambition other than to paint. In her eyes, he wasn't good enough for my mother, who was her only and treasured grandchild. That's why he was eliminated from family shots.

As to why my great-grandmother would cut her one and only child, Rosemary, out of the picture, I can only guess. Maybe she thought it was an unflattering picture. Or she was angry at Rosemary for being such a disappointment. My grand-mother Rosemary never lived up to Dena's expectations as a star or a person. I imagine my grandmother always wanting her mother's affirmation and never getting it. That made me feel more connected to her, as if we both shared that struggle and disappointment. Dena, my great-grandmother, thought Rose-mary was self-centered and lazy. Lazy is something Dena found particularly abhorrent, industrious as she was. Dena's achieve-ments and high-profile connections were many. My great-grandmother was the first female political reporter for a major Chicago newspaper, and then wrote for the *New Yorker* from Paris and Hollywood. In print, she dismissed Marlene Dietrich's slinky silver lamé gown as lovely but not memorable and cred-ited Miriam Hopkins for being devastatingly witty in spite of a head cold. Dena hung out with the brilliant thinkers and writ-ers of her day. She spent a decade in Shanghai with her fourth husband, where she founded the International Arts Theatre and developed a deep love for Eastern religion and culture. It was my great-grandmother Dena who introduced my mother to the teachings of the Buddha.

I met my great-grandmother Dena only once, and she didn't strike me as anyone special—just an older woman, in her eight-ies, frail, with emphysema and a lisp. Her long hair was knotted up and held in place with chopsticks. The nails of her strong Hungarian hands were painted bright red. She had a long, sharp nose, deep dimples, and wobbly earlobes stretched thin from years of wearing heavy hoops. Even when she had no outing planned, Dena put on red lipstick and wore huge Oriental rings and necklaces. Every morning she'd take an eyebrow pencil and draw arched eyebrows in the place of her actual ones, which she had completely plucked. With her shakier hands and fading eyesight the eyebrows were crooked, often with one quite a bit higher than the other.

Apparently she had a huge impact on my mother, Feather,

and by default, me. If not for my great-grandmother, my mother says, she might not have explored Eastern religions or been so open-minded. Without Dena, my mother might have ended up an alcoholic like her parents. Dena, she insists, made up completely for her own absent parents. At one point in my life, I might have agreed that it was possible not to miss a parent and to think their absence meaningless. Now I don't. There's no making up for the loss of parents.

Feather was the only child of John and Rosemary Meston, a handsome, well-known Hollywood couple. My grandfather John grew up riding horses and fishing for trout near his Colorado mountain home. His mother was a devout Episcopalian, uptight and conventional, who taught Feather the Lord's Prayer and how to make fudge. His father was a successful businessman who didn't want his son spending the rest of his life riding horses and sent him to an exclusive academy in New Hampshire for high school and then to Dartmouth and the Sorbonne, in France. My grandfather John was a gifted listener and storyteller and used those skills, along with his Western upbringing, to help him create the radio and television show *Gunsmoke*. When I left the monastery and came to the States as a teenager in 1987, I wanted to be an American and distance myself from my Tibetan past. I didn't like the strange last name Greeneye and changed it to Meston on my marriage certificate to be connected to my grandfather and what I sensed was an American icon he had helped create. I had no clue what *Gunsmoke* was about. But other people did and I latched on to that connection, thinking it would give me some credibility in the United States.

As a young woman, my grandmother, the willowy and beautiful Rosemary, modeled for *Vogue* and doubled for Katharine Hepburn. She loved the beach and flirting with tanned, handsome men and could rattle off a half dozen bawdry limericks. In many ways, Rosemary had a privileged youth. Educated at the best schools, she learned to ski in France and traveled around the world. Dena—her mother and my great-grandmother—was proud of Rosemary's beauty and talent and pushed her to be a star. In black-and-white studio photos, Rosemary's smile is wide and her dimples deep, but her eyes look sad. Knowing what I do now, I can't imagine she was happy.

Most of my grandmother's childhood was spent in boarding schools, first in Chicago and then in Europe, and at summer camp, while her mother, Dena, traveled and began and ended four marriages. None of Dena's husbands were interested in being fathers to Rosemary. Dena's first husband, Rosemary's biological father, left when Rosemary was two years old. Dena's fourth, a millionaire bank executive and polo player, didn't like children in general and Rosemary in particular because she cost so much to educate and entertain. While Rosemary was in boarding school, she confided to her diary how much she missed Dena's attention.

I came across some nude studio pictures, perhaps taken for a modeling portfolio, of slender, undeveloped, nymphlike Rosemary when she was about ten years old. In one, she faces the camera, standing perfectly straight, her feet together, and holds a branch with a few sparse white flowers in front of her bare chest. In a second shot, her body is turned sideways, but she is looking over her shoulder directly at the camera. Her bangs are cut neatly across her forehead. The branch is slung over her shoulder. When I first saw the photos several years ago, I was shocked to think that my grandmother was posing naked in front of a camera. Now when I look at them, I think of her own mother, my great-grandmother Dena, who allowed or subjected her young daughter to being photographed like that in the name of art. Dena did the same thing to my own mother. Posing naked in front of the photographer at Dena's request made Feather uncomfortable for a few minutes, but she insisted it had no impact on her. I suspect it did and she's unwilling to admit it.

My grandmother Rosemary ended up in therapy for much of her short adult life. She made her first of several suicide attempts when my mother was two years old. Rosemary's unhappy and lonely childhood didn't necessarily make her suicidal or an alcoholic, my mother told me. Other people have lousy childhoods and don't try to kill themselves, she says. Instead, my mother says Rosemary had bad karma. Maybe that's true, but it didn't excuse Dena for being an absent mother to Rosemary or for exploiting her.

❈

My mother's name, Feather, had been the affectionate nickname my grandfather John gave to my grandmother.

My mother doesn't remember instances of affection from either of her parents. They were talented and well regarded among their peers, but when it came to their only child, they were absent and cold. They spent much time going to parties and leaving my mother in the care of my great-grandmother Dena, who was my mother's only source of love. Neither John nor Rosemary was around to teach my mother momentous childhood achievements, like how to ride a bike or swim—she learned those kinds of things on her own or at camp.

My grandfather John was an evening alcoholic. Sober, hardworking, and uncommunicative during the day, he became drunk and loud at the dinner hour. After several martinis, he would begin slurring maudlin words and stumbling around the kitchen. Rosemary drank along with him. They weren't cruel or mean to my mother. They just weren't there for her. The only time my mother remembers being spanked was when Rosemary, a health freak who banned desserts and candy, found out that my mother had eaten some Valentine's Day chocolates. Rosemary put my mother over her knee and spanked her.

With no brothers or sisters, my mother was often alone, except for her blue parakeet named Beau, an amazing little bird that survived a few landings in the toilet and trips into a lit burner on the stove. In most photos my mother is by herself— sitting on the grass in the backyard or on the sand at the beach, petting the neighbor's dog through the fence, or dressing up in Dena's fancy capes. In a few family group shots, she is the only child, a little girl wearing cowboy chaps and a vest. She lived in nine different places growing up and never went to the same school two years in a row, which made it difficult to make friends. At the end of one year in high school, classmates wrote in her yearbook the type of messages reserved for people they don't really know. "To a real sweet girl. Hope you like the next school you go to."

As a little girl, she assumed that her parents were madly in love, and she remembers quite clearly the day she found out they weren't. She was about five or six, and my grandmother Rosemary had taken her out to buy new shoes. They arrived at the store. My grandmother parked the car, turned off the ignition, and sat for a few minutes. Then she looked at my mother and said my grandfather John was moving out of the house. My mother began to cry, somehow sensing at that young age that it was an important event and a loss to what had been her family life. A few minutes passed. My grandmother asked my mother if she still wanted to buy shoes. My mother said yes.

From then on, my mother lived with my grandmother, who was then probably in her early thirties, in a series of small apartments in the Burbank area. The first was a sullen, dingy, four-room apartment with a tiny kitchen, living room, and two bedrooms. My grandmother would send my mother off on her bicycle to Bill's Liquor Store on Riverside Drive with a note for the owner. He would put a half pint of bourbon and a pack of Pall Mall cigarettes into a paper bag. My mother deposited the bag into the front basket on her bike, and rode back to the apartment to deliver the package to her mother.

She was only six and learning how to read "Run, Jane, run" and "Sit, Spot, sit" when she began looking at her own mother as a sick person rather than a parent. My grandmother would disappear into her dark bedroom for weeks, eating little. The room had a stale, sick smell to it. One time, they were in the kitchen and my grandmother took a swig from the bourbon bottle.

My mother looked up at her. "Why do you drink that?"

"Because it feels good going down," my grandmother answered. Most of my grandmother's friends were also divorced women who drank too much. She had a boyfriend, too. He was a trombonist she met at a jazz bar. They had a rocky relationship that lasted eight years.

As a little girl, my mother missed her father's attention. The only thing she felt from him was distance. On the rare occasions when he took her out to dinner, he would start and end the meal with martinis. My grandfather dated various women, including the actress who played Kitty on *Gunsmoke.* Later, he marred Bette Ford, a famous American bullfighter. He and Bette spent much of their time in Mexico, attending bullfights. He wrote short missives to my mother on Thanksgiving, telling her to keep up with her studies. He would visit, he promised, but was never sure when.

My mother's happiest times were weekends. Every Friday afternoon, my great-grandmother Dena waited in front of my mother's school in her yellow Pontiac convertible to take my mother home with her. They established a comforting routine. Dena gave my mother an after-school snack of applesauce or a sandwich, followed by a bubble bath. A heated terry cloth bathrobe waited for my mother when she stepped out of the tub. They ate dinner side by side on the couch, watching TV and holding hands. As a special outing, Dena took my mother to a small amusement park in the middle of Hollywood, and watched my mother ride a small pony and the Ferris wheel and merry-go-round, smiling and waving at each pass.

My mother adored Dena, and was understandably shaped by Dena's own passions and beliefs, especially her love of the Far East. The two of them went through Dena's old, heavy leather trunk filled with beautiful silk scarves and skirts from India, Bali, and Thailand, and jewelry from China and India. My mother dressed up, putting on bright lipstick and eyebrow pencil, and danced around Dena's garden, pretending to be an Indian princess or a Balinese dancer. In the evenings, Dena read passages to my mother from the Chinese philosopher Laozi, Buddha, and Confucius and talked about reincarnation. Sometimes the two of them would get on the floor and try various yoga positions. The entire house, filled with Chinese furniture covered in beige silk and Chinese lacquer screens embossed with tiny hand-carved figurines, had a Far East feel to it. A three-foot-tall statue of Laozi with a long beard made of real hair guarded the front hallway, silently greeting Dena's guests. Dena had an impressive list of friends—the Hemingways, Henry Miller, the nearly blind Aldous Huxley, Sherwood Anderson. Autographed photos of Anaïs Nin and Gertrude Stein and other writers and actors lined one wall in her TV room. She liked to impress, dropping names of well-known friends. Her affected British accent became more pronounced at dinner parties.

My great-grandmother often brought my mother to fancy Hollywood and Beverly Hills gatherings, introducing her to movie stars, famous directors, producers, and writers. They would include my young mother in the conversations. She was only in grade school and didn't really know what they were talking about or care. She'd pluck fancy hors d'oeuvres from platters carried by maids dressed in black dresses and white aprons and watch people, cocktail in one hand, cigarette in the other, talking and laughing loudly. About the only time she had fun was when she played Ping-Pong at Henry Miller's house.

With my great-grandmother Dena, my mother felt that she

was the light in someone's life, special and worthwhile. She never felt that from her own parents. Only once does my mother remember crying as a child. She was alone in her bedroom, sobbing. My grandmother Rosemary opened the door and asked what was wrong. "I'm so, so sad because I'm thinking that maybe Dena will die one day." My mother never felt enough love from or for her own parents to cry over them, even when they died. Why Dena was such an attentive grandmother to my own mother, but such an absent mother to Rosemary, I can't say. Maybe by the time her grandchild arrived, she was willing to settle down and give of herself.

When Sunday evening arrived, my mother would go back home with my grandmother Rosemary. During her self-conscious teen years, Feather began resenting her mother's drinking binges. She couldn't bring friends home. My grandmother's jazz musician boyfriend was often snoring on the couch and my grandmother herself was locked in her bedroom, drinking. Soon my mother was spending less and less time at home and more time out with her friends, drinking wine and missing school.

At one point, my great-grandmother Dena arranged to have my mother, then about thirteen years old, sent to a posh boarding school to get her away from my grandmother. Rosemary begged my mother not to go, telling her that she needed her. My young mother, wanting desperately for my grandmother to be well and feeling guilty about abandoning her in need, agreed to stay on one condition. Rosemary had to start going to AA meetings and stop drinking.

My grandmother swore to my mother she would. Instead, Rosemary only began drinking more. The fights with her boyfriend grew more physical. When my mother was a freshman at Laguna Beach High School, she arrived home from school to find my grandmother nearly dead after trying to overdose on pills. My mother, though terrified, called the ambulance and tried to comfort my grandmother until paramedics arrived. All the promises my grandmother made to get help and stop drinking were broken. The dream that she would change was shattered. My mother felt betrayed.

It was settled. My mother had to leave my grandmother. Just fourteen years old, petite but resolute, my mother boarded the *Queen Elizabeth* by herself and sailed to Europe to join my grandfather John and his second wife, Bette Ford, the bullfighter. She spent the next two years in Europe, attending boarding school and traveling with John and Bette around Spain following the bullfights. Every night, the three of them would get drunk on wine and Pernod. Although she was spending more time with her father, he didn't show much interest in her.

"All I felt from John was distance, which did make me sad and yearn for his love and attention. As I grew older, I gave up on him and his love. Totally," Feather says. In what my mother felt was a last act of rejection, my grandfather left her nothing in his will. When she wrote letters home, they were to Dena, not to her father.

By the time my mother returned to the United States—she was in twelfth grade—she had a drinking problem. One drink was never enough. She had to keep going until she was completely drunk. To this day she doesn't know how she managed to graduate from Occidental College with her degree in comparative literature, let alone get good grades.

❊

My father, Larry, grew up in Los Angeles, the youngest of the five Greenberg children.

His parents, Sam and Sarah Greenberg, were Jewish, their families coming from Eastern Europe. My great-grandfather was a rabbi and circumcised my father on the dining room table.

Growing up, I didn't know what Jewish was. I think the first time I heard the word was when I was a boy and overheard my mother describing me to one of her nun friends and saying I had a Jewish nose. I associated Jewish with undesirable big noses.

The Greenbergs lived in a poor South Central Los Angeles neighborhood. Their run-down, big-framed wooden house, with a big walnut tree out back, had holes in the walls the size of soccer balls. Stuffing oozed out the bottom of the sofa and chairs that their father brought home from his secondhand store. They slept on dark, scratchy, unbleached muslin sheets. Their clothes and food were government handouts. The boys wore the same white corduroy pants that all poor kids did. The girls wore shapeless seersucker dresses that hung on them like drapes. When they were sick, they took free streetcars to the free clinic on the other side of Los Angeles, waiting in lines for three to four hours. Red and yellow arrows on the floor herded them along proper hallways and rooms, where they would wait with other poor people, painfully aware and embarrassed that they were charity cases.

The house might not have seemed so awful if it had been clean. But my grandmother Sarah was a terrible housekeeper. Beds weren't made. Dirty dishes sat unwashed in the sink and on the table. If the kids didn't pick up their clothes or clean their room, she didn't mind or even seem to notice.

The chaos was beyond carefree. Something wasn't quite right about Sarah. On the one hand, she was witty and charming to people who didn't have to live with her. At the bus stop, she would sit down and begin a conversation and within minutes have people laughing. A newshound, she read the newspaper and listened to the radio and could talk intelligently about nearly every subject. With little money, she knew how to make a single chicken linger through several meals—a roast one night, a stew the next, leaving only scrawny chicken feet, which had just enough flavor to make soup. Hunched over her sewing machine, she made clothes for herself and her daughters, trying to update fashionless government handouts.

But for all that apparent competence, she seemed forever on the verge of a breakdown. The youngest Greenberg daughter, Aunt Rhoda, remembers my grandmother walking around the house, saying how nervous she was and taking bromides. When the children misbehaved, or made too much noise, she seemed unable to respond in any controlled way, and began screaming wildly at them. The Greenberg children don't know if their mother suffered from some undiagnosed mental illness, but they do know she seemed unusually fragile. "My mother was a screaming maniac," says Aunt Rhoda.

If Sarah and Sam ever got along, it was before their children formed memories. What the Greenberg children recall is their parents slamming doors and yelling at each other about their respective shortcomings. Sarah was a nag. Sam couldn't hold a job. The family lived on welfare. Early in their marriage, he would peddle oranges to Japanese-American fishermen repairing their nets on nearby Terminal Island and sell secondhand furniture from a storefront. Whatever wasn't good enough to sell, he brought home. If someone wanted to buy the sofa right out from under them, he would sell it. Once, he sold the player out of the player piano. To top it off, he smoked constantly, which my grandmother hated. She nagged him on all points—money, holes in the walls, broken-down furniture, and smoking.

On more than one occasion, after an argument, my grandmother would pack a bag and storm out of the house, taking my Aunt Rhoda, then the only child at home, with her. They'd walk briskly to the nearest cheap boardinghouse, where they would stay only a night or two. My grandfather would come pick them up. My embarrassed grandmother lied to the boardinghouse owner, saying her brother was picking her up. Police came to the Greenberg house one time when my grandmother was ready to leave home with Aunt Rhoda in tow. My grandfather grabbed Aunt Rhoda's other arm. Little Aunt Rhoda, all of five or six years old, stood between her screaming parents, her thin little arms being jerked back and forth. My grandmother called the police and insisted that they make Aunt Rhoda come with her. "Ma'am," they said politely, "this is her home and her father. We can't make her leave."

As much as they argued, their children said they knew their parents loved each other and loved their children. Aunt Rhoda remembers her father lying down in bed with her and telling her stories about the little boy who slid down the hill with his shoes on and arrived at the bottom with his soles worn off. Her mother took her on daylong trips on the free streetcar, pointing out different neighborhoods and interesting buildings, to get them both out of the house on a free and fun adventure. "They loved their kids. They just didn't know how to take care of them," says Uncle Al, the third Greenberg child.

Education was not a big priority. They never encouraged their children to go to college and make a better life for themselves, although the oldest, Aunt Frances, did put herself through college. What motivated the Greenberg children was a desire to get away from their crazed parents and their wreck of a house. The two oldest boys enlisted as soon as they were eligible. Uncle Hal served in the merchant marine as an engineering officer. Uncle Al was a combat cameraman with the air force. Aunt Rhoda married when she was sixteen.

Though the family was essentially estranged, the children going their own ways at young ages, they were a tight band. Uncle Al and Uncle Hal went into business together. Commercials for Hal and Al's Tires ran with such frequency on local TV and radio that they became a household name. Uncle Al was always trying to get his baby sister, my aunt Rhoda, who was six years younger, to the Jewish community center to meet people outside their poor neighborhood.

Unfortunately, by the time my father was born, his two big brothers were in the service and his oldest sister was married. The only one at home was my aunt Rhoda, then eleven. She told me later that it was too bad that she and my father were born when they were. By then, her parents were older and weary of the arguing. Two more children meant more strain on my already fragile grandmother. Aunt Rhoda was tougher, though. "I'm a survivor. Larry isn't. He doesn't have that push," Aunt Rhoda said.

When my father was six months old, my grandmother left home, leaving him and eleven-year-old Rhoda with their father. Where my grandmother lived was a mystery. One night she climbed through the window of the tiny back bedroom, stepped onto the bed, and tiptoed in to check on the sleeping Rhoda and Larry. When my grandfather found out, he nailed the windows shut. After only a few weeks, my grandmother came back home. She missed her children and my grandfather couldn't handle them on his own. But by then, the marriage was over. My grandfather moved out. My grandmother asked for a divorce. Apparently, she didn't worry about losing my grandfather's income because there wasn't much anyway. My grandfather sent her $5 a week for child support. My grandmother relied on her own sisters for money.

My stubborn grandfather never spoke to my grandmother again. When he wanted to see the children, he had a code. Call and hang up after one ring. Hearing the signal, Aunt Rhoda took my father by the hand and walked him down to the corner, where their father would be waiting. Other times, she pulled my father in a wagon to Sam's secondhand store several blocks away, where they would watch him try to repair an old couch or TV.

Aunt Rhoda ended up being like a mother to my father. Not wanting to leave him home with their increasingly agitated mother, Aunt Rhoda took him with her to the beach or to her friends' houses. When posing for pictures, she stands close to him, holding on to his arm with one hand and resting her other hand on his shoulder, protectively.

My father didn't have many friends. On one occasion, when he was about four or five, he went outside to play. My grandmother grew worried because he hadn't come home, and sent Uncle Harold to look for him. Uncle Harold found my father at a neighbor's house down the street where two older boys lived. One of the boys was holding my father down, while the other boy was hitting him. The boys' father watched, calling my father a "dirty Jew." The Greenbergs were the only Jewish family in the neighborhood. Most of their neighbors had come to California from the Bible Belt to work in defense plants. Jews to them were Christ killers. With a name like Greenberg, everyone knew the family was Jewish even if they didn't tell them.

❉

When Aunt Rhoda was sixteen, she married, leaving my father, then five years old, alone with my grandmother. My grandfather died the following year. No one knows why, but my grandmother sent my father to live in Vista Del Mar, an orphanage for Jewish children, when he was about eight. His brothers and sisters could only speculate. Larry was a little boy, testing his limits. He got on Sarah's already frail nerves. If she said, "Don't bang on the piano," he banged on it. Aunt Rhoda wasn't in any shape to take him. She wasn't even twenty and had two small children. Aunt Frances offered to take my father in, but my grandmother refused.

For the next several years, my father lived in one of six cottages at the orphanage, each with a housemother, sharing a room with five other boys. They ate in a mess hall with the hundred other children there. A local Jewish bakery donated pastries. Out back was a wooded area. My father would go there and play, climbing trees and exploring the hilly acres. His older brothers bought him his first bike, which he rode down a hill on a dare before crashing into a wall and breaking his wrists. At first, the orphanage was nice, my father said. But then one of the boys started beating him up, so he ran away to his mother's house. It is hard to tell what he thought of my grandmother or how they got along. She isn't alive. His own mental illness leaves him uncommunicative. "She was a nice person. She cooked for me, gave me a bath, sent me to school," is all he would say when I asked about her.

A few years later, my father went to live with his older brother my uncle Harold, who had three younger sons. That didn't work out either. My father never felt he belonged. Uncle Harold loved my father but wasn't communicative or warm. His wife liked her home clean. My father was not. He fished at the ocean and brought home his fresh catch, thinking it would be a welcome meal. She shrieked.

As a teen, he was a loner. While other teenagers were dating, driving, and playing sports, he listened to classical music, read, and sketched pictures. Tall and thin, he had dark eyes and long lashes. His face was a little lopsided. The dentist found that half his jaw was missing and had to use bones from the other side to reconstruct it, making one side of his face smaller than the other. He has had a beard for as long as I can remember, the thick curls covering the scar and the concave side.

When he was seventeen, he dropped out of high school and joined the navy. He spent the next four years on the aircraft carrier *Midway*, mostly in his own little room, sketching intricate designs in black ink, of birdlike creatures and patterns for silver necklaces. After he got out of the service, Uncle Al and Uncle Hal made my father a generous offer. "Come work at Hal and Al's Tires, and after a year, we'll make you an equal partner at no cost or investment on your part." It was my father's first offer of solid work. It was a chance to settle down, maybe buy a house and start his own life. It was also a terrible fit. Cars didn't interest him. He didn't learn to drive until he was twenty-one. He didn't like grease, was clumsy with tools, and too shy to be a salesman. He would confide in his sister, my aunt Rhoda, that he felt guilty being paid good money and not doing a good job.

After several months, my father told his brothers that it wasn't working out. He quit and began driving a taxi in a gritty neighborhood where people often got robbed. In the summer, he took art classes. At some point, he befriended an artist who owned a psychedelic art gallery called the Art Emporium on a busy street in downtown Los Angeles. The man offered to sell it to Larry for $600. His older brothers loaned him some money and my father bought it. Since he never made enough money selling paintings and elaborate jewelry to rent an apartment, he lived in the back of the gallery. He didn't have a dresser or closet. His clothes were piled in a heap on the floor. He'd wear whatever was on top as long as it wasn't too dirty. He began hanging around with other artists and hippies, taking LSD and smoking dope.

As with his mother, something wasn't quite right with my father. His older brothers and sisters thought he was different from everyone else because he was artistic and quiet. The first hint that he had other problems was when he suddenly disappeared and ended up in the northern part of the state. Uncle Al received a telephone call from a mental health hospital saying his younger brother was there. My father wasn't coherent enough to tell them where he lived but apparently kept mentioning Hal and Al's. By then, the tire business was so successful that many people knew who Hal and Al were. Someone at the hospital tracked down Uncle Al.

After graduating from college, my mother worked Monday through Friday at a Head Start program for children in Watts. On weekends, she changed into a hippie, sorting through Dena's closets for long, flowing skirts from the Far East. On Friday and Saturday nights, she dropped acid and went to the Shrine Auditorium to see Janis Joplin, Led Zeppelin, and Traffic, dancing in a wide open space and "blissed out," as she would say.

She was making good money for the time and earned enough to drive a white Karmann Ghia. She could afford a kilo of marijuana and would share it with her friends or sell it for $10 an ounce. One morning her car was missing. She reported the theft to the police. Shortly after, police knocked at her door, telling her they had found her car. Then they arrested her for possession of marijuana, which was in her car. My grandfather John bailed her out. But because of the arrest, she lost her job and, with it, her confidence.

Shortly after, she met a forty-year-old with longish red hair who convinced her to move into his awful apartment. He worked occasionally in the "movie business," which meant he edited film for porn movies. Most of the time, he smoked hash and drank strong coffee. As time wore on, my mother did the same, growing thin and paranoid. If the phone rang, she let it ring. If people came over, she'd sit in the corner of the couch and try to sink into it.

That's what she was doing when she first met my father. He stopped by to visit her boyfriend, whom he had met through some hippie friends. My father saw her looking withdrawn and depressed and began talking to her. "You have to learn to celebrate life. You need to learn to enjoy life," my father told her. He showed her his drawings.

When my father left, she turned to her boyfriend and said, "What a nice man."

A few weeks later, my mother attended a wedding. At the reception, she went to get a drink and saw my father near the bar. They began talking like long-lost friends. Suddenly, my father grabbed her with one hand and grabbed a bottle of champagne in the other and told her to come outside with him. They sat on the lawn and talked. She told him how unhappy she was, and that her boyfriend was such a genius. No, he told her. She was the special and beautiful one.

That night he took my mother back to his gallery, the Art Emporium. He told her, "If you marry me, you can help me become a great artist." After that night, they became inseparable and eventually engaged. My mother took my father to meet my great-grandmother, her beloved Dena. Dena didn't approve. My father was uneducated and from a poor family. Selling tires and driving a taxi would have been too lacking in status. His art gallery didn't make any money. To her credit, though, Dena agreed to host their wedding in her long and narrow backyard filled with flowers and ivy. A harpist played. My parents wore matching tie-dyed orange-and-purple outfits. A woman in a blue flowered robe stood next to them and read the vows they had written on a long scroll of white paper. Couples in psychedelic prints drank champagne.

Thinking the wedding and reception would be a fancy Beverly Hills affair, my father's side of the family dressed up in their finest outfits. My uncles wore suits and ties. My aunts wore dresses and necklaces and carried small black purses. The minute they walked into the backyard, they glanced at one another. "We were definitely not in sync with the gang," Uncle Al later recalled. Noticeably missing was my grandmother Rosemary.

At one point, my father took off his shirt so that my mother could sew a fabric penis on the back of it. Over daiquiris, my grandfather John Meston told my father to be careful with his daughter. Then, knowing my father had no real money, my grandfather slipped him $400 for a honeymoon. The day before they left, my grandmother Rosemary called my mother. It was a strange conversation. Rosemary was unusually animated, talking nonstop. Later my mother realized that Rosemary knew it would be their last conversation.

After the wedding, my parents moved to Hog Farm, a hippie commune near Taos, New Mexico. They lived in a broken-down adobe house with only a wood stove for heating and cooking. My mother began feeling nauseous and lost her appetite. She had no idea what was going on and finally decided to see a doctor. To her surprise, the doctor said she was pregnant. A few nights later, she had a dream that she had given birth to a happy, smiling, handsome boy. From that point on, she knew in her heart that she would have a son and always referred to the tiny being inside of her as "him" or "he."

My parents didn't have a phone. Whenever they made or received telephone calls, they went to the local gas station. That fall, the phone rang at the gas station. The caller wanted to talk to my mother. My grandmother Rosemary had committed suicide. My mother didn't cry. She went about the day as she normally would, cooking, eating, drinking, washing, and laughing. She didn't return for the memorial service and has never been to my grandmother's grave.

I asked her once whether she misses her parents. Never, she says. Even years later, with time and perspective, she doesn't grieve their loss. "I wasn't close to my mother or my father either. We didn't have much in common," she told me once. My grandmother's drinking and depression left Feather without a mother or sense of what a mother should be, which in turn left me without the same. All she wanted from her father was attention and affection, and she never felt she got it.

After one cold winter in New Mexico, my mother decided to go to Europe. My father, passive and agreeable by nature, went along with everything my mother wanted to do. Plus she had the money to call the shots, thanks to Dena's financial support. With my mother five months pregnant, my parents took off.

Chapter Three
Himalayas

They ended up in Greece. My mother started reading the works of Meher Baba, a spiritual master from India whose message of love and compassion, and of letting go of selfishness, struck something deep within her.

By then we had moved out of the little house by the beach because the owner hiked the rent for the summer season. One of the families that had befriended us offered their olive grove and a working well and showed my parents how to build a hut out of trees and ferns. During the harvest season, transient workers fashioned those huts because they were cheap and convenient. We lived in the leafy hut for the next few months.

Each morning, my mother would pull water from the nearby well and cook over an open fire. Other hippies passing through the area would hear about the young Gypsy-like American family in the grove, and park their vans nearby. At night, they joined us around the campfire. I would sleep on a blanket while they smoked dope and played tambourines, bongos, and guitars.

During the day, my father painted or went on long walks. My mother read her spiritual books, some sent to her by my great-grandmother Dena. The more she read, the more immersed she became in meditation and yoga. For a while, she kept her growing passion to herself, thinking no one would understand or relate. But eventually my father started reading the spiritual books along with her.

Toward the end of that summer, my mother decided reading wasn't enough. She was convinced she had to go to India to find her own spiritual guru. My father returned from his daily walk. My mother informed him the family was going to India.

"OK," he said. That's how their relationship went. She had the will and the money. He had neither. He packed up the VW van with a kerosene stove, pots and pans, clothing, his paints and easel, my mother's books and macramé, their tambourines, and our parrot. Off we went.

Guided by a map in *The Whole Earth Catalog*, we drove through Yugoslavia, Turkey, Iraq, Iran, and Pakistan, where the van broke down. A group of Germans came by in a jeep. They stopped and asked where we were going. By coincidence, they too were on their way to India and offered to take us with them. Unsure whether we should go with them, my mother consulted the *I Ching*, an ancient Chinese text filled with hexagrams that is believed to help people understand and even control future events. When she was a young girl, she and Dena hovered over the book, like fortune-tellers. The book said we should go with the Germans. Days later, we arrived in

Dharamsala, India, home of the Dalai Lama and his government in exile, where we spent a year. I was not yet two years old.

My parents had heard about a special and well-known monthlong retreat at the Kopan, a Tibetan Buddhist monastery on a hillside overlooking the lush Kathmandu valley in Nepal. Many Tibetans had left their homeland to escape the Chinese occupation and settled in Nepal and India. After they settled in one location, they built shrines and monasteries, some of which were replicas of the ones in Tibet, and dedicated to Tibetan Buddhism, a particular strain of Buddhism. Once a year, several hundred people from all over the world descended on the valley, carrying backpacks, seeking enlightenment and a chance to hear the lamas. My parents found a local Tibetan family to take care of me. I remember nothing of them, but apparently, while there, I picked up a nasty habit of spitting at people.

Determined to have an intense experience, my mother told my father that she wouldn't talk to him or anyone the entire month and that she wasn't going to sit near him. When the hundred people gathered in the tent made of bamboo poles and straw mats, my mother found a spot in the front row. Incense made of a special plant found in the Mount Everest region burned sweetly. Day after day, she settled rapt in front of Lama Zopa Rinpoche. With his eyes closed, he talked about the path to enlightenment, compassion, and impermanence, the hot and cold hells, hungry ghosts, and death. She felt connected to him in ways she couldn't explain or understand. After a particularly stirring session, she took a small black-and-white picture of the lama and made a tiny altar to him, propping his photo up against the windowsill of her room and lighting a candle in front of it. By then, she had made up her mind to become a Buddhist nun.

There, our paths would diverge and our fragile little family unravel. I've spent years trying to find the reason why and discovered there's no such thing as a single reason in human affairs. What happened to us is the result of hundreds of small events, occurring well before the day I was born, and before my parents even met. Long-buried grandparents and great-grandparents and distant cultures played some supporting roles in shaping our fate. I suspect my great-grandmother Dena's influence and the absence of my grandparents in my mother's own life weighed heavily, as did my father's own delicate mind and his family. Whether our unraveling was inevitable, I don't know. Do two dysfunctional families automatically beget a third? My mother would say it was karma, that in past lives she was Buddhist and was destined to be Buddhist in this one. Doing so meant leaving her old life and all that went with it behind, my father and me included. I could never accept that explanation. Karma doesn't absolve people from responsibilities. Buddhism doesn't mean turning your back on family in the name of disavowing relationships and attachments. That is a convoluted understanding of Buddhism.

❈

At one point, toward the end of the retreat, she looked over at my father. He was leaning back with his mouth open, wearing a strange look on his face. She broke her silence to ask him what was going on. He started babbling about seeing psychic energies between people and the realms of hell, and that he was communicating directly with His Holiness the Dalai Lama.

My father had snapped.

After that, he began roaming the monastery through the night. He gave away his watch and his shoes. Then, one day before the retreat was over, he was gone. A voice in his head promised to explain death to him, but only if he left the monastery and went to the mountains. The voice, he said, belonged to Lama Zopa. "You are my slave. I am your Buddha," it told him. "Walk off to the mountains. Don't look back. Keep going." My father obeyed.

Weeks later, thin and drawn, he reappeared at the monastery with an intestinal infection. Sores covered his feet from wandering barefoot in the mountains. The monks gave him a tiny room and bandaged his feet. The skin between his eyebrows was burned. He had scalded himself trying to demonstrate his psychic powers by pouring tea into his forehead.

What caused my father to break down will always be a mystery. The mind is wonderfully complex but fragile. Maybe the sum of unnerving events in his life simply became unbearable—being sent to the orphanage as a young boy, years of smoking hash, my mother bringing him to a remote part of the world and then slipping away, leaving him rudderless in a totally foreign culture. Having relied on her for direction and guidance, he was suddenly unmoored, with nothing to hang on to other than these voices in his head. His own mother seemed to have some sort of mental fragility. Perhaps there was a genetic element that manifested itself in my father in the form of schizophrenia. I sometimes wondered, too, whether he was one of those mad geniuses. Once he resumed painting later in his life, he couldn't stop. It was as if his mind was churning out so many ideas that his hands could not rest. His images look distorted but are wonderfully complex and poetic.

When the retreat was over, my mother came running down the hill toward the home where I had been staying. "Mommy," I yelled, getting up and tumbling into her arms. She was surprised that I looked so happy to see her and that she meant so much to me.

There being no novitiate, my mother was ordained a nun and began wearing maroon robes that hung down to her feet. Her head was shaved and she took a new name, Thubten Wongmo. At first I went with her to the monastery where she lived with other nuns. It was an awkward situation. Only two years old, I couldn't understand why I couldn't be with her. She tried to get me to play with the young monks, but I ended up wandering around the monastery halls looking for her. She shared a room with other nuns, their sleeping bags spread out on the floor. There was no place, literally or figuratively, for a toddler among meditating nuns. A fellow nun told her, "You have to let go of attachment to your child and live like a nun now."

My mother was torn between feeling protective of me and feeling committed to her new life as a Buddhist nun. I needed someone to feed, dress, and comfort me, someone to nurse my scrapes, teach me to talk and read, and how to be a good person. I needed someone to make me feel secure and loved, and to explain that kids stared at me because they had never seen a white boy before, not because there was something wrong with me. A Buddhist nun needed to be devoted to studying and meditating. She needed to live free of attachments, children included.

At least, that is how she saw it at the time. I often wondered whether she was simply young and lacking a firm grasp of Buddhism, whether she could comprehend at that young age and with a relatively limited study and exposure to Buddhism what Buddhism was really all about. True, attachment is an important concern for Buddhists because it can cause suffering. But Buddhists don't disavow caring for one's own child. As far as I know, no paradigms existed for her to follow. There was no model at the time, no precedent of an American woman in Nepal becoming a nun after being married and having a child. Advice given to her by her lamas and fellow nuns, while well-meaning, could never take into consideration the issues confronting her or her feelings. They weren't mothers. Plus, she was so insecure about her ability to be a good mother that she thought she would be a much better nun than mother. She had no idea what I would go through without her.

My mother devoted herself fully to her vocation. Returning to the United States was out of the question. Nepal and India were her home.

Shortly after her ordination, she wanted to go with the other new nuns on a three-month retreat held in the mountains of Solu Khumbu, in the Everest region. The retreat is done in silence. I would be a distraction and confused by my mother's inability to talk. Not knowing what to do with me, she asked her main guru, Lama Thubten Yeshe, for advice. He had a solution. He knew of a large Tibetan family, the Trinleys, that would take me in. I would be in good hands, he assured her. The father was himself a former Buddhist monk who had studied with Lama Yeshe in Lhasa, Tibet.

Three months later, my mother returned from her retreat. After conferring with her lama, she decided it was best that I stay with the Trinleys. They lived in Kathmandu valley, only about ten miles from the monastery. She would visit when she could.

❀

The ancient city of Kathmandu, founded two thousand years ago, spreads across a bowl-shaped valley ringed by snow-topped Himalayan Mountains. It is a holy city, named after a temple built out of a single tree. Tens of thousands of people make pilgrimages to its white and gold-domed Hindu and Buddhist temples and shrines. Narrow alleyways connect a maze of neighborhoods. Tibetan Buddhists and Nepalese Hindus live side by side, rising at 4 A.M. to begin their respective rituals. The Hindus ring small bells to wake the gods and offer them music and oil lamps. The Buddhists walk to a sacred hill topped by a huge temple and circle the base of the hill clockwise, their prayer beads in their hands, and return home to offer seven bowls of water, representing the seven limbs of prayer, to the deities on the altars of their private prayer rooms.

At the center of the city is a lively, noisy, and dirty main market area called Asan Tole. By early morning, its streets are chaotic. Makeshift stalls burst with every sort of household good. Plastic toys, brassware, sugar, oil, spices, fruits, vegetables, clothing, and shoes. Tourists, monks, local villagers, Tibetans, Nepalese, and Westerners on pilgrimages to the holy temples swarm the streets. Cows run from one open-air stall to another, eating vegetables until shrieking vendors chase them away with brooms and sticks. Rickshaw drivers dodge bicycles and scream for luminescent silky white goats to get out of the way. Ornery monkeys squat on wood-carved windowsills and taunt in high-pitched squeals. During the three-month monsoon season, a thick muck of mud, trash, and feces slicks the streets.

My little corner of the teeming city was Jampa Trinley's pink, two-story stucco house, which sat on a narrow muddy road four short blocks from the main market area.

The Trinley family consisted of the father, a tall man with huge hands, the two mothers, and their collective eleven children. The mothers were sisters. Both wore their long hair braided in a single plait down the back. The older mother was a bit heavier, her face longer and creased. I liked the younger one better. She laughed easily and her eyes twinkled. Babu, their youngest, was about my age, but shorter. We were both happy to have a playmate. He and I assembled teams of rocks in the little patch of dirt in the front yard. Taking turns, we pitched our best rock at the other's best rock. The only real toy in the house was a six-inch-long shiny black motorcycle that a relative or friend from the States had sent the Trinley family. It was locked in a glass-doored cabinet. I would stare at it, wanting to run its wheels through tiny dirt paths and turn the handlebars back and forth, but knew better than to ask. I don't think anyone ever played with it.

Since we were the youngest, we held no real standing in the house. Adults ate at the table. Babu and I crossed our legs on the concrete floor, quietly chewing our rice and lentils for lunch and dough balls made of roasted barley flour, yak butter, and sugar mixed with tea for breakfast. Neither of us spoke during meals unless we were spoken to. I rarely was, which I considered a good thing. I kept my head down, averting any looks from the parents. I began doing that after hearing them talk about me. It may have been when I wet my pants. Cloth diapers had to be washed. The mothers were frustrated, saying I was big enough to know better and would have to learn quickly to use the bathroom. Having another child in the house, let alone one who was already two and not toilet trained, was a burden. My face flushed with shame. I felt like a problem that had to be dealt with.

I called the father *Pa la,* Tibetan for Father, and the mothers *Ama la,* Tibetan for Mother. On special holy days, we went together as a family to the monastery for prayers. I accompanied the older Ama la to the market daily to buy fruit, vegetables, and meat. Water buffalo carcasses rested on slabs of concrete. Ama la pointed to legs, shoulders, ribs, and the vendor began cutting, the blood dripping down a drain. At home, I sat in the kitchen, watching her cut the chewy meat into small cubes and stir-fry it with garlic, ginger, tomatoes, and onions. When I wasn't with her, I'd be outside. When the older brothers flew kites, I cheered them on as one of my own, hoping their kite would knock down the other swooping red, white, and yellow squares that dotted the sky.

On other days, I'd wander down to Jampa's noodle factory by the main market, where the huge machines both fascinated and frightened me. One of his daughters got too close to one that was flattening the dough. The machine ripped out a clump of her hair and cut her eye. After that, I stayed away from the factory and watched men boiling bean curd to make tofu at the small building next door.

I had my own chores and responsibilities. The Trinley parents taught me Tibetan, and how to perform some of the morn-

ing rituals and special prayers. Every morning, I would go out
to the yard and fetch a bucket of water from the well. I carried a
jug up the steps, trying hard not to spill, and into the prayer
room. Carefully, I took a stack of seven silver and brass bowls,
small enough to sit in the palm of my hand, and lined them up
on the altar in a row. Keep them a grain's width apart from one
another, I was told. Pour a little water in the first bowl, and
then pour some of that water into each of the other bowls. Fill
each bowl with water from the bucket, careful not to drip. Hold
your breath so as not to breathe on the water. I bowed my head
and recited the Four Measurables:

> May all sentient beings have equanimity, free from
> attachment, aggression, and prejudice.
> May they be happy and have the causes for happiness.
> May they be free from suffering and causes for suffering.
> May they never be separated from the happiness that is
> free from suffering.

Jampa, a former monk, insisted that I know my prayers. I
was too young to read, so he took a seat next to me and pointed
to the words. He read them aloud. I recited them after. If I
failed, he would hit me with his belt or stinging nettle branches
that made my skin itch. On one occasion, when I was about
three or four, he took me up to the prayer room and took off his
belt. The younger mother followed. We stood at the far end of
the room, by the window and away from the sacred altar. He
stood over me, lifted his arm, and began hitting my legs with
the leather strap. Trembling, I wet myself. Then more terrified
and ashamed because I had wet myself and made a mess, I
began walking in little circles, trying to outrace his blows but
not daring to run away. I don't remember what I did wrong.

I tried to avoid him as much as I could. When I heard his
motorbike leave the yard, I felt safe. Once I took money from

under Jampa's bed, planning to go to the market and buy some food. I don't think I considered it stealing. I was simply doing what I saw others do. People got money and spent it at the market. I bought a few pieces of hard candy and a thumb-size piece of fruit called *lapsi*, with green skin and sour white flesh that tasted like tamarind. The fruit's real attraction to a little boy was a big seed that if sharpened into a point served as a spinning top. Kids would gather around a flat piece of wood and spin their seeds and try to knock the others off the wood. I never got around to that. After I arrived home, one of the mothers, or maybe it was a sister, asked what I had in my hand. Not knowing enough to lie or that I had done something wrong, I told them. They asked how I paid for it. Again, not cunning enough to spin a story about finding money in the dirt or on the street, I confessed to taking it from under the father's bed. Thankfully, they didn't tell him. Instead, they sent me back to the store to return my purchases and replenish the money stash.

Our two-story house was bigger than many in the neighborhood. A fence surrounded our yard. A redbrick walk led from the dirt street to our front door. We had an indoor bathroom with two holes in a slab of concrete. Our neighbors had outdoor holes in the ground. Older houses had dirt floors. Ours was concrete with a shiny polish. Along the walls of the living room hung elaborate ancient paintings of deities, protected by a plastic see-through sheet. Indian craftsmen came into the house with sticks and bows, whipping cotton into soft tufts that went into futonlike cushions for the wood boards that served as couches during the day and beds at night. We didn't sleep on sheets. We slept under blankets, unrolled at night and put away each morning.

As in other Tibetan homes, we had a prayer room. Ours was especially fine, filled with sacred antique statues that the Trinleys, who were a noble family in Tibet, had brought with them. Cabinetlike wooden altars housed two-foot-tall statues of the

Buddha and Green Tara, the goddess who represents compassion. Precious scriptures were wrapped in yellow-orange cloth. Smoke from dried juniper and frankincense cloaked the air. We had a local boy from a poor family, Ramji, cook and wash clothes. I'd sit on the kitchen floor, watching him chop potatoes into uniform chunks, mesmerized by the rhythmic up-and-down blur of the knife. He'd brush back his long dark hair when it fell into his eyes as he stirred a pot of lentils simmering on a kerosene stove. While he cooked, he told me about his own family and what he was making for dinner. Sometimes, he would give me a spoonful of *tsampa,* a roasted barley flour.

The street outside the front gate led to the banks of the Bagmati River. The river was considered sacred because it ran at the base of a hill that housed a massive monastery. Local Hindus cremated their dead on its banks and sprinkled the ashes on its clear blue surface to be carried away to a new, holy afterlife. Funeral processions passed by our house frequently, sometime twice a day, en route to the river. I could hear a procession approaching from a half mile away. The haunting sounds of women wailing and crying, men banging small cymbals and drums, drowned out the barking of stray dogs. I'd run to the front gate and watch as the priest, dressed in a Gandhi-like dhoti, approached. Behind him, a line of men wearing white from head to toe carried the corpse on a stretcher made of bamboo and cloth. Behind the corpse, a train of women shrieked.

The haunting scene terrified and excited me. I studied the corpse, shrouded in a white or red gauzy mesh. It was thin enough that I could make out the features, the stiff bony nose and swollen chest. I tried to see if it was an adult or a child. If it was a child, I began worrying that I might be next. The procession never lasted long. The mourners, though weighted by grief, moved quickly, rushing to the cremation site to avoid the curses that surrounded death. Dead bodies would turn into demons if they weren't cremated fast enough. I had heard stories of corpses coming back to life as evil, hungry ghosts that would have to be stoned to death. The night after a procession passed, I had nightmares of ugly beings with big stomachs and tiny necks chasing me and eating me alive.

At one point, Jampa Trinley's frail father came to live with us. He died in the room next to mine. The following three days, his body rested in his bed. I couldn't sleep at night, picturing his thin, lifeless corpse on the other side of my bedroom wall. Afraid, I recited mantras to keep demons away. Monks from nearby monasteries came and surrounded the corpse, chanting and burning pine needle incense. Villagers lined up outside the front door, waiting their turn to go upstairs and offer prayers. For months after, the thick smell of pine needles filled the house. All mirrors were covered or turned to face the wall. Each of the forty-nine following mornings, we went to the balcony, where incense burned, and added wheat flour and butter to the fire to feed the grandfather's soul while it was in purgatory. For a year, no one was allowed to utter the grandfather's name.

In Kathmandu, death was not an event reserved only for the very old. Unbiased, it struck playful children and vigorous men and women. Disease was common and medical treatment was not. There were few hospitals and doctors. Sickness was attributed to offending the gods and thus treated by offering bowls of fruit or eggs to make amends and hopefully earn recovery. I had to be especially vigilant not to irk the nagas, powerful spirits who lived in water, stones, and trees. I was careful not to pee on a rock or tree. If I had to, or did so by mistake, I quickly uttered the phrase *Benabe,* the equivalent of "Excuse me."

Some of our Hindu neighbors went further in trying to please the gods, slashing the throats of chickens, goats, ducks, sheep, and water buffalo, and squirting the warm blood on doorways, car engines, wheels, and any other machinery to bring health and good fortune. When they did, I stood on the balcony to get a good view, watching our neighbor lift a glinting axe and smash it into the temple of the buffalo. Blood squirted in an arc. The buffalo fell over with a thud. Its legs were bound with ropes made of straw. Women gathered wood for the fire and hauled huge brass pots and pans to boil water and cook. A quick death was a good sacrifice. Not everyone had a sharp axe. Poorer families with blunt knives would hack at the necks of goats. Blood trickled. The doomed half-dead animals ran in dazed circles as men tried to grab hold of their horns and necks. I felt sorry for the animals and repeatedly whispered the Great Compassion Mantra, *Om Mani Pedme Hung*. It means "Hail the jewel in the lotus," and it invokes the deity Chenrezig to relieve suffering.

As the days stretched into weeks, months, and years, I came to believe that I was a member of the Trinley family, one of their younger sons. What I couldn't figure out is why I looked different from everyone else in the family. I didn't notice it at first. Over time, though, I became increasingly aware and troubled that I was odd. The Trinleys were more fair-skinned than other Tibetans because they didn't work in the fields. But even so, they were darker skinned than I was. My face was longer than the round-faced Trinleys'. My hair was blond. Maybe I wouldn't have been aware of the differences if people didn't stare at me. Tagging along with the older Ama la to the market, I began noticing heads turning and eyes following me. I looked down at myself to see if my clothes had holes in them or to make sure no huge insect was clinging to them. If a police officer approached, my older Ama la worried that he might ask for my immigration documents, which she didn't have, and told me to run and hide. My heart racing, I would slip inside a nearby store or behind bamboo stalks that thankfully grew in thick clusters. I was perhaps four or five years old, worried they would take me away because I didn't belong. I stood out even more after the older mother took me to a barber, who cut my hair shorter than anyone else's in the family. They were following the wishes of my mother, who wanted me to become a monk. My white bald skull looked like a white onion. From that point on, I was allowed to wear only pants and shirts that were red in preparation for the robes I would wear. That made me unlike Babu, who wore blues, blacks, and whites. I had always considered the two of us as similar. We had that common bond of being little boys who liked to play the same games. We belonged together. Now I was different.

People were always dropping by the house, seeking Jampa's advice or help. Jampa's family in Tibet was wealthy and had been well connected in the government. Tibetans wanted to pay their respects to him, especially when they first arrived in town. Groups gathered out front, smoking Nepalese Yak cigarettes, which came in a pink box. Their conversation would halt when I walked by. They looked puzzled. Their eyebrows furrowed as they studied my arms, legs, and face. Everyone gave the same look. It wasn't just one visitor, but all of them. Young, old. Men, women, and children. Occasionally, they had seen an adult from the States or Europe. A white child, though, was a true novelty. I heard snatches of unsettling words that would follow me for years. "Blond hair." "White skin."

"Who is this little boy?" they would ask. I couldn't figure out why they would ask such a question. I was a part of the Trinley family. The older mother jokingly said I was her own child. Everyone laughed. What was so funny? I wondered. Once, the younger mother told me to show the visitors how I could meditate. I obeyed, sitting in the middle of the room and crossing my legs in the lotus position. They nodded, impressed that a little white boy could sit like a Tibetan. Rather than feel good or proud of the accomplishment, I felt more freakish. Babu didn't perform in front of other people.

My response to the unwanted attention was to be as unnoticed and invisible as possible. That became my approach to life. I walked quickly in the streets, hoping no one would have enough time to study me. I looked down at my feet, figuring if I couldn't see people, they couldn't see me.

The only person who resembled me at all was my mother.

❊

By the time my mother returned after her three-month-long retreat, I was four years old, speaking Tibetan, calling the brothers *Chocho la* and the sister *Acha la*. Shy after not seeing her for so long, I stood several feet away from her. She glanced over at me and smiled as she drank tea with Ama la. That night, the older Ama la told me I was to share a bed with my mother.

As we lay in the dark, my mother hugged me and talked to me in quiet whispers. I felt special, feeling her warm breath, her arms around me, surrounded by the smell of her perfumed robes. I didn't understand what she was saying. All I knew was that she treated me special. No one else whispered to me or held me in bed. I woke the next morning alone. She was up, drinking tea. I could hear her voice, her English and broken Tibetan, mixing with those of the other mothers, their laughs. I ran in the kitchen just as she was gathering up the red cloth bag she wore over her shoulder. She was getting ready to leave. I was certain I was going with her, that she had come to collect me.

She said good-bye and turned to go out the door. I started crying and clinging to her soft cotton robes. Jampa scooped me up and held me firmly in his arms. He rocked me, talking softly to me. He took me upstairs to the prayer room and pointed to the Buddha statues on the long altar and the wall hangings of deities. Slowly and deliberately, he named all the colors and flowers in the brocade, mentioning the reds, blues, and yellows and trying to distract me as long as he could. He gave me an apple.

My mother's heart had sunk looking at my face before she left. But she knew she had to go and had by this time learned to shut off her feelings and to rationalize that my new home was the best place for me. I had children to play with here and I was well taken care of.

Over the next few years, my mother visited every few months. Though the distance between the Trinleys' and the monastery where she was living wasn't far, the journey was difficult. Taxis wouldn't drive up to the monastery because the road and terrain were too rocky. The fare wasn't worth the damage to their cars and tires. Monsoons washed out the roads each year. When she knew that one of the monks needed to drive the monastery jeep to town to buy hundred-pound sacks of rice and flour in the market, she asked for a ride and through messengers alerted the Trinleys to let them know she was coming.

My older Ama la would announce, "Mummy is coming." I got excited because Mummy treated me kindly. She hugged me and brought me little gifts. I wasn't quite sure how we were connected, but figured she must be a doting aunt or godmother. Not my Ama la. I'd look out the front door, waiting for her robed figure to appear, and run down the redbrick path covered with moss to meet her. The house became festive when she was there. A little more meat was served with vegetables. She was an honored guest. Having some connection to her, I got special treatment too. My face and hands were scrubbed. I wore freshly laundered clothes. Once tea was prepared and my mother was seated, Jampa would direct me to the middle of the room. "Meditate," he said. Obedient, I crossed my bony legs into a lotus position. I smiled, not too broadly, but proud. I searched her eyes for approval. She seemed pleased. I continued, knowing it was time to recite prayers I had memorized.

At night, the two of us nestled under a blanket. Her soft white arms wrapped me. I began thinking this time she would take me. No matter how many times she left, every time she visited, I dreamed she would take my hand and we would walk out the gate together to her home, where we would live together and be happy. One day in particular, I woke at daybreak and jumped out of bed and joined my mother and the parents in the kitchen. The tea was hot and the wheat dough balls sweet. My mother got up from the table and picked up her red cotton bag, and slung it over her shoulder. She was smiling. I went out the front door, waiting for her to come outside, so we could both leave. Several minutes passed. I suddenly realized that I no longer heard my mother's voice, her distinctive broken Tibetan.

I ran toward the house, calling, "Mummy, Mummy," and tripped over the brick, cutting my chin. Blood gushed. Inside, Pa la and the older Ama la rinsed my wound and told me my mother had gone out the back door. I cried harder, standing at the doorstep, salty tears streaming down my cheeks, my nose running.

From that point on, whenever it was time for my mother to leave, Pa la and one of the two Ama las or some of the older brothers and sisters would trick me, calling me to another part of the house to see a kite or an animal passing by. When I was out of sight, my mother sneaked out. I returned to the room where I last saw my mother standing. She was gone. All the eminence of the day disappeared. I was no longer important and celebrated.

My mother became like the tide, ebbing into my little world and then receding. I could chase after her, and try to hold her, but she vanished. I couldn't understand why she always left me there. The two of us had something in common, I thought. We were alike, she and I. In the village and market, I searched the crowds for people who had white skin and eyes likes mine. Out of hundreds of people, there were none except her. We had to be connected in some way.

The only answer I could come up with was that something was wrong with me. Maybe she knew I wet my pants. Maybe I didn't recite my prayers well enough. Every time she left, I promised myself I would do better, and be better. Then she would want me. She never did. I was never worthy enough to go home with her.

She always seemed happy when it was time to go, smiling, joking, and laughing. I thought it was because she was with me and we were about to leave with each other. I didn't realize until later why she was happy. In her mind I was thriving. I lived in a clean, big house with good food, a bed to sleep on, brothers and sisters to play with, and a father who helped me memorize scriptures. She could go back to her monastery to meditate and meet with her lamas in good conscience. She didn't know that when she left, I felt rejected, that I would want or need her. She learned to deliberately chase away any thoughts that I might long for her.

"I don't dare think of how much you must miss me," she wrote me in a letter decades later. Like me, she had grown to doubt that she was worthy of being wanted. "It doesn't even cross my mind that anyone, even my own child, would miss me or need me."

These comings and goings lasted for more than three years. I had turned six by then and figured out that she would never want me with her.

Chapter Four
Ordination

Disillusioned about her own unhappy childhood, my mother was determined that I would not grow up as she or anyone in her family had, seduced by wealth and fame, drugs and booze. The surest way was to physically remove me from her childhood home. Temptations that haunted her in Beverly Hills would never be a part of my life in one of the poorest countries in the world.

She could think of nothing better for me than memorizing scriptures, sitting at the feet of the lamas, and one day, after having mastered English in classes, traveling around the world with them as their able translator. In her eyes, I could be a Buddhist teacher, greatly appreciated and respected. Wearing maroon robes and going barefoot, I wouldn't be troubled with appearances. My days would be deliciously spent buried in spiritual texts, exploring questions that really mattered—like "What is compassion?"—and engaging in lively debates with wise men. As a monk, I would learn morality, empathy, suffering, and the nature of impermanence, things she says she never learned in school. Protecting me from evil was her way of showing love for me.

And so, after consulting with her lama, my mother arranged to have me sent to the monastery at the age of six to spend the rest of my life as a Buddhist monk. In the Tibetan culture, it's not unusual for young boys to go into the monastery. She thought I would learn not to need her, as she had learned not to need her own mother.

I can't help but feel there was the matter of convenience. She being a nun, I being a monk, we would both be consumed with spiritual studies and she wouldn't have to worry about being a mother to me in the traditional sense. We could grow blissfully spiritual, but independently, without me needing her guidance or affirmation, she assumed. Our lives could follow parallel paths and never have to intersect and intertwine. I would get what I needed from the monastery and the teachers there and not have to bother her. Moreover, I would be so isolated I wouldn't even realize I was missing something.

There was only one problem: I shared none of my mother's aspirations for myself and she never supported mine. We were pursuing the exact opposites.

❁

I was ordained on December 27, 1976. A fog had settled that morning, draping the valley in a gauzy shroud. I stood in the front room of the Trinley home, holding my arms up as the older Ama la adjusted my new robe. Normally serious, she was even more so that morning. Her eyes narrowed with concentration. The robe had to be folded a certain way so the bottom fell loosely, like a skirt. Two folds on the left and one on the right. A long beltlike piece of cloth tied at the waist to hold the material in place. There was enough cloth to wrap around my skinny body twice, maybe three times. Frustrated, she called her older son, who had already joined the monastery, to come help. I was in awe of him. He has been recognized as a reincarnated lama. I paid no attention to what they were doing with my robe, not knowing I would soon have to do so by myself. It seemed like a fun game of dress-up.

Standing in front of the mirror, I looked at my new robe with its curtainlike, perfectly smooth folds and rubbed my prickly scalp. The day before, a Nepalese barber had shaved my head, leaving only a thin batch of blondish hair in the middle of my skull. I liked looking like a monk and felt important and grown up. Whether I thought about it or not, I'm sure I assumed I could go back to being a child tomorrow and that life would return to what it was before. I would sleep in my own bed, wake in the morning for tea with Babu and a game of pitching rocks in the dirt. There was no trepidation, only excitement, because I didn't know this was permanent. I had no idea what permanent was, anyway.

We climbed into a clunky Toyota taxi. The older Ama la sat next to me. I stared out the window, watching the city market and the narrow alleyways give way to fields of rice and corn and huts made of crumbling gray mud and straw. The sun had burned off the mist, and the fields shimmered in the wind. We rattled over a bumpy dirt road up a slow, winding hill toward the village of Kopan and, just beyond it, the Kopan Monastery. It was the same monastery my parents had attended for the monthlong retreat four years earlier that changed all of our lives. I had been to the monastery while living with the Trinleys. Two of the boys were monks there. On important religious holy days, the family went to the Kopan Monastery. The mood would be festive, with people laughing and smiling and hundreds of candles flickering. Villagers offered young monks gifts and money to earn special merit. I thought it would be fun to run around with all those young, smiling monks.

My ordination day was also the anniversary of the birth of a famous lama and cause for great celebration each year. When we arrived, crimson blurs of monks dashed up and down cracked concrete steps, and in and out of the main temple. One group of young monks clustered around a mud incense vase, taking turns puffing into the small opening to ignite a tiny pile of wood sticks. A wisp of smoke appeared. The spicy smell of juniper incense spread.

The lamas were expecting me. A wise-looking man with several strands of thin mustache, named Lama Lhundrup, greeted us. He exchanged a few words with the Trinleys. I was too busy looking at the activity around me to hear what they said. When they were done, he led me away.

We passed the flower garden and walked to a three-story yellow building, which housed the temple on the first floor and the lamas' living quarters above. Climbing a dark narrow set of steps, Lama Lhundrup coached me, telling me what I should do when I met the monastery's two highest lamas. He opened the door of a small room, cramped with sacred statues, books, and paintings. Inside, Lama Zopa Rinpoche was perched on a platform covered by a small, flowered wool rug in shades of red, yellow, and green. A table piled with books and long scriptures sat in front of him. Immediately, I prostrated. Half kneeling, my right knee on the floor and my left knee up, I leaned my near-bald head over to the lama. Reciting a series of mantras and prayers, Lama Zopa Rinpoche clipped the remaining strands of hair to signify my detachment from the lay world. I kept my head bowed and heard the scissors snip. My last bit of blond hair dropped, scattering on the polished wood floor like strands of fine silk. He spoke in a low guttural voice that made him seem more serious and holy and otherworldly.

"Repeat after me, three times," Lama Zopa Rinpoche said.

"I take refuge in the Buddha.

"I take refuge in the dharma"—the teachings of the Lord Buddha.

"I take refuge in the sangha"—the monastic community.

In barely a whisper, I repeated the affirmations three times. He asked me if I vowed to renounce all trappings of worldly existence.

"I do," I swore.

"Do you vow to be celibate, not to take the life of another living thing, not to steal or lie?"

"I do," I said, having no idea what celibate was but not even thinking to ask.

To show I was leaving one life behind, I was given the new name of Thubten Wangchuk, which means "Powerful One." At the end, Lama Zopa Rinpoche draped a white scarf, signifying pure intentions, around my neck. I fingered it gently. I didn't know then that Lama Zopa Rinpoche was the same lama who had left my mother so enrapt that she built a tiny altar devoted to him four years earlier.

After, Lama Lhundrup led me by the hand down to the main temple, where all the monks and people from the city, including the Trinleys, had assembled. The air above the altar glimmered from hundreds of butter lamps and candles. The lama nodded to the front row, where the older monks were sitting cross-legged on the floor. A space was left for me. "Sit there," Lama Lhundrup said. Though I would rather have been with boys my age, I sensed I was an honored guest, and proud.

When evening fell, I received a small, thin white candle and lined up with the eighty other monks. We walked outside around the hillside surrounding the monastery, singing and chanting under the stars. The flames flickered, illuminating solemn profiles and casting shadows against the hillside. I spoke quietly so as not to blow out my candle and followed lockstep the monks around me. It was a beautiful night. I looked up and saw hundreds of stars and felt very small.

As momentous as all this was, I didn't want or expect to stay. I planned on returning to what had been my home.

My mother was not there for my ordination. She was out of the country, perhaps in England conducting retreats. "Had I been in Nepal," she assured me years later when I asked, "I would have been at the ceremony." At the time, I didn't expect her to be there or even think of her. She had already become remote.

Those first days were disorienting. A loud brass bell began clanging at five-thirty the next morning, startling me out of my sleep. It took a few moments to remember where I was. Someone kicked our door and banged on the tin wall. It was the monk police, elected each month to supervise all the other monks. Warned that they would throw a bucket of cold water on a monk who wouldn't get up, I scrambled into my robes. Unable to get them the right length, I tied them up as best I could and followed the other monks out the door. A crowd of robed figures circled a communal water pot, splashing cold water on their faces before rushing up the steps to get to the main temple for morning prayers. On the way, I tripped over my robes. The top slipped off my bony shoulders.

The morning sun poured through the temple windows. Looking around, I saw only one other white monk. He was older. I tried to cover my white legs with my robe. No one came up and introduced himself or welcomed me.

Not knowing what was expected those first few days, I watched closely what other monks did and tried to do the same. I bowed my head when they did. After meals, I saw them pick up their dish and walk over to a basin of water, dip the dish in water, and clean it. I did the same. I was given a tree branch and shown a plot of dirt. Watching other monks bend over and sweep the dirt, I did the same. It was tiring, having to be ever watchful. Slowly, it dawned on me that I was on my own. The life I had known was over. I wanted to cry but was afraid of being teased.

My whiteness was immediately an issue. Everyone else was darker skinned. Some might be a little fairer, depending on whether he was Sherpa, Tibetan, or Nepalese. But all were essentially different shades of brown. Each group of monks soon adopted its own derogatory name for me. Sherpa monks called me Mik Karpo, or "White Eye." Their own eyes were dark brown pools surrounded by yellow. I didn't have a mirror to look at my eyeballs so I imagined they were eerily colorless. Dark-haired Tibetan monks, pointing at my head, called me Gopserr, or "Yellow-Haired." Nepalese monks said my white skin meant I had decayed and called me Qure, which literally means "Rotten." Get a piece of charcoal and rub it all over your skin, they teased. One monk in particular enjoyed picking on me, remarking on the size, color, and shape of my eyes. "Big Eye," he taunted.

Sometimes I cried and hated myself for being weak. "Go back to your mother's womb," some older monks said. Even though I didn't know what they meant, I knew they were mocking me. Around this time, I began to dislike my mother and be embarrassed by her.

Other monks had nicknames. "Africa" was the boy with the big lips. Two monks were called "Mouse," one because he had a small, sharp lip and another because he was so short and had large ears. To tell them apart, we called one "Nepali Mouse." But those nicknames were used differently. The tone was collegial not hurtful. The nicknamed monks may have had one distinguishing trait, but otherwise they looked like everyone else. They were in a group. I was in a group that consisted of me.

I was sitting with a group of young boy monks on a log next to a bunch of kerosene drums when one of the older monks started cracking jokes about the origin of white people. "You come from monkeys, right?" he asked as he played with a twig in the dust. The other monks laughed.

"That's why they have so much hair," one of them said.

I hated the blond hair on my arms. At least most of my head was shaved, but I couldn't hide the hair on my arms.

Another monk with a long jaw looked at me. "Isn't it true that yellow-hair people have tails?"

I looked away, trying to show that I wasn't fazed. Privately I thought, They're right. I did have hair on my arms and it was yellow. My six-year-old mind couldn't distinguish between empty taunts and truth. Most of the monks were older, so I thought they must be right. Something was wrong with me.

I didn't know why I was different and what I could do to change it. I spoke the same language, recited the same prayers, and wore the same robes. I had two Ama las. I grew up in Kathmandu, knew the marketplace as well as they did. I was too young to know that I was white because of genetics, that the nun Wongmo had given birth to me and was my true mother. At one point, the monks began telling me stories about my father. Villagers had found him wandering in the mountains barefoot and mumbling incoherently. I didn't know what they were talking about. My father was Jampa Trinley. The person they talked about couldn't possibly exist. They were lying just to be mean.

Not only did I look different, but I spoke differently, too. One morning shortly after I arrived, I was standing with a group of monks. We had just finished our memorization session and were waiting to be called in front of the teacher and tested. Turning to one of the other monks, I asked when it would be my turn. From all around me, I heard monks whisper and giggle. One imitated what I had just said, exaggerating in a singsong voice. My eyes watered. I didn't understand what was so funny and felt like a fool. If I could have disappeared, melted into the ground, I would have.

Until then, I didn't know that I was speaking a dialect used by upper-class, aristocratic Tibetans. I spoke the way the Trinleys had taught me to speak, which was different from the way the other monks spoke because they didn't come from noble families. From then on, I listened closely to their subtle inflection and figures of speech, and tried to imitate them. I picked up slang and dialect that had been discouraged at the Trinleys'. I was confused as to what was right, but wanted to fit in. When I returned to the Trinleys' home for a weekend visit, they were horrified I had become so vulgar.

One of the few monks who didn't mock me was a quiet Tibetan boy about my age named Thubten Osel. With his round face, soft eyes, and quiet voice, he seemed gentler than the other monks. I didn't have to be afraid of him. At one point, we shared a room. During the night, we'd talk in the dark about which monks got in trouble and how many days off we had for the next holiday. His entire family was killed while making a pilgrimage when a bus traveling to India tumbled over the edge of a cliff. After that, he kept to himself. Other than him, I had no close friends. Since I was the object of taunts, the other monks probably were uncomfortable getting close to me, fearing they might be targeted, too.

The main monastery, a three-story building painted yellow with a gold-colored roof, rested on a hillside overlooking the Kathmandu valley. Sprinkled around it were various other buildings that housed classrooms, sleeping quarters, and the library. A large vegetable garden grew on one side of the monastery. Bir Bahadur, a thin local Nepalese man with dark, dry, leathery skin, tended it. All day long he would dig and turn soil. A spring ran at the bottom of a steep hill. To fetch water for the garden, he walked down the hill with a long pole, buckets dangling from each end, resting on his shoulder. After filling the

buckets, he trudged back up, careful not to spill. Cows and buffaloes grazed in an area circled by a barbed-wire fence. Groves of
tall bushy mango trees clung to the side of a hill. Pumpkins,
weeds, and clusters of bamboo grew wild. Just before special
holy days and the influx of visitors, young monks were dis-
patched to beat the disheveled weeds down with sticks. Beyond
the monastery stretched expanses of corn and rice fields and an
occasional house with a straw-thatched roof.

All the young monks slept in a two-story, motel-like complex with thin walls and a tin roof built with cheap materials by
Nepalese workers. Torn screens sagged from the windows. Our
beds consisted of thin, itchy straw mats woven by local farmers.
We slept on the flimsy wood floor, wondering whether we
might fall through the thin planks that creaked when we
moved. Eventually, bunk beds were built. I had two robes. The
one I wasn't wearing became my pillow. Both robes were filled
with lice that laid their eggs along the seams by the waists, arms,
and collar. When my nose dripped, I blew it on the inside of my
robe. Some monks had a tin box and kept their shoes, pens, and
paper locked inside. I didn't. I put everything under my robe
pillow.

Even though the rooms were small and there wasn't much in
them, they were impossible to keep clean. Mice scurried across
our floors and beds, leaving a trail of hard little pellets. Fleas in-
fested the bed mats. If there was water in the spring at the bottom of the hill, we bathed once a month. Monks who had soap
used it. Many didn't. A stench of urine, vomit, and sweat hung
in the room. I woke one night to something dripping on me
from the ceiling above. It couldn't be rain, since I was on the
first floor of a two-story building. We didn't have any running
water in the building either. So it wasn't a leaky pipe. I smelled
it and jumped out of the way. The young monk above me had
peed clear through his mattress and the cracks in the wooden
floor onto me. Humidity made the rancid air even heavier. Lit-

tle breeze came through the two tiny windows, and when it did, it wasn't fresh. Diarrhea was common because of the unpurified water. The bathrooms were in a separate building. Often, when a monk couldn't run fast enough, he just went in the dirt or weeds outside our windows.

Every morning, monks had to sweep the grounds. Bending over close to the ground, I brushed the dirt with my stubby branch, raising a swirling cloud that settled and coated my feet with a fine brown grit. I was given a pair of shoes, but didn't know there was a left and right foot. When I put them on the wrong feet, I decided they were too uncomfortable to wear. I had a pair of shoes that laced, but didn't know how to tie them, so they kept falling off. I preferred going shoeless. Thorns dug into the bottoms of my bare feet. I waited for the area around the thorn to get red and infected. The tender swollen flesh lifted the thorn to the surface and I would just yank it. Gradually I developed thick calluses.

Once I had been at the monastery for a few weeks, a dull routine of prayers and chores settled in, making each day excruciatingly long. At dawn I hurried over to the main meditation hall and prostrated three times on the floor before sitting on a mat in a back row. Monks who had been at the monastery the longest took the front row. A narrow path was kept open in the center, leading to the main throne, which was covered in gold brocade. The distinguished seat was reserved for the high lama, Lama Yeshe. If he was traveling, his picture rested in his place, with white scarves draping the frame. Sometimes a robe was stuffed and formed into a sitting position. The headless, lumpy proxy was seated in the throne. The message was that the lama was present even when out of the country. Altars stood on either side of the throne, covered with clay statues of Buddha and holy scriptures. Several sets of seven silver and copper water bowls, filled with rice grains, flowers, and water, rested on the altar's carved-wood ledge.

I sat in a lotus position, back rigid, hands folded. Invariably, as the minutes grew into an hour, my back curved, my shoulders hunched. The wood floor seemed to grow harder. Half asleep, I moved my lips and murmured sounds rather than formal prayers. My legs tingled. Monk police roamed the rows, pinching or slapping sleeping monks. To keep awake, I chewed the tip of my shawl, sucking the red color until it turned pale, mildly enjoying the taste of wet cotton. Out of boredom, I tried to wedge my finger in between the wood planks of the floor to dislodge a piece of candy or coin that had fallen through. Behind me, monks waged spitball fights. Tiny wads of paper shot across the rows before dropping silently to the floor. I snatched those that landed by me and put them in my mouth. When the monk police passed, I returned fire. Guilt washed over me when I looked up and saw the translucent eyes of the Buddha statues staring right into my brain, reading my thoughts about safely returning spitball fire.

I tried to concentrate on the chants, but my mind wandered. A curious painting hung on the wall. In it, a bloated red creature with big white eyes and long, pointed nails held a huge wheel. The wheel was filled with various images of gods, humans, animals, hungry ghosts, and hell. In the center were three animals, representing greed, hatred, and ignorance. I stared at the hungry ghosts and at a dark path in the center where naked people were being dragged to hell. On a lighted path, holy people were robed and on their way to a better afterlife. I wondered where the hell realm existed. Somewhere inside the earth, I suspected, but how far down?

Unable to solve that riddle, I turned my eyes to the statue of the emaciated Buddha that depicted him prior to his enlightenment. His skin was pulled tight over his bony knees and elbows. I imagined he must have been pretty hungry sitting under the bodhi tree, refusing to eat. My stomach growled. I wondered how much longer we had to wait for breakfast.

It was the one meal we ate in the meditation hall, rather than the dining room. Groups of monks ran back and forth between the kitchen and the hall, shuttling hot aluminum kettles of sugared tea and baskets of pita bread. As we chanted prayers, several monks walked along the rows filling our cups and handing out bread. At the proper time, the chant leader led us into a blessing of the food. After the blessing, we ate in silence, the stillness interrupted only by coughs and sneezes muffled in our robes, and the occasional and excruciatingly embarrassing and sacrilegious passing of gas. The offending monk was teased for days.

Midmorning became my least favorite part of the day. We spent an hour memorizing scripture. I took a spot on dirt outside the meditation hall with a few other monks, holding my prayer book in my hands. Never sure what I was supposed to memorize, I blindly opened the prayer book and stared at the words, which didn't make sense to me. I kept my head down, pretending to read. When monk police passed, I chanted. Each day, we were tested on what we had memorized. If we failed the test, we were beaten. That was an expected and accepted way of discipline. I even considered it lucky at times.

Once a lama hit me with the *mala,* or rosary beads, for not being able to recite a prayer from memory. He was my favorite teacher and seemed to take special interest in me. He showed me how to meditate and imagine the light of the deities flowing down, purifying me. He could tell when something was wrong and would invite me into his room to talk. I thought it was good that I was hit. It would make me a better person.

Lama Yeshe, the founder of the monastery, terrified me simply because he seemed so holy. I was convinced he could read my mind. He was taller than most monks and had a round face. When he took slow strolls around the monastery, everyone ran inside his room and stayed quiet. It was Lama Yeshe who had arranged for me to live with the Trinleys and who agreed that I was old enough to be admitted to the monastery. When he died, the monastery had a twenty-four-hour vigil in the meditation hall, with each of us assigned a time to sit and pray. It was eerie, sitting by myself, surrounded by a few flickering candles and small lamps. The only sounds came from the occasional popping from the unfortunate beetle that flew into the butter lamp.

Lama Passang, an ugly man with a protruding chin, scared me because he had a black electrical cord hanging on his bedpost. He used it to whip the heads of misbehaving monks, leaving red welts. I could feel his fingers digging into my scalp when he rested his hand on my head.

In contrast, even when Lama Lhundrup scolded a group of monks, he was good-natured. After one particularly noisy night, he stood in front of us during the morning prayers and gave a long lecture about proper monk behavior. Demanding to know why there was so much commotion during the night, he asked, "Were you all being chased by demons?"

The person who terrified me most was not a lama or a monk, but a lay Tibetan teacher with coarse hair and thick lips. Grammar, English, and math were occasionally taught by lay teachers in the afternoon. The classes were irregular, depending on whether a teacher was available. Unfortunately, this particular teacher was frequently available. I had two run-ins with him, both painful.

He was reviewing the rules of grammar and asked me to recite one rule governing vowels. I stood there in embarrassed silence, not knowing the rule. Armed with a thick piece of wood, he told me to come to the front of the class.

"Hold out your hands, palms up," he told me. I slowly extended my hands. He lifted the stick over his head and with alarming force and speed brought it down with a loud, stinging whack. Then he did it again and again, until he had hit me ten times on each palm. My palms puffed and turned red. As hard as I tried not to, I stood there crying from the pain.

But the real beating came one day when groups of us were in the meditation hall. We stood in a row and he went from monk to monk, asking a question. After he passed me, I followed him, mocking the way he walked. He wheeled around and caught me. I froze and knew I was in big trouble. He glared at me and then dismissed the rest of the monks, saying they could go early to lunch. Once we were alone, he began hitting me, first with his fist, then with a wooden broom and a stick. When he was done and dismissed me, I was too ashamed to join the other monks for lunch. Instead I went crying to my room. A part of my spirit broke that day. I have never been so frightened of someone. I hated Tibetan grammar after that.

Actually, writing in general intimidated me. Once a piece of scripture was found on the bathroom floor—a huge offense and grounds for another long lecture. All writing, even a single letter of the alphabet, should be respected, our teacher said. Don't ever walk over the written word, or sit on it, we were scolded. I came away convinced that the written word was so sacred that only the holiest of men could write. Later in life, I would stare blankly at pieces of paper or a computer terminal, feeling totally inadequate and unworthy to put words together.

Sometimes I would go off by myself to a small, triangular-shaped pond. A statue of Green Tara, the goddess of compassion, stood at its edge. Her reflection wavered in the dark green-blue pond filled with frogs. Sitting on the cold bricks at the tip of the triangle, I looked up at her. Perched on a white moon disk, with outstretched hands, she seemed to invite me to offer my fears. I asked her to help me do a better job memorizing. I felt certain that she was listening to me. Sometimes I recited prayers without any special request. The more I suffered discomfort from sitting on the cold, hard bricks, the more merit I was accumulating.

When we weren't praying or attending classes, we were doing chores. I mopped floors. I dug in the garden. I fetched tea and milk for the lamas and delivered it to their rooms. I hauled the bins filled with meal scraps to the fields and fed the cows and buffaloes. I volunteered for anything that would get me out of studying and involve food. Kitchen duty, for instance. The monastery had only two Nepalese cooks. It was impossible for them to make all the bread, peel the potatoes, and chop vegetables for the entire monastery. They needed help and I was happy to oblige. The kitchen was a dark place. Soot covered the walls and ceiling. The heavy smoke from the wood fire burned my eyes. Some days, I made pita, kneading and rolling the dough with a long cylindrical piece of wood, then cooking it on a large flat griddle. Squinting through the haze, I watched carefully as one side of the bread gently puffed. As soon as it did, I flipped it over, the top now golden brown. Other times, I squatted on the ground with three other monks around a pile of potatoes, peeling them, chopping them, and tossing them into the pot. Any opportunity I could, I scooped sugar, butter, or roasted barley flour from nearby bins into my mouth. I hung around until it was time to clean the pots used to boil unpasteurized milk and then volunteered to do so. With a spoon, I scraped the dried cream from the sides and bottom of the pan. The paper-thin slivers of sweet milk melted on my tongue.

While working in the kitchen, I came across ginger beer crates stored in the room next to the dining room. Some Westerners came up with the idea of making and selling ginger beer, saying it would be a way for the monastery to earn extra money. The crates were used to store the bottles. Eyeing an empty crate, I figured I could fit inside if I curled up in a ball, and sleep. I was obsessed with sleeping. Waking at 5:30 A.M. and studying until 10 P.M., I never felt rested. Sleeping was the only time I was left alone and didn't have to worry about memorizing, or monks picking on me. The crate looked like a good escape.

After dinner, I waited for the monk police to look away and then slipped outside the dining room, hiding in the dark bushes. Once the room emptied out, I hunched over and crept into the storeroom. It was cold inside. Bottles of ginger beer were stacked along the wall and in crates. My stomach hurt from the spicy rice porridge. I drank bottle after bottle until I could drink no more and climbed into the wooden crate. The hard wood pressed against my skin, but was only slightly harder than sleeping on woven mats on the floor. I didn't have to worry about being missed because we didn't have roll call at that point. I fell into a deep sleep.

The next morning, the sound of barking dogs woke me. It was dawn. I climbed out and tiptoed quietly outside. My bare feet tingled against the cold grass, wet with dew. I crept down the long series of brick steps to my room. Careful not to wake the other two monks, I climbed into my empty bed, feeling rested. I would return to the crates again and again, skipping evening prayers and enjoying an extended sleep.

One night the ginger crates had been cleared out to make room for buffalo meat, so I had to find another place to nap. A dented steel drum that held kerosene for cooking was sitting outside. I looked inside. It was empty. The bottom was black and the sides dented. Nearby, a pile of straw mattresses that were worn through in places waited to be thrown out. Glancing around to see if anyone was looking, I picked up a mat and ran with it to the drum, dropping it inside. I dragged the drum behind a large pile of bricks. That night, I snuck out after dinner and climbed inside the drum. It was cold and cramped. I pulled my legs to my chest to keep warm and have enough room. The straw mattress provided a little bit of warmth, protecting me from the cold, hard metal.

When the kerosene drum was thrown out, I tried the monastery's old Russian jeep—a workhorse used to haul hundred-pound burlap sacks of rice, potatoes, and meat back to the monastery from the markets of Kathmandu. The open-air jeep was colder than the crates and barrel. But it was also more reliable. I knew it wasn't going to be thrown away or disappear.

Unfortunately, the monastery began roll calls soon after I began sleeping in the jeep. One morning, the head monk called roll. He got to my name and I didn't answer. He came looking for me. I was asleep on the floor in the backseat of the jeep, tightly bundled in my cotton robes. I was dreaming about losing a fight with a monk who had been bullying me.

A voice woke me up. "Mik Karpo, are you in there?" A bright circle of light from a flashlight passed over the driver's seat. I jumped out the back of the jeep and crouched down. When the light came closer to me, I crept around to the other side. I circled the jeep, trying to keep ahead of the light before the head monk caught me. He pulled me by the ear, dragging me to the main temple, and ordered me to prostrate in front of all the other monks.

My other obsession was food. I could never get enough of that either. Meals were predictable and bland. Pita and tea for breakfast. Rice and dal for lunch. I learned to sort through my rice after taking a mouthful and biting into a stone. Steamed dough and vegetables for dinner. I especially hated the pumpkins, which unfortunately grew wild and were plentiful. Occasionally someone made special offerings of meat. When they did, word traveled quickly around the dining room, prompting cheers.

We were all aware that better food was served in another dining room, reserved for anyone who came from the United States, Australia, or Europe. Most were laypeople and teachers, but a few monks and nuns ate there too, including my mother. That side also had four basins filled with hot, soapy water to clean dishes. We cleaned our own dishes in the cold water outside. Their side had purified water. Ours didn't, the assumption being that we were used to dirty water and wouldn't get dysentery. It didn't dawn on me until later that I might get away with eating there since I was American.

Our dining room itself was a dark place. Although the walls, like most on the grounds, were painted with lime whitewash, soot from the kitchen streaked them ashen gray. The redbrick floors wore a stubborn, black film from years of dirty bare feet and spilled food and drink. No matter how much we swept and mopped, which we did every day, it looked dingy.

A thin plywood wall separated the dining room from the kitchen. The two Nepalese cooks passed tin buckets and large aluminum pots filled with food through openings in the wall. We sat on benches, saying prayers while older monks ladled a pile of vegetables onto our plates. We weren't supposed to talk. Once the revered Lama Yeshe walked through and heard us talking during the meal. He scolded us, saying we sounded like cows, and ordered us to eat in complete silence.

After dinner, I was always hungry. I'd take leftover pieces of bread and stash them under my pillow, eating the stale pieces at night. During the free hour in the afternoon, I hunted for food, combing the dump close to where the Westerners stayed. Every once in a while I'd find pieces of unopened candy. I scraped hard, masticated pieces of red- or green-colored gum off the brick and popped them into my mouth. I climbed tall mango trees and plucked fruit from the branches, whether it was ripe or raw. Raw mangoes were bitter. They needed spices. Determined to eat them, I waited until the Nepalese cooks took their afternoon break and climbed the bricks piled outside the kitchen window. Pushing through a screen that had been loosely nailed in place, I bent over and quietly stepped through. I grabbed a few pinches of spices and climbed back out the window. Outside, I sprinkled the raw mangoes with salt and dried hot chili and sank my teeth into the hard flesh. On those evenings, my neck and lip broke out into a rash from the sap of the unripe fruit.

Usually I went foraging on my own. But every once in a while I went with a monk who had a huge appetite. He didn't mind the mushy vegetables and offered to eat what other monks didn't finish, scooping their leftovers into his bowl. When the corn in neighboring fields was ready to harvest, he asked me if I wanted to steal some. He rounded up a few other monks. That night, we ran, bent over to blend in with the low bushes and weeds, to the fields behind the monastery grounds. By the light of the moon we pulled firm yams from the ground and ears of corn off their stalks and brought them to a small clearing behind an empty brick building. We gathered sticks and dry leaves and piled them high. Once the fire was lit, I threw the vegetables in the middle of the flames. As I watched them char, my mouth watered. The skin on the yams crunched, giving way to the sweet orange flesh. I ripped the husk off the corn and peeled as much of the silky strands away before biting into the ear. Juicy corn kernels exploded.

Even as I ate, I felt guilty for disobeying the vows not to steal. I knew I would spend more time in hell than nonmonks because I was supposed to know better. My thoughts had to be more pure than laypeople's because the powerful deities and the high lamas, with their omniscient powers, could read my mind. Luckily, when I turned eight, I moved to the next stage of being a monk, which meant an additional thirty-six vows, but also the chance to go to confession, admit wrongdoings, and be cleansed.

Lama Lhundrup sometimes asked me to lead the confession chant called Sojong. I would clear my throat and, in a high-pitched voice, sing out: CHO OOO CHUNA SHOOKPAY SANGAY DHANG JANCHUP SEMPA THAMCHE DHANG GENDUN TSUNPANAM DAKLA GONSOSOL DAK GETSUL MING DHE THUBTEN WANGCHUK SHIGEWAY . . . ("All you Buddhas and bodhisattvas of the ten directions and the venerable sangha, please pay attention to me. I, who am named Thubten Wangchuk, have created unwholesome actions from the following sections of vows . . .")

Along with the other monks, I recited the vows I had broken. I confessed that I had killed insects and stolen food. It didn't matter if the sins were committed knowingly or not. Before we could be absolved, we had to go in groups of three to a fully ordained monk. The three of us prostrated three more times, squatted with one knee down, and recited some verses. I walked out of confession feeling refreshed and forgiven.

On Sundays and holidays, those monks who could go home did so. Those first few years, from the age of six to about eight, I would go back to the Trinley house, still believing they were my family. Jampa would engage me in debate to see how well I was learning. I would watch the younger Ama la and the others in a game of cards. But gradually I began to sense something. They didn't seem all that happy to see me. No one came to the gate to welcome me. No special welcome-home meals waited. None of the Trinleys said anything about me not being family. They were too kind to say anything directly. But I think they wanted me to know the truth. For my own good, I needed to realize they were simply caregivers.

When I finally came to understand I was not their son, I felt hurt and ashamed that I had been a fool for so long. For years, I had assumed they were my mother and father. They weren't. From that point on, I felt like my weekend and holiday visits would be an imposition. At times, I paused outside the front gate and never went in. If I did stop in to say hello and the older Ama la gave me *khapse,* or fried dough, I felt guilty for eating the family's food. A distance developed. Gradually, I quit going back.

One day, Nepali Mouse asked me if I wanted to go to his house. We didn't have permission, and we took a back way so no one would see us on the road leading up to the monastery. We walked through rice paddies and marshes, and crossed a small river. Neither of us knew whether we were going in the right direction, but we kept on going because we didn't want to go back. After several hours, we finally reached the house where he lived. His parents weren't home. Upstairs, we ate and drank a whole jug of rice wine and passed out drunk. His parents came home and kicked us out, telling us to go back to the monastery. Lama Passang found out. He whipped the tops of our heads with his black electrical cord. Red welts rose. It stung but I refused to cry and give him any satisfaction.

Sometimes I just stayed at the monastery on weekends or walked into Boudhanath, a nearby village with a famous pagoda-like stupa. One particular day, I went to the village with five rupees in my pocket from people who had asked me to pray for them. It was a bright, sunny morning. On a corner of a back alley, I saw a sign for a movie.

Outside, an older Nepalese woman was hunched on a stool.

I asked her what movie was showing.

"English movie. English movie," she said. I paid her five rupees and went inside. The room was dark and filled with cigarette smoke. I found a spot on a straw mat on the dirt floor and sat in a lotus position. I turned to the television screen. A huge image of a penis flickered on it. After a few more minutes, I stood up and walked out.

The old Nepalese woman watched me leave.

"I'm a monk and can't watch that," I explained and asked if I could have my money back. She gave it to me. I used it to buy a plate of buffalo *momos,* a dumpling made of chopped meat, onion, and cilantro. I remember hearing other monks talk about pornographic movies and how terrible they were. Shameless, immoral Americans made them. I was embarrassed to have white skin like them.

On the way back, I passed the stupa. Looking up, I saw the big, four-sided pagoda trimmed in gold and copper and filled with relics. A pair of huge eyes stared out from each side. I was sure they saw me walk into that evil place, and I prayed for mercy.

One road led in and out of the monastery. Monks with nothing better to do would sit on the hillside above and watch to see who was coming and going. They all knew Nun Wongmo because only a handful of nuns ever stayed at the monastery and only one had a son who was a monk. They grasped the connection between the two of us better than I did. Those first years, I knew she was a special person in my life. The Trinley mothers were my Ama las, so she didn't register in my mind as my mother. She was Mummy to me, a special person, who happened to be foreigner, or Inji, as we called them. At the monastery, the lamas and all the monks called her Ani Wongmo, or Nun Wongmo. I started calling her that, too, instead of Mummy.

One day, one of the monks told me that Wongmo was staying in a small house on the far end of the monastery grounds. I was about seven or eight years old and couldn't wait to see her. I imagined that I could stay with her in a nicer house. I could go to my studies and she could go to hers. She used to bring me gifts when she visited me at the Trinleys'. Maybe she had something for me.

She was staying in an area with several buildings reserved for Westerners and off-limits to monks. From their third-floor rooms, the lamas had a clear view of the dirt path that led to the area. So I avoided the path, darting from one bush to another. I wasn't sure where she was, so I crept close to each building and peeked into windows.

Finally I found her. She hugged me and told me to come in. I don't recall what we talked about. It couldn't have been much because I didn't speak English very well and she didn't speak Tibetan very well either. I just felt happy to see her and that we were together. She was typing a letter. I watched, fascinated. I had the hiccups. She showed me how to hold my breath to make them stop. After a while, she sent me back to my classes.

I visited her several times. During one visit, one of the Westerners took a picture of us, sitting cross-legged on the ground, side by side, our hands in our laps. I'm grinning. She's grinning. We're both squinting in the bright sun. I had this curious sense of being both content to be with her and uncomfortable because I knew I wasn't supposed to be there. The conflicting emotions of that moment would come to characterize much of our time together.

During one of her silent retreats in a small brick room on the back of the hill, I went and waited outside her door for her to finish her meditation session and come out. I didn't know she was supposed to be in strict silence and didn't really care. I just wanted to see her. She heard me outside her front door and opened it. She looked surprised and not happy to see me. She didn't say a word and motioned me to go away. I didn't move. "I'm not allowed to talk," she whispered. I left. The next day, I returned and waited.

She opened the door and gestured for me to leave. I walked back across the hillside. Looking down at my feet, I wondered why she didn't want me. I couldn't concentrate on my studies. All through the evening chants, I wondered why. I was confused. She was the only person who ever came to see me. She brought me little gifts. Once, she had a pair of sandals for me. Now she wanted me to go away.

Unbeknownst to me, my mother was under pressure from her lamas not to pay too much attention to me. It would spoil me, her lamas told her. She gave me a watch once and they scolded her gently, saying the other monks would get jealous and that I would become demanding. It was far better to treat me like all the other monks, they said, and not someone special. "That made me a bit colder than I would have been toward you," she said years later. She had to cut off her feelings.

She wished she had explained things better and reassured me that she loved me. It never occurred to her that I always felt like an outsider and couldn't find a place or group of people that made me feel comfortable. Tibetans and Nepalese stared at me because I was white. But then white people stared, too. A white boy monk was an oddity. She was totally at home and thought I would be as well. Maybe, she says, she was too trusting of the monastery and the lamas to make sure I was happy. Since I spoke perfect Tibetan and Nepalese, she thought I would be accepted, not shunned because of the way I looked.

The day after she motioned me to leave, I went back again. I waited and waited. She didn't come out. I knocked on the door and slowly went inside. She wasn't there. Earlier that day, she had gone to a monk who was treating a painful boil on her chin. I looked around her room. A small crystal pyramid prism stood on her altar. I picked it up and turned it around, examining all of its sides and colors. It was pretty and I decided I wanted to keep it. When I turned around, something shiny and red caught my eye on her dresser. I picked it up. It was a Swiss army knife. I had never seen one before and played with the little knife, pulling it out and then sliding it back into place. I walked out of her house with both the prism and knife. I don't recall thinking I had actually stolen something.

My mother immediately noticed the missing items and guessed that I had taken them. She was upset that I would steal from her and told Lama Lhundrup what I had done. He told her to let it go, that I was very young, so it wasn't a big issue. Later I returned the prism on my own, but kept the Swiss army knife. Whether I took the prism and knife because I wanted her attention, I don't know. That was her theory.

When I was about eight, my mother was sent with a few other nuns and monks to live in London for two years to establish a Buddhist center. The day she was leaving, I came to her room and walked with her as far as I could down the hill. I didn't tell her I wanted her to stay or that I would miss her. But she could sense my grief.

"It broke my heart," she told me years later. "But my guru had told me to finally go to the West as a nun to teach and study and help spread the dharma."

I had my room, my studies, and other young monks to live with, she reasoned, and would be fine.

Chapter Five

Girl in a Green Sari

In 1980, at the age of ten, I bought a pair of jeans in the marketplace of Kathmandu where vendors sold goods imported from Singapore and Hong Kong. I had been a monk for four years. Compared to my loose robes, the denim was stiff and uncomfortable. I fumbled with the button, trying to pass it through a small hole, and tugged at the zipper. When I looked down, my legs looked strange, like two blue sticks. The waist felt tight.

I went by myself. My mother was still in London.

The occasion was an upcoming trip to the United States. Lama Lhundrup told me I was going to the United States to meet my great-grandmother Dena for the first, and what turned out to be the last, time. I didn't want to wear robes. Some Americans in retreats at the monastery wore blue jeans. Wanting to make sure I fit in, I was willing to endure a little discomfort to do so.

The trip was filled with one remarkable event after another. I tasted soda pop for the first time, went trick-or-treating, and saw Mickey Mouse. Instead of waking up to hours of memorizing chants and sweeping dirt plots, I splashed in a pool and played with children who had fair skin like me. At night, I slept on a bed with sheets and pillows. I rode in a plane and was awed by the cottony floor of clouds below us and the endless horizon.

As unforgettable as all those adventures were, I experienced something far more memorable. For the first time in my short life, I fit in. People were white. I was the center of attention, and that made me feel good and welcome, not freakish. In the States, I could let down my guard and the vigilance that made me weary. No one told me to run and hide when I saw the police. I could nap without fear of punishment. Family fussed over me, embracing me in a sense of comfort that had eluded me thus far. The trip turned out to be a turning point in my life, opening my eyes to a world and family I never knew existed.

Going to California was Lama Yeshe's idea. My great-grandmother Dena was ill. My mother, who adored Dena, told the lamas about her poor health and asked what to do. Take me to visit her before she dies, Lama Yeshe told her. Ever since she has been a nun, my mother has consulted her lamas about all major decisions, asking them where she should live and whether she should have surgery. She asks them to do a Mo, a Tibetan practice to extract omens, and follows their orders.

If it were up to her, I don't think she would have taken me. I can think of several reasons. She was more concerned with me being a monk and didn't want me to have distractions. The thought of spending time with me made her uncomfortable. I was a child. Having spent the last decade consumed with her studies and teachers, she didn't know how to relate to kids. My being her son didn't make much of a difference.

Then there was the whole American lifestyle, which she thought was amoral. A trip to the United States would expose me to apparent ease and a way of life that she had deliberately kept from me. Our lives would be easier if I thought the only option for me was the one she chose. I wouldn't know enough to question her decision to send me to a monastery. Plus, she felt safer in India and Nepal and England, surrounded by her Buddhist community. The United States frightened her. It represented all the haunting temptations and disappointments in her life. Going back to the childhood home she abandoned meant confronting a painful history that shaped her and, ultimately, me. Whenever I would ask her about her personal life, she would be evasive. As educated as she was, she seemed to believe that ignorance was bliss when it came to her life before becoming a nun. Don't dwell on or cling to the past, she told me again and again. The present is all that matters.

We argued for years about the value of understanding the past. She stubbornly insisted I was living in the past. I stubbornly insisted she was denying it.

❧

The plan was for me to fly by myself to England and meet up with my mother. The two of us would then fly to California. On the plane ride to England, the flight attendant invited me to sit in the cockpit. The kind pilots in their white shirts explained the rows of glowing dials. I couldn't understand a word they said. It didn't matter. Being selected and invited to sit with them in an honored place, while everyone else sat in ordinary seats, was enough.

My mother was in northern England, living in a tiny room at a large, eight-hundred-year-old stone building that looked like a Gothic cathedral. The building had had many incarnations. Once a hospital for the poor, a private home, and a hotel, it was now a Buddhist center. With fancy gardens, vaulted ceilings, and ornate woodwork, it was impressive, formal, and no place for a ten-year-old. Everything about it was imposing, including the people inside. All fairly serious adults, they were consumed with classes and studying. My mother had been there for two years. For fun and diversion, she took long drives in the English countryside, hardly enough to engage a boy.

I had not seen my mother in two years. And before then, our visits had been infrequent and short. As strange as it may sound, we didn't know each other. Understanding someone, knowing her likes and dislikes, her personality, her frailties and sensitivities, requires countless hours together, not just in conversation but in observation. If you watch someone work and play, you can learn about that person's interests and strengths, whether she is determined or defeated. My mother didn't know if I was funny, if I was interested in planes, machines, or the stars, whether I had a way with words or numbers, whether I was meticulous or sloppy. She didn't know what I liked to do for fun. At times, when she would see me make a silly face or imitate a pronounced walk, making people laugh, she would be surprised—pleasantly—that I had a sense of humor. Sharing the day's small victories and defeats creates a bond and trust, as well as a certain level of comfort. That takes time, and my mother had little time for me. She was busy, doing the work her lamas told her to do, traveling to England and Hong Kong.

I had grown since she had seen me. My face was thinner; all the fullness that rounds a little boy's cheeks was gone. Standing next to her, I almost reached her shoulders. The thought of entertaining an energetic and enigmatic boy terrified her. What was she supposed to do with me? I'd be bored. We'd end up staring at each other in awkward silence. She couldn't draw inspiration from her own childhood and pull from that reservoir any fond memories of fun outings with her parents. They hadn't known what to do with her either.

Rather than bore me (in her eyes) or get to know me better (in mine), she enlisted the help of the Redhead family to entertain me. I stayed with them for a few weeks while my mother finished up her classes.

The Redheads had children. The mother, Sue, was a kind and playful woman with long, brown hair and a disarming, gentle face. On warm afternoons, she loaded us up in her Volkswagen Beetle and set off for the community pool. On the way, she turned the steering wheel back and forth, making the car waddle. I sat in the backseat, howling with laughter at each swerve. Cool, clear water glistened in the pool. The bottom was painted sky blue. I inhaled the strong chlorine smell again and again, finding it refreshing. In Nepal, when we wanted to cool off, we splashed in the river with water buffaloes, dodging their floating dung piles. I didn't know how to swim. Mrs. Redhead slipped little red inflatable circles on my arms so I wouldn't sink. They felt tight against my skin, but I liked wearing them. They made me feel special because they were given to me by Mrs. Redhead. She seemed to care about me. When I got water in my ear, she showed me how to bounce on one foot to get it out.

Since no one in the family spoke Tibetan or Nepalese, I was immersed in English. I began picking up certain words and phrases. Please. Thank you. You're welcome. Where are we going? Bedroom, bathroom, kitchen. Delicious. Swimming. I developed a fondness for red and orange pop, delivered by a truck every week, and creamy yogurt.

I saw my mother rarely during those few weeks. She stayed at the cathedral, taking classes and studying.

Finally it was time to leave for the States and visit my great-grandmother Dena. Dena knew about me through my mother's letters. Every so often, I sent my great-grandmother postcards. My mother helped me with the words. "I'm fine. I'm happy. I'm studying." I drew pictures of lotus flowers on them. My mother wanted to assure my great-grandmother and other relatives back home that I was a thriving, well-adjusted monk, not a forlorn little waif, alone, without my parent, in one of the poorest countries of the world.

I had no great expectations of America because I had no concept of it. Knowing only Nepal, where some people lived on patches of dirt on the sides of the road, I could not begin to imagine Beverly Hills with its flower-lined boulevards. The entire landscape looked as if it had been freshly painted the day before I arrived. Whether it was the bright sun or the manicured landscape, the grass looked greener and the flowers more vibrant than in Nepal. Melon-sized purple flowers bloomed on bushes. The streets were clean and smooth as glass. People walked on concrete sidewalks, not dirt paths. Giant hamburgers beckoned from huge billboards. Women wore high heels and men wore crisp white shirts. Children skipped in bright pinks and yellows. Behind shiny storefront windows, mannequins wore gowns and suit coats.

There was something about what I saw that made me feel secure. It was hard to put my finger on it. Structures weren't crumbling. Streets weren't washed out. A sense of order and permanence prevailed. This new place was bountiful. I saw no families sitting shoeless and filthy by the roadside. Nepal, in contrast, felt unstable, random and disheveled.

My great-grandmother lived in a comfortable ranch house. Her street wound gently around small hills. When my mother and I arrived at her house, a small, frail woman came outside, her hair tied up on top of her head. She had a long, narrow nose. Her forehead rippled with creases. She wore bright red lipstick and a sweeping flowered robe. A wide toothy smile spread across her face. She had dimples like my mother.

I might have recognized my great-grandmother if I had kept the batch of photos mailed to me at the monastery. I'm not sure who sent them. I was sick with chickenpox, quarantined in my room when they arrived. Looking through them, I saw a variety of adults, some tall, others short, a few stout, and the rest thin. They wore knee-length dresses or pressed pants and shirts. The hairstyles were twofold: short curls for women, slicked-back for men. The people in the photos weren't doing anything interesting, just standing in yards or sitting in a house, smiling. I wasn't sure what I was supposed to do with the photos. As far as I could tell, only one amusing purpose existed for them. I could tear them up into pieces and see if I could stuff them between the floorboards, which I did.

I never knew I had an aunt and cousins, but they came over to meet me. A few friends of my mother and great-grandmother dropped by. Mainly I sat and listened. I couldn't really engage in too much conversation because my English was weak. One older woman walked funny. I watched, quietly amused. The minute she left the room and was far enough down the hall that I knew she wouldn't see me, I got up and imitated her strange walk. My mother began laughing hysterically. I felt proud that I could make her laugh.

Everyone seemed kind. For once, I could do no wrong. The only time I was reprimanded was when my great-grandmother, my mother, and I were eating dinner in her study, sitting at a low table and watching television. Either my mother or great-grandmother wanted the channel changed. Thinking I was being helpful, I began switching the channels. My agitated great-grandmother, fretting that I was going to break something, told me to sit down. I didn't switch stations after that.

Worried that she couldn't entertain me any better in her native California than in England, my mother arranged to have a

Chinese man pick me up nearly every morning for an outing to a park with swings and a slide. Wanting me to have someone to play with, she took me to the home of a friend who had two young daughters. Both girls had long, wavy brown hair. By then, my hair had grown out a bit, so I didn't look like my head was shaved. The three of us were sent to their room. We sat on the floor. They opened their toy chest and pulled out games, toys, and books, asking what I would like to play. The sturdy colorful boards and little plastic pieces baffled me. Figuring bingo was easiest, they handed me a cardboard square and a bunch of flat blue chips. They explained what I should do if someone said, "B-fifteen." I wanted to play each game and look at every brightly colored picture in the books, but held back because I didn't want to be impolite.

One night while we were there, my mother announced it was Halloween and gave me a white sheet with two jagged peepholes. She helped me put it over my head and adjusted the holes to my eyes. I peered out. Handing me a bag, she explained how Halloween worked. Go to the house next door, ring the bell, and say, "Trick or treat." Outside, children were running up and down the sidewalks wearing masks, strange hats, long gowns, and baggy one-piece outfits that tied in the back. I went up to a house and pushed the doorbell. Watching through two little circles, I saw a woman open the door. "Trick or treat," I said. She dropped a chocolate candy bar in my bag. I didn't ask her for it. I didn't have to pay for it. She didn't even know me. Not only that, but everyone up and down the street did the same. By the end of the evening, my bag was filled with candy I had never seen before. Chocolate bars, Life Savers, brightly colored M&M's. There was hard candy, chewy candy, round discs, and chocolate squares.

I thought Halloween was special, but nothing sharpened the contrast between life in Nepal and life in the United States more completely than Disneyland. Passing through the gates of the Magic Kingdom, with flags waving from staggered pink towers, I felt as if I had entered a place where I was allowed to be the ten-year-old child I was. I darted from one ride to the next, from the flying elephants to a little green convertible I could drive myself. I floated on a narrow boat through a tiny enchanted kingdom where a chorus of high-pitched children sang, "It's a small world." I descended into a submarine, taking my seat beside a porthole, listening as the captain guided us through a lagoon filled with fake giant eels and clams. I climbed the tree that housed the shipwrecked Swiss Family Robinson.

Everywhere I looked, kids were running, laughing, and screaming happily. Parents snapped pictures of them standing with Snow White. I was with my mother, a great-aunt, and cousins. My mother insisted on wearing her robes. People stared at her and us. I tried to ignore it. Maybe people would think she was a performer, I hoped. At least, I looked like the other kids in my jeans and red shirt. My mother insisted I wear red shirts while in the States, red being close to the color of my robes. Someone bought me a Mickey Mouse mask. At lunch, the waitress put my Coke on the table. I put the straw through the opening in the Mickey Mouse face and bobbed my head in a comical way and started drinking, so it looked like Mickey Mouse was enjoying a Coke. Everyone laughed. My mother beamed at me, proud that I was so well behaved and funny. She felt vindicated. It was clear to any relative who questioned her decision to send me to a monastery that I was a well-adjusted boy.

When it was time to go that day, I didn't want to leave. I hadn't gone on every ride and couldn't understand the hurry. Walking out, I looked back at the spinning cars and elevated trains growing smaller, and longed to stay. Around me, I could hear other children begging their parents for one more ride. I wanted to beg along with them, but didn't.

That night, in a warm, soft bed, I wondered why I had been singled out by the deities for such good fortune. The daily funeral processions in Kathmandu, the agonizing memorization, the drudgery of sweeping dirt and mopping filthy floors, the constant hunger, the same food day after day, and the teasing all seemed like another life. Never before had I felt so happy and people been so attentive.

One morning, my mother said we were going to visit my father. With dread, I remembered young monks telling me my father was a crazy man who had to be carried out of the mountain by villagers. I wasn't interested in meeting him.

He lived in a halfway house in Santa Monica and was taking medicine for schizophrenia. My mother knocked at his door. A man answered. He had thick glasses and curly hair and a beard. He opened the door and let us in. I sat down awkwardly on a dirty couch, between my mother in her robes and my father in smelly clothes. His eyes looked a little wild. He strummed on a guitar. After a while, he looked up. "Do you have any money?" he asked my mother.

"No," she told him. I knew she had her maroon sack. There was probably some money in it, but I didn't say a word.

He was quiet. He didn't seem interested in me. I wasn't even sure he knew who I was. I wanted to get away from him, get out of his gloomy room and back to the sunshine and the smell of the ocean. Finally, he mumbled that it was time for us to go. Relieved, I stood up and walked out the door. I didn't even say hello and good-bye to him.

I woke one morning to find my mother packing. She said it was time to go back to Nepal. My heart sank. I wanted to cry, but was afraid of appearing selfish and whiny. Privately, though, I felt betrayed. It almost seemed cruel to have been brought to the United States, shown a wonderful life, and introduced to people who cared about me, only to be whisked away from it. I didn't understand why I had to go back. I belonged here. People liked me. They looked like me and made me feel special.

I never told my mother how I felt. By then, I had fallen into the role of obedient monk and good child. I never challenged or questioned adults, and accepted uncritically whatever they said. From her perspective I was not lonely. Buddhism taught me that all beings were interdependent, so how could I feel alone? Maybe that was a way of rationalizing and reassuring herself that I was not missing a thing.

Telling her I wanted to stay wouldn't have made a difference. Even though she seemed to be enjoying herself, staying in America never occurred to her. Her home was in India and Nepal. Her entire circle of friends, her vocation, and her spiritual, emotional, and intellectual support system were there. In her mind, so, too, was mine. I appeared sweet and funny. I never complained.

How was she to know I felt uncomfortable in my own skin?

My cousin's husband gave me a sleeping bag to take back. I had told them the monk on the floor above peed on me. The sleeping bag would keep me dry. Before we left, my mother took me to Target. I bought a red vest with pockets, buttons, and short sleeves that I would be allowed to wear with my robes. I packed my Halloween candy in a plastic bag. My mother said I should share it with the other monks, which I really did not want to do. It was gone within minutes. The other monks, like me, had never seen so much candy and such variety. While it lasted, I was popular.

From then on, I longed to return to America. It seemed like such a happy place compared to where I was, superficially anyway. Despite the summer heat in Nepal, I wore my red vest from Target as a reminder of my trip. As long as I had it, I was still connected to the United States.

After spending a month in a place that was clean, shiny, and bright, the monastery seemed even drabber. I felt lonelier. The things I had seen, the food I had tasted, and the comfort I had felt were indescribable. What words could I use to convey the bubbling feel and taste of red soda pop or a submarine ride, or sparkling clean? I wanted to tell the other monks how wonderful all those things were and have them understand why, but I couldn't. So I kept it to myself.

While mopping dingy floors and trying to memorize scripture, I thought of the airplane cockpit and fizzy drinks and paper-smooth roads. Taking my daily exam, I wished I were running carefree at Disneyland. At dinner, eating stewed pumpkin prepared in a huge pot for eighty monks, I thought of sitting in my great-grandmother's cozy study, eating a juicy hamburger and watching TV. Going to bed on the wood floor, I thought of the soft mattress. Walking through Kathmandu's market in my robes and sensing heads turning to stare as I passed, I remembered being blissfully unnoticed at restaurants and stores. At the sound of "White Eye," and "Yellow Hair" and "Rotten," tender smiles of people I barely knew flashed by me.

Each pleasant memory was coupled with guilt. Everything I wanted and enjoyed conflicted with the vows I had taken when I was eight years old. At that time, I had promised to avoid maintaining a layperson's lifestyle and all that went with it, nice clothes, rich food, and leisure. I was to avoid all kinds of singing and dancing. I was not to play musical instruments except during ceremonies. In a young monk's life, there was no room for Disneyland or even longing for it.

The lamas, the humble emaciated Buddha, the deity of compassion were all reading my mind and knew I was being childish. Maybe it was good seeing such wonderful things and not being able to have them. The harder the sacrifice, the better person I would be, I told myself. I tried to drown out the questions that kept popping up in my head. Why couldn't I stay where I was wanted and liked? Why go back to a place that was such a struggle for me?

Rather than forget what I saw and the people I met, I found that they took on a new life in my mind. I fantasized about living in their homes. I imagined relatives clustered around me, and playing games with them, having them read to me and treat me to ice cream. I dreamed of them waking me gently in the morning, of sitting at their dinner tables, talking and telling stories, making them laugh. It never occurred to me that I didn't really know these people or what they were like. Altogether, I probably spent less than seventy-two hours with any one of them. The fantasies were really about a sense of belonging rather than a specific cousin or aunt.

Shortly after I returned to the monastery, two people came to see me, an American writer and a photographer. I didn't know what they wanted and was embarrassed at being singled out from all the monks. All day long, they followed me, taking pictures of me doing odd things like taking a shower at the spring and kneading bread dough. They had me sit in the library holding a Tibetan grammar book and stare out a window. They said they were from *People* magazine, which I had never heard of. My well-connected great-grandmother must have contacted the magazine, saying her ten-year-old great-grandson was a Buddhist monk.

Months later, a package arrived in the mail. Inside was the *People* magazine story with the headline "For an American Boy Monk in Nepal, the Path to Buddhism Began in Beverly Hills." I studied the picture of me showering. My face grew hot. I threw it away. I didn't want anyone else to see it and tease me. I couldn't read it anyway. If I could have, I would have discovered my grandfather John Meston was famous, that my parents were Jewish, and that I was related to a well-known woman who had founded Hadassah. I would have known that my great-grandmother Dena paid the $11.53 a month for my room and board, that my mother thought life apart from me was better for us both, and that she didn't think I missed her.

❈

My great-grandmother Dena died two years later, in 1982. After she died, some of the relatives I met on my trip tried to get me back to the States, apparently thinking I would be better off there. I knew nothing of their efforts and assumed all adults thought the monastery was the best place for me and perfectly normal. But apparently, my relatives contacted the U.S. embassy in Nepal and wrote to the head lamas at the Kopan Monastery, trying to determine who had legal custody of me— my mother or the monastery. Turns out, my mother did. They also enlisted the help of a born-again Christian missionary from the States who was in Nepal trying to convert people to Christianity.

She had long blond hair, parted to one side, which fell halfway down her back. She was pretty and had a sweet smile. She tracked me down and invited me to spend a religious holiday in her rented house near the monastery. I had nowhere else to go and was eager to get away from the monastery. She bought me pants and a blue shirt with a Coca-Cola emblem on it and took me swimming in a hotel pool. I spent the afternoon floating dreamily on a blue air mattress. Imitating Westerners, who were lounging on chairs to get a tan, I got a nasty sunburn. We ate at Annapurna, a fancy hotel owned by a relative of the king of Nepal. From what I learned later, the plan was for the missionary essentially to kidnap me and bring me back to the States. Not knowing who she was or why she was interested in me, or her agenda, I was confused. I liked being with her because I ate good food and played in a pool. When the holiday ended, I decided to stay.

As each day with her passed, I became terrified and con-flicted. I was afraid of going back to the monastery because I knew I would be in trouble. But I was also growing more un-comfortable with this strange woman. She invited groups of local Nepalese to her home. I'd sit on the steps leading to the second floor of her house and watch them playing guitars and drums, shouting "Hallelujah" and "Praise the Lord," and jump-ing up and down. At one point, the missionary asked me to talk in Tibetan to an old local woman who was dying. Tell the old woman that if she accepts Jesus as her savior, she will go to heaven. If she doesn't, the old woman will go to hell. Horrified, I turned to the old woman. Speaking in Tibetan, I assured her that everything would be fine and that she had nothing to worry about. Turning to the missionary, I lied and said the old woman had accepted Jesus.

I told the missionary that I wanted to see my mother, who was in India. She arranged the trip. Lama Yeshe was in India at the time and knew that I had been missing. He scolded me. "You're behaving like a big elephant," he told me. Being repri-manded by the highest lama deeply shamed me. I returned to the monastery, vowing to avoid the missionary woman.

The episode caused enough of a stir that my mother wrote to reassure relatives that I was fine. Contacting the embassy set off a chain of distracting calls and letters that she didn't want to repeat. "There is absolutely no reason to worry about him. In fact, he is the luckiest boy in the world," she wrote.

"Just because something is different than what one is expect-ing or used to, doesn't mean that thing is inferior or untrustwor-thy. Often the unconventional is the superior way. Be joyful that he has a basis in nonviolence, honesty, good heart, compas-sion for all beings, profound philosophy, abstinence from all drugs and alcohol. How I wish I had been blessed with such a healthy upbringing."

Lest they doubt her resolve, she added, "The main point is

that he is a monk and that is that. Being a monk, he must live in a monastery or in seclusion."

❄

By the time I was fifteen years old, I was becoming rebellious. I started goofing off and seeing what I could get away with. While visiting India, I snuck off with another monk to watch beautiful Tibetan women singing onstage at the Tibetan Institute of Performing Arts, a famous school for aspiring Tibetan singers and dancers. After, we went off to the woods, scaling over large rocks, through the rhododendron trees overrun by taunting monkeys, and downed a tall bottle of Taj Mahal beer that he bought at a roadside shack and hid in his robes. I slacked off in my studies.

The confidence I had in my mother to know what was best began wavering. She became a source of embarrassment for me for reasons that other kids didn't have to deal with. Nobody else had a mother who shaved her head and wore robes. When she came to the monastery for occasional retreats, she waved and smiled at me. Rudely, I'd look the other way or glance at her with disdain. "What are you doing here?" I demanded saucily in front of other monks. I was curt, offering only yes or no answers to her questions. I didn't want to engage in conversation. I wanted her to leave. It must have hurt her, although I didn't think or care about it at the time. I had declared my independence from her and my own credulous childhood.

My private little mutiny took on other forms. I refused to eat. The noodle soup with pumpkin and turnips stewed together in one big pot became so unappealing that I lost my former voracious appetite. During mealtime, I'd go for walks or stay in my dormitory. Already gangly, I got skinnier and skinnier. My thin arms looked like they might snap. My ribs started to show. Concerned that I might get sick, the lamas made a special exception and told the cooks to give me an egg a day. One of the monk police who liked to pick on me tried to steal it. We tussled for it and rather than let him get it, I threw it as far as I could so neither of us could eat it.

Food was better in the dining room where the Westerners ate. Fresh fruits, vegetables, and desserts were served cafeteria style. Meat was more plentiful. The floors and tables were wiped clean to avoid illness. The special accommodations were made because the Westerners weren't used to our foods and paid extra money to stay at the monastery. Switching to our diet and water would have made them sick. Being American, I decided I would eat there or not eat at all.

Boldly, I went to the Western dining room, took a plate, and piled it high with buffalo meat and fried rice. No one said a word. I ate until I was full. As much as I rationalized eating there, I was never quite sure whether I was entitled to good food. I kept looking around to see if anyone was watching me. I felt like a sneak. The sense that I was somehow undeserving followed me. Being an immigrant no matter where I went, I was always the intruder. In Nepal, I was the American. Later, in America, I was the white Tibetan.

About that time, my mother gave me some money. I bought a tape player and Canon camera, which made me immediately popular. A group of monks crammed into my room. We replayed the same Michael Jackson and American break-dance tapes, snuffed the best of Punjabi tobacco, and looked through old issues of *Time* magazine, one with Madonna on the cover.

Women were a complete mystery to me. As a monk, I was not even supposed to look into the eye of a female for fear it would lead to attachment and suffering. But as a fifteen-year-old boy, I couldn't help noticing the young Nepalese girl.

Every Sunday, she brought her family's laundry tied up in a bundle to the spring at the bottom of the monastery hill. She was a young girl, with long, dark hair, smooth skin, and large eyes. She smiled often when she saw me. For all I knew, she might have smiled at everyone or was just curious about my white skin, but I took her smiles as a sign that she might be interested in me. She lived in a straw-thatched house with her parents and brothers and sisters. They rarely came with her.

One day I was by the spring and saw her walking down the hill. As she came closer, I could hear her singing a local folk song in a sweet, high voice. A glittery brass water jug rested on her hip. A dozen villagers stood in line, waiting their turn at the spring. Knowing it would be a while before she could fill her jug, she sat on a knoll and plucked a blade of grass from the ground. She put it in her mouth and absentmindedly chewed on the end as if dreaming.

When it was her turn, she slowly got up and washed her face, hands, and feet before taking the brass jug and filling it with water. With one smooth motion, she lifted the heavy jug. I watched her turn and leave. Later that day, she returned with a large bamboo basket filled with colorful saris, dhotis, and long, white, beltlike strips of cloth worn around the waist. She set the basket down and began beating the clothes under the water with a wood plank. She rinsed each piece under the cool stream and wrung it with her strong hands. Water dripped sensually down her leg onto the well-worn black stone slabs under the spring.

That week, she came to the monastery with a basket of eggs and clay jugs filled with fresh warm cow's milk to sell. It was a sunny afternoon. When most of the monks were in the temple chanting, I was outside the main square in front of the temple, chopping wood for cooking. I looked up and saw her coming up the road, barefoot. Her light green sari clung to her body. She stopped when she saw me. We stood ten feet apart under a giant pipal tree, its branches growing long and extending out like outstretched arms. I was tall for my age and might have looked older than my fifteen years. I didn't know how old she was. I knew she wasn't married because she didn't wear red dye. Married women dye a red strip down the center of their heads showing they are off-limits.

"*Mua sangai aowni?*" I asked in Nepalese, wanting to know whether she would come with me. I wasn't really thinking where I wanted to go or what I wanted do to. The words came out before I had a chance to come up with a plan. I probably should have asked her name first or made small talk about the eggs in her basket. But I wasn't used to talking to girls and didn't know the polite or right thing to say. Keeping her head down, she said nothing. I continued, politely urging her to come.

"*Eakchin aownus na?* Just come for a moment, will you?" I asked. She looked up. I motioned for her to follow me. We walked in silence. My heart raced with a rush of adrenaline. I glanced around, making sure no one was watching, and walked quickly. Part of me wished she hadn't come that day. I regretted opening my mouth and daring to talk to her in the first place. The other part of me was sky high. I led her to a room belonging to a friend of mine. I knew it was empty. I opened the door for her. The window looked out onto the Green Tara pond and the steps leading up to the main temple. We could hear the chorus of deep guttural chants emanating from the brightly colored temple. She stepped inside. I reached for her arm. Seeing no one inside, only a dark bed, she was startled. She quickly slipped out and left. I never saw her again, but dreamed of her often.

Lama Lhundrup was concerned about me because I clearly didn't care about my studies. One afternoon, shortly after the Nepalese girl incident, he called me up to his room on the top floor of the main temple. Convinced he could read my mind, I was sure he knew I was dreaming about a girl. Frankincense burned in his mud vase. Ancient, holy brocaded paintings hung on his wall. Statues of sacred deities lined his small altar. Pictures of high lamas, draped in white scarves, hung on his walls. Walking through the door was like stepping into a tiny temple. I glanced out the glass window at the Kathmandu valley with its white-domed Boudhanath stupa and the airport runway.

I prostrated to the lama three times before sitting cross-legged on the wool carpet.

He thumbed his well-worn sandalwood rosary, murmured his usual mantras, and delicately asked: "What is going on with you? What kind of problems are you having? Is it with desires? Is it women or something?"

I was not going to lie to him.

"Yes," I answered, embarrassed and relieved at the same time that he was the one who brought it up.

His eyes widened with understanding.

"Oh, let me help you through this."

Before he began his teachings, he asked, "Who is it?"

I said nothing.

He didn't prod me. Instead, he nodded. "I see . . . I see . . . ," he said. "Now imagine the girl."

I closed my eyes tightly. I imagined the milk girl in her green sari walking barefoot.

"Now begin peeling her skin, starting from the head. Think about the bones, the veins, the blood, and all the fatty tissues."

I hesitated. I did not want to go beyond her beautiful skin, but was worried that my teacher, with his clairvoyant powers, would be able to read my mind and know how badly I was be-having.

The lama went silent, too.

I tried to force myself to think of the red flesh and muscle, the blood and skin. I had never seen any human anatomy pic-tures to know what veins and fatty tissue look like, so I just thought of the red insides of animals I had seen sacrificed or raw buffalo meat.

I peeked. He was also sitting in a meditative position with his eyes closed. I quickly closed my eyes again and tried to go back to thinking about the beautiful milk girl in all her guts and gore, but could not.

After ten minutes of this, he looked down at me, gleaming, and asked, "Did it work? Did you come to realize that the girl is just a mass of flesh and bones, that there is nothing really to get so attached to?"

I bowed my head, indicating that I had indeed come to that realization.

To purify me, he guided me through a series of meditative rituals. Envision the deity Chenrezig with his thousand eyes and thousand arms hovering above your head. Visualize the clear white light pouring from the deity, streaming down upon your head. Let the light come through you, washing over your entire body, and ridding your soul of everything negative.

When he was finished, he said, "You are not learning much here. You might do better in a more disciplined environment."

At the time I had no idea what he was referring to and dismissed it as a warning that I had better start studying. In fact, Lama Lhundrup had begun making arrangements for me to be sent away to a much larger monastery around twelve hundred miles away called Sera, in the Indian state of Karnataka. Sera was well respected and known for turning monks into skilled debaters and good teachers. The lamas thought I had a future as a *geshe,* the equivalent of a monk with a doctorate, but that I needed more discipline. Sera would provide that.

Sera was the last place I wanted to go. Monks told stories of the unbearably hot temperatures there. The heat turned food rancid and made people violently ill. The massive grounds themselves were unfriendly and intimidating, rising from a flat field like a small city. Huge prayer halls and study centers towered over the maze of interconnected small sleeping rooms for thousands of monks.

I had become relatively comfortable in Nepal, knew my

way around Kathmandu, and had picked up some tricks to survive at the monastery. I regularly ate in the Western dining room and found chores that freed me from memorizing scriptures.

Sera would mean starting all over again as the new monk, the focus of the same stares and "White Eye" taunts and monkey comments. Even though I was a monk for ten years, I would be relegated to the last row because I was a novice there.

But I had no choice and in 1985 went by bus and train with my new lama to Sera. The living conditions were harder and more brutal than I expected. At the main temple hall, I watched one of the monks who didn't know his lesson get beaten by the teacher. The teacher started hitting the monk with a broom used to clean the floor. After the broom broke, he whipped the monk with his rosary beads, which fell apart. Blood appeared on the monk's face. Sitting on the floor at the end of the line with all the other novice monks, I was terrified.

Dry, hot weather spoiled the water buffalo meat that we were given for lunch. Within days after I arrived, I became ill with dysentery. For the first time in my life, I stood up for myself and decided I was not going to stay. I didn't care if I had to run away on my own in the dark of night. The only problem with my plan was that the lama who was supposed to be watching over me had my citizenship papers. I needed those to cross the border from India back into Nepal.

I knocked on his door. "Come in," he said. I prostrated three times and sat on a carpet in front of his mini wooden throne draped in colorful Chinese brocade.

"I want my papers," I told him.

"What's the matter?" he asked.

"I am not happy here. I have been sick all the time and I have not been able to eat."

"Everyone goes through that, you will get used to it," the lama answered.

"I cannot live here like this. I am too sick and not getting better."

"Why don't you stay on for a while longer?"

"Those papers are mine and I want them back."

I was determined to leave as quickly as I could with or without the papers, and I told him so. There was nothing the lama could say to change my mind.

"What is the hurry? Why don't you wait until I speak to your mother about this?" Beads of sweat covered his forehead. My mother was his financial supporter and benefactor. As her son, I was supposed to have better food, and not be miserable with nausea and diarrhea. If he failed to keep me at Sera, it might jeopardize his financial support. On the other hand, if I got caught crossing the border without papers and jailed, he would be in bigger trouble.

I left him abruptly and went back to my room. I was determined to leave immediately, but needed money to buy train and bus tickets to cross the entire country of India and return to Kathmandu. I looked around and gathered whatever could be sold at the marketplace. Luckily, I had the sleeping bag from the States, a rare find in southern India. By the time I sold that, along with pens, an extra pair of black Chinese kung fu shoes, and a robe of polyester, which was considered fancy fabric, I had enough to buy the tickets. I exchanged a pair of my robes for a pair of gray Indian cotton pants.

Around five that evening, while I was eating noodle soup in the dining room with the other monks, the lama approached me. He lifted his hand to his shirt pocket and took out a tiny blue booklet. His lips stretched in a slight uncomfortable smile as he handed me the booklet. Inside, the fragile citizenship document made of fine rice paper showed a picture of me wearing a traditional Nepalese hat called a *topi*. The hat looked like a small lamp shade.

Later that night, I met up with two streetwise monks known

for goofing off and gambling. They agreed to take me to the train station. The three of us hitched a ride in the trailer of a green farm tractor. Sitting on a burlap sack, I stared back at the sprawling Sera Monastery. Its lights faded as we bumped over the red dirt path, filling me with a mix of relief and anxiety. Relief about getting away and anxiety about making it back and deciding what to do when I returned to Kopan. Enough worrying, I told myself, and joined the happy conversation of the monks with me.

We hopped off the tractor and took a bus to the ancient city of Mysore and then a train to the great south Indian city of Bangalore, arriving just after midnight. The three of us walked through the streets to a shabby hotel and checked in. Women stood outside. I knew they were prostitutes: they wore extra makeup and looked directly at us, rather than averting their glances as other women would. "If you want one, just ask," one of the monks said, half jokingly.

I looked at them. Why not? I had already made up my mind that I didn't want to be a monk any longer. I wanted to leave monastery life for good. If I sleep with a prostitute, I would break my vow of celibacy and be disrobed. My lamas at Kopan would be upset. So would my mother. But they wouldn't be able to do anything about it. This was my chance at automatic expulsion. But the fact is, I was too afraid. The closest I got to sex that night was dreaming about prostitutes.

Early the next morning, loud Indian pop songs about love rattled the thin glasses on the bedroom window. The two monks and I quickly packed up and walked to the Bangalore railway station. Passengers slept on the concrete floor. Coolies in red shirts and turbans hustled by with heavy burlap sacks on their heads, fighting their way through the mob to get sleeper cars. Stray puppies sniffed the platform for crumbs. A crowd of fat black crows huddled over paper sacks. Rats the size of my foot scurried past, dodging sleeping bodies. It reeked. The two monks showed me where to buy a train ticket. I handed over 750 rupees and bought my third-class train ticket to Varanasi, the holy Indian city next to the Ganges River.

I turned to ask the monks a question about where the train was boarding, but they were gone. I saw them in the distance, walking through the metal gates to begin their trip back to Sera. I was alone, ticket in hand, standing by the magazine stand. There was no place to sit. I didn't know where to go. A conductor stood farther down the platform. I walked over to him and began talking. He gave me special treatment, apparently because I looked like a Western tourist, and led me to my third-class section of the train. I put my backpack on the smooth wooden plank, sat next to the iron-barred window, and began reciting mantras, praying that I was on the right train. I asked the middle-aged Indian couple sitting across from me whether the train was going to Varanasi. They assured me it was. They were traveling there, too.

The trip took three days. I developed a huge boil on my right leg and could barely walk. The Indian couple watched out for me. They shared the food and drinks they brought with them. They watched my bags when I went to the bathroom at the end of the coach so no one would take them. If anyone tried to take my seat, they chased them away. At the last stop, they helped me off. I took a rickshaw to the bus station. Waiting there was a bus that would take me to Kathmandu.

I returned to Kopan, dressed in lay clothes, with a sense of shame. I scolded myself for being unable to handle Sera. Maybe I left too soon. Most of the other monks from Kopan had toughed it out. Why couldn't I? I wondered.

Lama Lhundrup wanted to see me and was waiting in a small room off the library, where the librarian slept. I had already decided on the train to lie to him and tell him a story about being seduced by a prostitute. I couldn't just say I didn't want to be a monk anymore. That was too equivocal. I wanted to make sure that I would be automatically disrobed. I rehearsed my words again and again.

He was sitting on the bed. I walked in and sat down. I kept my head down, not wanting to look at him and unsure about how to begin. My stomach was churning. I was embarrassed to even mention the word "prostitute." The fact that it was a lie made me feel even guiltier. I was betraying my loyal teacher.

I described arriving after midnight at the shabby hotel where we stayed and prostitutes milling outside. "I was seduced by a prostitute in Bangalore. I had no choice," I said, feebly trying to make the offense seem less my fault.

"What did you do?" he said.

The room fell silent. I could hear him breathing quietly. My stomach was in knots. I said nothing and kept my head down in remorse and shame.

After a few minutes, he began to speak in his ever gentle manner. "It's OK. You can start a new life. Nothing will happen. You will be OK."

I got up to leave. I was relieved that confrontation was over, but felt terrible for having lied to the one man who was always good to me. I had disappointed him. He once thought I could become a great teacher. I wondered whether I had done the right thing. Others had left the monastery. I knew what monks said about them behind their backs. The same would be said of me, that I was too weak to avoid the lure of lay life. In later years, I have one recurring nightmare. I return to my room at the monastery, trying to be allowed back in. My things are strewn about. I am told to leave. The monks don't want me. I'm frantic because I don't know where to go. I'm not sure what to do. I can't find anyplace to belong.

My departure certain, I wrestled with complicated and conflicting emotions. The monastery, the routines, the chores, the temple, the rituals were the only world I knew. Though I loathed the tedium of rote memorization, there was also an element of familiarity. I knew what to expect and what was expected of me. A discomforting hollowness filled me.

Sixteen years old and officially an ex-monk, I felt obliged to become a member of the lay community, which I assumed required sex. Within days after I had told my concocted story, I walked to a nearby town that had several brothels. I walked up and down the streets, slowing at seedy doorsteps, trying to work up enough courage to go in. After several passes, I left.

My mother, I knew, would be devastated by the news. She was in Delhi when she received my short telegram telling her I was no longer a monk and had been disrobed after being with a prostitute. She had heard from the Kopan and Sera lamas that I had been misbehaving, but had no idea I would abandon the life she chose and thought best for me. In her eyes, we would go through life as a happy, well-educated mother-and-son Buddhist team, sharing the same ideals, religion, beliefs, interests, and gurus.

That ideal shattered, she had to figure out what to do with me. As long as I was in the monastery, she didn't worry about me. She could go about her studies and life. I would go about mine.

Now I would be adrift in a shameless world. Who would watch out for me and make sure I was OK? It never crossed her mind that she could or would be the person to watch over me. For one thing, I wanted to go to the United States. She was terrified of living away from her Buddhist supports. She had not lived in the States for sixteen years. She would have to find another caretaker for me.

As independent as my mother seemed, having chosen such an unconventional life, she had become totally dependent on her lamas to advise her. She asked her lama what to do. He began reciting mantras and prayers and shook two dice in a wood bowl. He looked at the numbers on the dice and read a special scripture passage that helped interpret the numbers. Within minutes, she had her answer. I should be sent to Istituto Lama Tzong Khapa, for now.

It was a Buddhist center operating in an old castle in Italy, affiliated with the Kopan Monastery. Going directly to America would be too great a culture shock, she and her lama decided. I was angry. I thought it was essentially a monastery with a different name. We argued and I lost. I had no money and no choice.

❁

Before my mother could take me to Italy, she had to complete some work in London. There, I celebrated my freedom. I rode a bicycle in a tank top, defiantly ignoring the cold rain, and listening to Madonna's "Like a Virgin" on a little Walkman. When I was hungry, I stopped at vendors and ate fish and chips with vinegar, wrapped in newspaper. I smoked cigarettes and drank pop out of a can. I went to my first nightclub and felt the vibrations of the heavy bass pounding in my chest. I began using silverware. Up until then, I rarely used a fork or knife. We ate with our hands or chopsticks and slurped soup from bowls. I realized I needed better manners in the lay world when a friend of my mother's took us out to dinner. When I was done eating, I picked up the plate and began licking it. After, I looked up and saw his eyes widen.

After about a month in England, we flew to Italy. The center was two hours away from Pisa. I stayed there for a year, picking up some Italian, as well as fashion and grooming tips. My guide to lay life was an ex-monk himself, named Jinpa, who had been at Sera Monastery years earlier and left.

Jinpa was a compact Tibetan with muddy brown skin. He and I lived together in a corner room on the top floor of the castlelike center.

Having lived in a monastery, he knew what I would have learned and not learned. He knew that I never used a comb or had to put together an outfit that matched. He took me to a storeroom filled with donated clothing. He picked out a wool jacket, a tie, and some jeans. He rummaged through the shoes and found a pair of slightly worn Italian leather boots. I tried on different combinations, looked at myself in the mirror. Most of the jackets, shirts, and pants hung loose, but I was still thrilled. He showed me how to tie a tie, which I wore with jeans like American movie stars.

Jinpa, whose mane of thick black hair swept down to his eyes, gave me a black comb. I had been letting my hair grow, and while not long, it could at least be parted. He showed me how to comb the top off to the side, the front sweeping over my forehead. I practiced in front of a mirror, changing my expressions, trying to perfect a cool look, a friendly look, a handsome look, a macho look.

He assumed correctly that I wasn't used to meeting girls and talking with them. He asked his girlfriend to introduce me to her Italian friend, a tall, slim girl with dark hair. He knew better than to send me out on a date alone, so the four of us drank red wine and talked for hours in our room with a loft. My date didn't speak English and I spoke little Italian, but I felt comfortable because Jinpa and his girlfriend were there to help translate.

Back in India, my mother was still hurt and angry. She told me she wouldn't send me much money and that I would have to work to pay for room and board. Her message was clear: if you want to disrobe, you can take care of yourself. She had better ways of spending money than on me, she told me. She was sponsoring a lama's education and her retreat center needed a new jeep.

I felt as if she was punishing me because I didn't want the life she chose for me. It was then that I first detected a flaw in her character. I had disagreed with her in the past, but respected her. The fact that she would support a lama and not support her own son hurt me. I would find out later that my grandfather had cut her out of his will. She was terribly hurt by that. I would have thought she wouldn't want to make me experience the same hurt she suffered. On the one hand, she had told me over the years that she didn't want me to make the same mistakes as she did. On the other hand, she seemed willing to repeat the same mistakes her parents made. I didn't even know at the time that Dena had left money for my care until I was eighteen. At that point, I was seventeen years old.

The first six months, I worked in the kitchen, making pasta and salads. After, I worked with a construction crew, renovating the entire face of the castle. Each day, I took a hammer and chisel and removed old mortar. I hauled bricks and operated a crane. My skinny arms became muscular and my chest thickened. Working shirtless, I grew tan. Some of the local Italians called me Rambo and John Travolta. I didn't take offense. Their tone was complimentary and I had seen Rambo movies in Nepal. I liked the work because I could see tangible results and because I was a hard worker and good at it.

Jinpa asked why I wasn't living in New York City in a tall building. "You're lucky," he said. "You're a U.S. citizen, you could go to school free there."

I never thought of it. The more he and others talked about how they wished they could go to school in the States, the more fortunate I felt and the more I wanted to go.

After I had been at the center about a year, my mother called from Hong Kong and asked how I was doing. "I'm not happy," I told her. "I want to go to the U.S. and get an education. It's free." We both knew I couldn't spend the rest of my life at the center.

Reluctantly, she agreed.

I packed a blue Samsonite suitcase with my belongings—a couple of pairs of jeans and shirts, UB40 tapes, the Swiss army knife I had stolen from my mother, my Tibetan prayer book, and a red plastic Camay soap dish I bought in Dharamsala that had become a good luck charm for me. The day I was to leave, I put on the gray silk suit that Jinpa and I found in the donation closet. The director of the center handed me a letter he had written in English, describing me as a good worker. When you try to get a job, he told me, give them this letter. Feeling a little sad and lonely, I took a bus to Milano, boarded a plane, and took off for Los Angeles.

Chapter Six

The Bullfighter

A woman named Bette Ford was picking me up at the LAX airport.

We had never met. She was the person who said yes when my mother frantically contacted the few remaining friends and relatives in the United States, looking for someone to take me in.

The first time I heard her name was when my mother telephoned me in Italy to let me know who was going to meet me when I landed. "She's your stepgrandmother," my mother said. The word "grandmother" failed to register any endearing emotions or images with me as it might with others who have a grandmother or wish they still did. I felt nothing. I didn't know what a grandmother was. I knew nothing of Bette Ford either. That unfamiliarity didn't bother me. I was used to random people assigned to my care. The Trinleys, the Redheads, the Chinese man in Beverly Hills, the lamas at Kopan, the lamas at Sera.

I wrote her name down on a piece of paper, folded it up, and put it in my wallet. My mother sent Bette my picture so she would know what I looked like and could flag me down. Coming out of Immigration, my suitcase in hand, my gray suit now crumpled, I heard my name being called. I looked over. A woman with abundant, dark brown hair falling in soft curls to her shoulder waved. Holding my picture in her hand, she walked toward me. A tall man with longish blond hair and a square jaw was with her. He must be Scott. My mother mentioned Bette had a friend named Scott. I smiled, relieved that we had connected. They looked nice enough.

Bette was the second of my grandfather John Meston's three wives. Two decades earlier, she had reached out to another rudderless teen—my mother. After she and John married, Bette invited my then fourteen-year-old mother to join them in Europe, to protect her from the despair of my suicidal and alcoholic grandmother, Rosemary. While my grandfather stayed in the room, writing episodes for *Gunsmoke,* Bette and my mother lounged by the hotel pool and beach, shopped, and went to the hair salon. Even when my mother was in college, Bette would call and invite her for dinner.

In retrospect, I must have been an inconvenience. Bette didn't have children. She worked hard establishing her own career, leaving a small steel town in western Pennsylvania in the 1940s for a modeling and acting career in New York City and Hollywood. While on a photo shoot in South America, she fell in love with bullfighting and went on to make history as the first American woman to fight in Plaza Mexico, the largest bullring in the world. She figured she killed four hundred bulls in three countries, Mexico, Panama, and the Philippines, and in the process broke her back once, dislocated both shoulders, and survived several gorings. At the time, I didn't know she fought bulls and I'd never even heard of bullfighting. I never fully appreciated that part of her life until many years later when I saw a Warner Bros. documentary following her from Los Angeles to the bullfighting rings of Mexico.

When I met Bette, she was in her late fifties but looked much younger. She worked out every morning on a stationary bike in the backyard, and dressed stylishly, wearing big belts and necklaces. She walked tall, her sharp chin thrust forward and her back straight. Maintaining good posture was important to her. If I unwittingly slouched, she let me know with a "Stand up straight." Slouching was a sign of weakness. Bette was not a weak woman. She had returned to her acting career and carved out a niche as the free-spirited, lusty older mother in television dramas. Scott, several years younger, sold expensive homes. They lived in a well-maintained, small, single-story stone house on a quiet street in the fashionable suburb of Toluca Lake, California. Every morning they pulled out of their paved driveway at 7 A.M., while the dew was still wet on the grass, and returned at dusk, when Bette would make a gourmet dinner. Their comfortable routine was established. They didn't have to worry about anyone depending on them, let alone a seventeen-year old who couldn't read or write English and was just learning table manners.

Before I arrived, they cleared out a space in their detached garage. Stacks of books, magazines, and boxes were pushed up against the wall, making room for a single bed. Bette showed me around the house and led me to the garage. She gave me fresh sheets and towels and a handheld black-and-white television set with a three-inch screen. Their house was more than fifty feet away. I was glad for the distance. Being in a separate building made me feel less like an intruder. I didn't want to be a burden. Falling asleep that first night in the cozy, warm, private garage, the rhythmic chirp of crickets outside, I thought about my good fortune. I didn't know what was going to happen next. I didn't really care. I was happy to have food and a place to sleep.

❧

The next morning, I woke up, went inside the house, and smelled hot bacon sizzling in a pan. Bette was in the kitchen, cutting fresh melon. Coffee dripped in a thin stream into a glass pot. Scott was in the backyard, sitting at a table under a small umbrella, smoking and reading a newspaper. I sat down. We exchanged "Good morning's." Bette carried a plate of eggs, bacon, and fruit outside and told me to help myself.

I spooned eggs onto a plate and poured a bowl of cereal. Bette handed me a section of the daily newspaper. She and Scott each had their own. I couldn't read and had never held a newspaper. In the monastery, I paged through *Time* magazine and Spider-Man comic books, looking at the pictures but unable to read the words. Even if I could sound out "Los Angeles Dodgers," it wouldn't have meant anything. I wasn't familiar with baseball. "Persian Gulf" was eleven letters strung together. For all I knew, it could have been an exotic flower or animal as well as a place.

Laying the newspaper on the table in front of me, I scanned the words, feigning interest. No one said anything. I tried to pour milk quietly, but it crashed on my toasty flakes. Self-conscious, I chewed slowly, hoping to squelch the crunch. With little to say, I said little. Mainly, I kept my comments to "Thank you" and "Please." After Bette and Scott were done eating, they got ready to leave. If I needed anything, I could call, Bette said. She showed me the phone and gave me her phone numbers. "You OK?"

"Yes. Thank you."

Scott went to sell homes and Bette drove off in her Mercedes to the television studio in nearby Burbank. I had no plans. I simply wanted to explore this new and bountiful place. I had always lived in sprawling structures—the multiroomed two-story Trinley house, two monasteries, and one castle. Their house was small in comparison. Its low ceilings and dark blue walls made it feel cozy and warm. End tables were employed as pedestals, rather than convenient depositories for the day's newspapers. My eyes darted from one tabletop to another. Each was mounted with gracefully curved vases and rocks glistening with shades of purple, green, and brown minerals. Regal bulls with fierce eyes stood in frozen prances on shelves. In the living room, a large, asymmetrically shaped piece of glass rested on a polished oak trunk surrounded by soft black leather sofas and chairs. Posters showing Bette in the bullring hung next to autographed photos of Clint Eastwood. Each was a cherished keepsake of the two loves of her life, bullfighting and acting. A large crucifix hung on the wall above the fireplace. Smaller ones were propped up on the mantelpiece

Though the house was crowded, I got the sense that each statue, rock, and photo had its place. All had been deliberately situated after long consideration of their significance and where they would look best. I kept my hands behind my back so as not to disturb anything. Neatness seemed to matter. Mantels, shelves, counters sparkled. I developed a habit of wiping away any water drips in the bathroom sink after washing my hands.

A string of shiny silver appliances lined the kitchen counter. Although I had worked in kitchens in Nepal and Italy, I had never seen a food processor or a toaster with settings for light and dark. Bette had electric devices that chopped, blended, and toasted. Little handheld devices crushed garlic, sliced cheese into thin strips, and removed an apple core with one swift stroke. Every evening, she prepared elaborate meals, paying attention to details like fresh parsley garnish. Melon was adorned with maraschino cherries. Delighting in variety, she served German food one night and Mexican the next. Courses, a new concept to me, were served in order, salad or soup first, each with a specific spoon or fork. A centerpiece of fresh flowers or candles ruled the middle of the table. A bottle of red or white wine was uncorked, depending on whether chicken or meat was served. I never thought of meals as a showcase, or eating as a formal affair. At the monastery, food was prepared in huge pots and ladled unceremoniously into bowls and slurped at barren tables. Such attention to detail struck me as unnecessarily involved. Americans live complicated lives, I would think to myself when trying to remember which fork or spoon to use.

Out back was a black bicycle-like machine. I had seen Bette riding it that morning. I sat on the seat and began to pedal. The wheel moved quickly, spinning with a quiet whirr. My feet pumped. After about a minute, I stopped. Peddling, going nowhere, and getting tired in the process felt like a waste of time. In Nepal, bicycles were a means of transportation. Most people had to walk several miles to get a jug of water. Getting through the day—finding food, washing clothes, carrying water up hills—required so much physical effort, no one would think of exertion for the sake of exertion.

The sun was shining. I went for a walk. The more houses I passed, the more I noticed that they bore a certain sameness and order. All were light cream or brownstone one-story homes, not ostentatious but tasteful. A few had gates out front. Bushes were uniformly cut and round. The trees, big and leafy, stood about the same height, their tops blending together into one green horizon. Velvety lawns, each the same rich shade of green, spread invariably from one property to another. Streams of water shot up from the grass and arced, crisscrossing the entire yard, and rotating with a steady rat-a-tat. I had never seen a lawn water itself and stopped and stared for several minutes. No matter how many different flowers one house had, all the yards started to look repetitive because nothing was out of place. An unkempt bush would have stood out. Dandelions, if allowed to grow, would have caught my attention. Even the sidewalks consisted of evenly spaced, perfectly square concrete slabs.

On Riverside Drive, the main street, it was much the same. Palm and coconut trees, all roughly one height and shape and equidistant, marched lockstep along the boulevard. Behind glistening windows, bright red, yellow, and orange cotton shirts and dresses hung in their proper sections, according to size and color. Silver necklaces dangled uniformly on racks. Books stood in an even row.

A small diner was serving lunch. I went inside and stood at the counter. A waitress handed me a menu. I scanned the selections, looking for the cheapest item.

"Pardon me. What is this?" I asked the waitress.

"A hot dog," she answered.

I had never heard of a hot dog and assumed it was a canine-based dish. My mother had two Pekingese puppies. I was quite fond of them. Nixing hot dog, I looked further down the menu and saw "hamburger." I ate a hamburger at the Yak & Yeti hotel in Nepal, where they served Western food. I ordered one.

As I walked down the street after lunch, I sensed something was missing in this orderly world. Except for me, the sidewalks were mostly empty. In Italy, village people gathered outside stores and restaurants. It was their meeting place. Their conversations hovered in one collective din in the air. Here it was quiet. I grew self-conscious, aware of the sound of my own footsteps. People drove by, parked their cars, went into a building, and came out, got in their cars, and left. Their car windows remained closed, keeping the cold air in and everything else out. There must have been hundreds of people within those few blocks, tucked inside stores and offices. I felt completely alone.

The neatness and order that impressed me when I was ten now felt regimented and compartmentalized. Everything, it seemed, was locked into its proper place. People had established routines. I was on the outside, looking in. I didn't know how I would break in or whether I would fit. No one looked at me strangely as they did in the East. Unlike in Nepal, where I stood out, on the streets of California I looked like thousands of other teenagers. A seventeen-year-old boy on the thin side, my once-blond hair now dark brown, blue eyes, fair skin, and eyeglasses. Yet I still felt foreign.

※

That feeling of alienation has never left me. I have come to realize that I will always feel like an outsider. No matter where I am or how much time I have lived in a certain place, whether I am so familiar with a city that I can walk the streets blindfolded, I don't feel like a full-fledged member of the citizenry.

When I lived in Nepal, I was an immigrant because I was white. In America, I was an immigrant because my language, demeanor, and worldview were Tibetan. Throw in the Buddhist monk perspective and mind-set, and I was even more an immigrant. Maybe not in the legal sense, since I am a U.S. citizen, but in every other sense of the word. Even though my parents were California born and raised, and my grandfather created an American icon, I knew nothing of American culture, customs, history, or traditions. American idioms and slang were not mine. The country's idols and fads and sports were alien. So were drive-through windows. Receiving a paycheck was a novel concept and so was leisure. A cousin took me for a ride in her boat. I couldn't understand why a person would have a boat if not for work or transportation.

Looking back, I realize that at the time I was like millions of people who are immigrants and share the same struggles of being on the outside looking in. They often find themselves relegated to certain parts of the city and certain occupations, like

domestic workers and landscapers. They sit alone in crowds and
are sent to classrooms for those who don't speak English. Interviewing for a job, we don't know what is too dressy. On ré-
sumés, we underestimate. The stuff of daily life—choosing a
school, paying taxes, getting a work permit, paying bills, or
finding an apartment—are more problematic for people who
don't speak basic English, let alone legal or bureaucratic jargon.

I did have some advantages over many immigrants. My skin
color allowed me to blend in with other Americans. I had people in the United States who were willing to help me. But I
lacked something that many other immigrants seemed to have:
a homeland. I straddled two worlds but belonged to neither. I
imagined that most immigrants have a place they refer to as
home. I would see groups of them gathered around a picnic
table, reminiscing about a common geography and past. They
seemed comfortable being able to swap stories, laugh, and cry
about the place they left, knowing that the others on the
wooden bench probably felt similarly connected. Belonging to
one nation provides an identity. No matter where they went, I
imagined they were anchored somewhere. In the back of my
mind was a constant thought: if I failed here, where would I return to?

Being in two worlds affects everything. When I first arrived
in the United States, I didn't know a red light meant stop and
could barely converse in English. I've accomplished many things
since then in my American world. But the immigrant in me still
feels undeserving. I can't shake the uneasy feeling that my
home, work, degree, and friends can be whisked away without
notice because they were never mine to begin with.

❊

Lying on my bed in the garage, I turned on my little television
set. I flipped through the channels and stopped at one. A white-

haired man in a long black robe was standing behind a big wooden desk. As he sat down, he said in a low voice, "You may be seated."

For the next half hour, I was mesmerized by Judge Wapner and *The People's Court*. This man seemed both wise and powerful. People called him "Your Honor." A hammer rested in his hand. When he slammed it down, everyone in the room hushed. Two people stood in front of him. He listened to their stories and told them what to do. They left and another two people came forward.

I listened intently as they talked about property lines, dented fenders, and barking dogs. Someone had a wrong topping on a pizza. I had no idea what any of that meant or that the squabbles were often petty. In the monastery, we debated less tangible questions, such as how cause, effect, and destiny are wrapped up in karma. After, we went to bed. Nothing changed or happened. But these were real people with real problems, whose lives were changed. Being on television lent it all credence. I felt privileged to have lucked upon significant teachings and studied television with more attention than I did scriptures. Gradually I picked up new words and phrases. "I object." "Your Honor." Overruled." "Fine."

The little television was hard to see, so I decided to watch the large color television set in Bette and Scott's bedroom. I didn't ask their permission and they didn't give it. Feeling somewhat sneaky, I waited until they left the house before going into their room. I passed Bette's open closet and glanced inside. Rows of high heels in red, white, black, yellow, and blue lined the floor. Above them hung dreamy gowns made of chiffon. They were so glamorous and impractical, I figured they must be costumes for her work. I turned on the television set and flipped the channel to *The People' Court*. A soft rich brown bedspread covered their bed. I sat down gingerly on the edge, trying not to wrinkle it. When *The People's Court* was over, I changed the station back to where it had been. I smoothed the bed and left. Doing so never seemed quite right or quite wrong.

Bette and Scott took me out whenever they could. Scott sold big homes to rich people. He was proud of all of his listings, but thought I would get a particular kick out of one house.

"You've got to see this one," he told me one afternoon. The asking price was $2 million, he added. We got into his car and drove several blocks to a sprawling white house with lots of glass windows. Inside, he pointed to a small camera near the ceiling and explained that it was a security camera. He flipped switches on a remote control lighting panel to make the room darker and lighter. Curtains and blinds opened and closed seemingly on their own. Most of what he showed me, I didn't understand. Our voices echoed. The floors squeaked under my shoes. I didn't want to tell him, but I thought the house was ugly and uncomfortable. I couldn't understand who could live in a place like that.

When Bette needed to see her agent, she invited me along for the drive. I would wait in her Mercedes, adjusting the air-conditioning, flipping through radio stations, and watching people. Women in short skirts and shoes with spindly heels walked by. Americans, I began to notice, were heavier. Stomachs bulged over belts cinched too tight.

On one occasion, Bette took a detour on the way home. She turned down one street and pointed to a house with an iron gate at the entrance. She slowed as we approached so I could get a good look at it.

"There's Bob Hope's house," she said, looking through dark sunglasses and nodding toward the house. I could tell his name was one I should have known.

"Who's Bob Hope?" I asked.

Later that summer, just before the school year was about to begin, I heard a knock at the door. I opened the door and saw a heavy-set man with a well-groomed reddish beard. His name was Doren Lee Harper. I recognized him from London. He was the man who took me out to eat the night I licked my plate. I didn't know it at the time, but he was trustee of my great-grandmother Dena's estate. He would become my legal guardian in the States. He also happened to be Buddhist.

Doren invited me to come live with his wife, Mary, and their two daughters, Alicia and Rochelle. With children in junior high, the Harpers were more familiar with the local school systems than Bette and Scott. Plus, their life and routine were more oriented toward kids—homework, driver's education, soccer games, and fast food. The arrangement with Bette and Scott was meant to be temporary anyway. Everyone agreed I should move in with the Harpers.

I was used to the winds shifting and taking me with them. I was too naive to worry about the future or know the obstacles ahead as I tried to fit in academically and socially with American teens. High school was an intimidating and not always welcoming world, especially for someone who was already seventeen and had never sat at a school desk before.

Doren lived in a modest home in Whittier. Compared to Toluca Lake and nearby Burbank, Whittier was a bland, working-class city. Homes had aluminum siding and shingled roofs. People worked in factories and warehouses. Doren's business, West Coast Lockwasher Company, distributed fasteners for nuts and bolts. Mary, a big-boned woman with a pretty smile and large, square glasses, was a secretary. They both put in long hours.

The closest school was La Habra High, a series of buildings and athletic fields connected by blacktopped walkways. A tennis court stretched alongside the student parking lot. Just beyond it were the football field and courts for handball, basketball, and volleyball. Baseball had two fields, one for varsity and one for junior varsity. Softball had a separate field, next to the track. The indoor pool and gym were next to the Senior Park, a grassy area. A dozen rows of long yellow buildings housed classrooms and offices, including one belonging to Robert Shoup, the guidance counselor.

Doren and Mary took me to meet him. A pleasant gray-haired man, Mr. Shoup shook my hand. He walked us past several cubicles to his office, a colorless square room with a desk, covered with papers, and a few chairs. We each took a seat, Mr. Shoup behind his desk and the three of us in front of it.

I presented a dilemma for him. On one hand, I was eager, well-spoken, thoughtful, and calm. Fluent in two languages, Tibetan and Nepalese, I knew a fair amount of English, Hindi, and Italian, and had studied philosophy, debate, and religion.

Yet I had no formal education. At seventeen, I couldn't multiply five times five. The world, as far as I knew, was flat. In the monastery, during the lunar eclipse, I ran outside with the other monks, banging pots and pans to scare away the demon that was eating the moon. We were convinced that the gods had heard our banging and slit the neck of the demon, releasing the half-swallowed moon and restoring it to the black sky. The faint images on the moon's surface were that of a rabbit, not craters and mountains, I always thought.

Mr. Shoup turned to me. "Did you have any math?"

"When a teacher was available," I said. In my lifetime, I probably had a total of four or five weeks' worth of math. I could count to 100 and add double-digit numbers, like 21 plus 32. I was just learning how to subtract when I left the monastery, and never learned to multiply or divide. Mr. Shoup and Doren exchanged glances.

He decided to enroll me as a freshman in classes with other immigrant students. School was already in session, so I would start that week. The morning of my first day of school, Mary packed me a turkey sandwich in a Ziploc bag, a can of soda, and some chips. I put the new notebooks, pencils, pens, and erasers into my black backpack.

Desperately wanting to fit in, I wore acid-faded jeans, a tight short-sleeve shirt, and an imitation black leather *Top Gun* jacket, with round, blue, fake U.S. Navy logos on the front, made famous and popular by Tom Cruise. With the help of a heavy dose of hair spray, I sculpted my bangs perfectly to the left side. Looking in the mirror, I saw a normal American teenager looking back.

I was tall for my age and on the thin side. The construction work in Italy had transformed me from scrawny to lean. After I began playing badminton, I would develop more leg and arm muscles.

I walked into American history for students who spoke English as a second language. Rows of desks faced the blackboard. Everyone was sitting at a desk except me. Up until then, I had always sat on the floor for classes. I saw an empty desk and slid onto the smooth seat. I held my breath, hoping I wasn't in trouble for taking my own seat.

Right after I sat down, everyone stood up and put their right hand over their chest. Looking around, I did the same. Without prompting, they began to recite a pledge. Not knowing the words, I moved my mouth to make it look like I was participating. By this time in my life, after having been dropped into many new situations without knowing the rules, I had become adept at imitating people around me. During the roll call, the teacher called out "Daja Greeneye." I cringed at the odd-sounding last name.

History presented a fundamental problem for me. No one told me it involved past events. I thought the battles in Gettysburg were being waged then and that General Robert E. Lee was at that very moment marching in the fields. When I realized we were studying something that happened over a hundred years ago, I couldn't understand why. At that point in my life, I had no appreciation of how the present is wrapped in the past, whether talking about America's history or my own.

A bell rang. Not sure what that meant, I watched. Doors opened and kids slung their backpacks over their shoulders and filed out of the classrooms. They formed pairs and threesomes and took off along the blacktopped walkways. Watching them, I would see one person break from the group, veering off into one of the dozens of classrooms. Another would merge into the twosome. The flow was uninterrupted.

I was the only one standing still, a piece of wood wedged in the rocks while water ran over me. My eyes darted along the series of classroom doors, looking for room numbers that matched the printout of my schedule. I was disoriented. Was I supposed to turn left, or right? Was math in the first row of buildings, or the second? Worried that I wouldn't get to my class and would be punished, I finally asked someone the way.

I found the math class, but felt more lost once I arrived. The teacher was a bulbous man with a deep voice. His round face was mottled with acne scars. Standing in front of the class, he spoke words I had never heard before. Fractions, denominators. Numerators. The fraction concept, stacking one number on top of another, was inscrutable to me. I sat low in my desk, trying not to be noticed and fearing an unfathomable question coming my way. At the monastery, where learning and punishment went hand in hand, failing to answer correctly meant a beating. I assumed it meant the same here. Fortunately he never called on me. Though totally confused, I didn't know it was OK to ask the teacher for help. At Kopan, teachers taught. There was limited give and take. When the dismissal bell rang, I slipped out of the room as fast as possible.

Mistakenly, I thought physical education class would be easier. It took a single gym class for me, my gym teacher, and my classmates to realize I was not an athlete. The gym teacher looked very physical indeed. I never saw him in pants, only shorts and a short-sleeve shirt that stretched taut over his biceps. He led the class to a baseball diamond. I had never seen a baseball, a bat, or a game. Most of my classmates, on the other hand, had been coached in the rules since they were in what I later learned were called peewee leagues. They had seen the L.A. Dodgers, memorized batting averages, and checked scores each morning in the newspaper. I lined up with the other boys and watched to see what I was supposed to do. One by one, each boy picked up a metal bat and walked over to a white square in the dirt. He stood there, waiting for another boy to throw a small white ball toward him, and then swung the bat at the approaching ball. If he hit it, the ball sailed into the air and landed a hundred feet away in the grass. I watched and listened to the series of thwacks, moving forward as each kid's turn came.

I was next. The boy in front of me handed me the bat. It was lighter and cooler than I expected. I walked over to the white plastic square in the dirt. Everyone watched. Afraid of the ball hitting me, I stood far from the plate and held the bat with my arms straight out as if it were diseased. The boy on the mound tossed the ball slowly to me. I watched it go right past me, swinging well past the appropriate time. The gym teacher came over.

"Hold it like this," he said, showing me how he held the bat behind his head with his arms bent.

"Stand like this," he said, planting his feet close to the plate and about a foot apart. He swung the bat slowly a few times and then handed it over to me. A boy pitched the ball toward me. I missed. Several more attempts were equally unsuccessful. Mercifully, the gym teacher told me I could stop.

I never went back to the baseball field again. I found out I could try other sports to fill my gym requirement. I chose badminton.

I was beginning to feel like school was impossible. No way could I pass, and I was foolish for even trying. Doren enrolled me in a speed reading class to help me read faster. It left me terrified. The teacher moved her finger down the middle of the page, supposedly reading and comprehending each paragraph along the way. I imitated her, my index finger breezing from the top to the bottom of each page, and not comprehending a single passage. I dropped out.

In my second semester, I took a class that gave me hope.

Typing.

I had been enamored of typing ever since I was a small boy and saw my mother seated at a table in the little house on the monastery grounds. In front of her was a typewriter. Her fingers flew from one square key to another. Tiny hammers pounded her paper. "What are you doing?" I asked.

"I'm typing a letter to Dena," she answered. Lines of crisp words marched uniformly down the page. Typing seemed such a singular skill and talent. Now I had the chance to learn the same.

That memory aside, typing appealed to me because I could see and measure my progress. If I typed twenty words a minute one day, the next day I would push myself to type twenty-one. My teacher, a tall, gray-haired man, encouraged me. When I looked down at the keys and my fingers, which I wasn't supposed to do, he reminded me to keep my eyes on the paper. Nothing more. He didn't humiliate or punish me. I began to relax. In America, learning and punishment didn't necessarily go hand in hand. Just being told not to make a mistake, rather than being punished or beaten, was liberating.

Soon I was doing better than the other typing students. I started coming to class early, arriving a half hour before everyone else, to begin my assignment. Content to be alone in the quiet, cool room, I turned on my sleek green electric typewriter. It warmed up, sounding like a small engine idling. I opened my practice book and began typing. The sound of my keys hitting the paper, the bell chiming at the end of the line, and the automatic cartridge zipping across the paper filled the silence. I could finish half of the next assignment before class began.

When I was done with the day's assignment, I'd ask for extra work. My zeal and progress were rewarded. In May, I was named the Business Department's Student of the Month. A school photographer took a picture of me, standing in front of a tree, smiling shyly, and wearing my *Top Gun* jacket. It hung on the school bulletin board for the month of May. Under it read, "Daja Greeneye. May Student of the Month. Business Department." I was worried the other students might be jealous. It was the only recognition or award I received during my year and a half of high school.

Socially, I remained pretty much a zero. No one invited me to their house or a movie. I wasn't bad-looking. I had good teeth and a nice smile. I wasn't overweight and was no longer scrawny. My arms and legs were becoming more muscular. But I was timid. My English was choppy. I struggled to find the right word for what I wanted to say, which led to awkward silences. The only time I initiated conversation was to find my classroom.

In the morning, I boarded the school bus that stopped at the corner of Tigarina Avenue and made my way to the back. Around me, kids threw wads of paper and stuck their feet out to trip whoever was coming down the aisle. I felt old. Their pranks and play seemed childish. At lunch, I sat by myself on a bench or on the ground under a tree. I tried the cafeteria once. Walking in and scanning the huge room filled with tables already occupied by small groups, I turned around and left. I'd rather sit alone outside under a tree, where it wasn't so obvious that I was alone.

Once, when I was eating lunch outside, a group of boys tried to strike up a conversation with me. One of the boys asked where I had gone to school.

"I went to a monastery in Nepal," I said. "I was a monk," trying to keep the explanation short and honest.

"Do you know any kung fu?" another boy asked.

"I don't," I said.

That was all they asked. Spirituality, scriptures, and meditating weren't subjects teenagers wanted to explore. I wanted to forget about them, too. It made me freakish. I was ready to be an American.

That was easier said than done. American teenagers were not like any teens I had ever met. As a seventeen-year-old U.S. citizen, I was technically an American teen. Physically I looked and dressed like one. But I had nothing in common with American teens. They were interested in dating and going to the mall on weekends. They had their own groups. The rich kids hung out with the rich kids, the jocks with the jocks, the band members with the band. There was no group for ex–Buddhist monks fluent in Tibetan who didn't know anything about baseball.

Girls, in particular, intimidated me. They moved as an ensemble, never alone, which made them all the more unapproachable. Their pants were tight and their lipstick bright and glossy. Their fingernails changed colors daily, moving from red to pink to purple. Their hair was remarkable. I had never seen such huge, unnatural curls. Tufts rose from their foreheads and then back down in perfect waves held stiffly in place by a thick coating of hair spray. I couldn't bring myself to begin a conversation. What would I say? "I used to walk barefoot to a marketplace filled with goats, wear robes, and swim with water buffalo. What about you?" Watching them walk by, and overhearing them talk about going to the mall, I told myself I had to find a Tibetan girl.

Once I passed my driver's test, I was finally able to escape the obvious fact that I had no friends. Doren lent me his old red Chevy Monte Carlo. At lunch, while the other students gathered in the cafeteria or courtyard, I drove to Carl's Jr, a fast-food restaurant and home of Happy, the yellow star mascot. At the drive-through window, I ordered a huge hamburger with bacon and cheese. I ate alone in my car, biting into the thick patty and soft bun moist with grease. The freedom of having my own car, coming and going, listening to music on the radio, was exhilarating.

Eventually, I gravitated toward other quiet kids, who more often than not tended to be Asian immigrants. My circle of friends consisted of an Indonesian, a Persian, and two Vietnamese boys. We verged on nerdy, didn't go to the mall or date. Each of us felt outside the mainstream because of our foreign culture. I was luckier than they were because my skin was white. I was tall and looked American. People didn't make racial remarks about me.

My Asian friends worried about grades and already knew what they wanted to study in college. Their worrying rubbed off on me. Up until then, I had been relatively relaxed about what I was going to do with my life. As a monk, I had lived in each moment. The whole concept of preparing for the future never crossed my mind. Hanging around them, it dawned on me that I didn't know what I was going to do and that I was behind.

Rudy Tanuwidjaja, a small, dark-skinned boy from Jakarta, was my best friend. He introduced me to badminton and invited me to play in local tournaments organized by Asian communities. His big glasses dwarfed his flat nose and lips and made him look bug-eyed. He looked younger than he was and had the beginnings of a mustache but not enough to shave. Rudy took life seriously. A math wizard, he wanted to be an engineer. Both of us were without parents. His were in Indonesia. He shared an apartment with his older brother. The brothers invited me to their apartment for dinner, cooking spicy dishes wrapped in banana leaves.

For the most part, I spent my free time with Doren and his family. They had converted their attached garage into a den and laundry room. I slept there. The washing machine and dryer hummed in the closet. Piles of clothes waiting to be washed sat in baskets. The family spent most of the time in the living room, which was dominated by a large-screen TV. A Dodgers fan, Doren watched baseball games on weekends and in between backyard projects. He built brick walls, installed a Jacuzzi, and planted bushes. I pitched in to help. I liked physical labor that produced something. In the monastery, so much of the day was spent in mental exercises, or in work that seemed futile—sweeping dirt plots that were disheveled minutes later, mopping floors that defied cleanliness.

He and Mary worked long hours. When they came home, both were too tired to make big meals. Soon I learned the various forms that American food assumed. Frozen dinners came in Weight Watchers and Stouffer's, takeout in Mexican and Chinese, pizza in thin crust, pan, or traditional. We could pick up, drive through, or tip the delivery boy, go out for soft-serve ice cream in the evening or doughnuts in the morning.

Food was a strange battleground. Mary seemed to be trying to limit and control what was eaten, but ice cream, chips, and frozen TV dinners were ever-present and consumed. I steered clear of the food arguments, hanging out in the den. I didn't understand what all the fuss was about. After spending much of my childhood hungry and scrounging for food, having more than enough seemed like a good thing. Or at least nothing to be ashamed of. I didn't know being heavy was a health concern or social stigma. Illness in Nepal was tied to rotten food or impure water, not to abundance.

In the summer, when I wasn't in school, I went with Doren in his brown van to the fastener company in the nearby city of Industry, California. Inside a huge warehouse, thousands of metal and plastic washers sat in bins, buckets, and boxes. Walking through, he explained that some were used in airplanes and others in jeeps. He showed me the different sizes and shapes and how to sort them according to size. I went to work moving boxes and counting fasteners, setting aside those that didn't belong in a certain bin. When I was done, he tried to pay me.

"No, thank you," I said. He was letting me stay at his house. The Harpers fed me, washed my clothes. Mary's mother, the ever-patient Grandma Orico, tutored me nightly, reviewing multiplication and division at the kitchen table. I had never received money for work. In Italy, I worked for room and board. The same should apply here.

During those half-hour drives to work, I would ask Doren one question after another. I had seen the science show *Nova* on television and was becoming more curious. By then I had learned that the earth was not flat and stationary but round and spinning. "How come we don't fall off the ground? Why don't we feel the spinning motion?" I asked.

Patiently, he answered, talking about gravity.

Each answer led to a new question. What is gravity? How did people get to the moon? How do heavy space shuttles make it that far? I leaped from science to business, asking how people get jobs and buy houses. I wanted to know how the president was elected and the difference between Republican and Democrat. What was Christmas and why do we celebrate the Fourth of July? To have a person willing and able to answer all my questions was almost liberating. I could freely air my ignorance and naïveté.

Doren was a devoted Buddhist. In a small room next to his bedroom, statues of Buddha rested on a small altar. Pictures of the Dalai Lama hung on the wall. Every morning before work, he meditated there. He and other local Buddhists met regularly for prayer sessions with a lama in Los Angeles. He assumed that, being a former monk, I would want to join him. Although it was the last thing I wanted to do, I thought it would be impolite to say no to a man who was gracious enough to give me food and a place to sleep and who answered my endless questions.

Two or three times a month we went to the Buddhist center, which was less a temple and more like a motel with an upstairs balcony. He introduced me to his lama, a small man with shaved head and dark eyebrows, who lived in a room upstairs. Knowing I had been a monk, his lama addressed me in Tibetan and then led us to the main meditation hall, which was a narrow rectangular room downstairs on the street level, next to La Cienega Avenue. He directed me to sit in the front row, a place of honor. A dozen or so people sat behind me. While Doren and the others were deep in prayer, I stewed. Here I was in the United States. I had finally escaped the monastery and drudgery of hours of meditation. Now I was back doing the same thing. Unable and unwilling to muster a single spiritual thought in my head, I waited for Doren to finish so we could leave. Any patience I had once had to sit for hours on the floor was gone.

❖

My mother came to the States for a monthlong stay in the fall of 1987. She was in between studies at a Buddhist center in London and one in Hong Kong. I had not seen her since she'd dropped me off at the center in Italy the year before. Since then, we had kept in touch with infrequent letters and phone calls.

Our relationship was different from Mary's relationship with her daughters. In some ways, I felt ours was better. The daily friction of family life, the little quarrels over what to wear or eat, didn't come between us. I didn't know that daily life also carries subtle moments of closeness and affection.

I wanted to look nice for her and wore a silky blue-and-white shirt, open at the collar. The minute I saw her at the airport, her face lit up and her dimpled smile spread across her face. I had hoped she wouldn't wear her robes, but she did. Her hair was closely cropped. I saw people turn their heads to stare at her and felt their eyes on me, too, when I gave her a hug. The uncomfortable feeling of being a novelty, which I had not felt for months, returned. Mary and Doren took our picture, our arms around each other's waist. I was anxious to get into the car, out of public view.

Aline, who was my great-grandmother's sister, invited us to her home in Pasadena. My mother's few cousins, Bette Ford and Scott, and some of my great-grandmother's friends were there. I sat on the living room couch, which evolved into center stage. One of my mother's cousins teased me about finding a girlfriend. My face grew hot. I couldn't even bring myself to talk to American girls, let alone have one as a girlfriend.

People I never met came up and asked questions.

"How's school?"

"Good," I lied.

"Are you driving?"

"Yes."

"What do you do for fun?"

I didn't have an answer for that. I wasn't sure what I did for fun.

"What do you plan to do?"

"I want to get an education."

"What do you want to do?"

"I want to help people."

I felt like I was making a formal presentation, rather than conversing. Someone handed me a pair of sunglasses, a visor, and a splashy short-sleeved shirt embellished with tiny cars. "Now that you're a kid in California, you have to look the part," a cousin said. I smiled sheepishly and said, "Thanks." I was hoping to fold up the gifts and put them away, but a chorus of "Put them on" erupted. I disappeared into the bathroom. After I dressed, I looked into the mirror and felt like a clown. I walked out and heard a burst of laughter. Cameras flashed. I laughed along with everyone else, not wanting to seem humorless or like a poor sport. I couldn't wait for the afternoon to end.

My mother, on the other hand, was jovial. She laughed hard and often. I was glad when the food arrived on the dining room table because it gave me something to do. My mother helped herself to everything but the silverware. She ate with her hands. I could see her relatives stare. In the monastery and Nepal, I did the same because we didn't have forks and knives. Here, we did. My mother knew how to use silverware. She had been raised with it. Why couldn't she use it here? Her stubbornness bothered me.

I don't think she had a clue as to how embarrassed I was. I didn't confide in her about anything at that point. It would never occur to me to share any fears, worries, or sadness with my mother.

Shortly after the party, my mother told me she didn't like me being teased about having a girlfriend. Girls were bad and impure influences, she told me. The girl issue led to an entire denouncement of my new life. I had made such a mistake leaving the monastery, she said. I had hurt her by rejecting what she thought was best for me. I didn't even realize how good I had it. American education was useless. It led only to materialistic and selfish goals—a job, a nice home on a comfortable street filled with the latest appliances, getting ahead—everything, she said, she had luckily escaped from and tried to protect me from. Her only consolation was seeing how different I was from the other kids. In her eyes, I was more gentle and respectful, which she credited to my Buddhist upbringing.

I didn't know what to say or do. I began to realize that we were on parallel paths, but in opposite directions. I had been surrounded by spirituality from an early age, but didn't have any practical life tools, like the ability to read and write English or multiply numbers. I didn't know what history was or why it mattered, or about the galaxy. I wanted and needed that knowledge. At that point, I had not even begun to comprehend the deeper things missing in my life, like a sense of rootedness that comes from having parents and family.

My mother was on another path. She had all the practical tools, having learned them in school, and was pursuing her spiritual goals. At one point, she had three circles burned into her forehead as part of the ceremony to become fully ordained as a higher-level, Bhikshuni nun. For her, being happy meant being locked inside a retreat house and speaking to no one for more than a year, reciting mantras, studying, and performing breathing exercises.

For a long time, neither of us saw the value in each other's pursuits. I was convinced that everything about my new life was good—technology and comforts in America, being white in a white society—and everything about my former existence as a misfit child monk was bad. She was equally convinced that everything about the United States was worthless and everything in the East was superior.

After staying in America for about a month, she left for Hong Kong and then Nepal, where her lamas would tell her what to do next. Before she left, she read some of her own mother, Rosemary's, diaries that had been left to Aline. "How she suffered and longed for Dena [Rosemary's mother] when she was in those boarding schools in Switzerland. I cried just reading the diaries," my mother said.

❈

While at Doren's, I had an unexpected visitor. Mary called for me. An older man with a graying goatee was sitting on the couch. He got up when I came into the room and introduced himself. He was Albert Greenberg, one of my father's two brothers. I didn't think to ask why his name was Greenberg and my name Greeneye. We visited for a little while. He had a disarming laugh. His dark brown eyes sparkled. With what seemed to be conviction, he said he was delighted to find me. He knew his younger brother, Larry, had a son named Daja, but he didn't know where I was and never thought we would meet. He tracked me down after a local newspaper wrote a story about me with the headline "Teen-Age Buddhist Monk Comes to Mother's Homeland." We went outside in the backyard. Mary took pictures of me standing with him, his arm draped over my shoulders.

A few weeks passed and my Uncle Albert called and invited me to join him and his wife, Charlotte, at their condominium in Santa Monica for a Jewish seder. I didn't know what a seder was, and didn't want to go. Though Uncle Albert was pleasant and a nonthreatening person, I wasn't interested in any connection with my strange father or his family. But I said yes. I didn't want to hurt his feelings and didn't know how to voice mine.

My uncle and Aunt Charlotte, a slim woman with a sharp nose and chin, greeted me in their driveway. We came through the garage, which was divided into two. Their car took up one half. The other side was cluttered with paintings my father had done and tables where Uncle Al sculpted tiny Jewish figures. He pointed to a hard-shelled brown leather suitcase on a shelf in the back of the garage. "That's your parents'," he said. They left it with him before they went to Europe. It was filled with letters and paintings, and pictures of my mother as a young woman and of my father as a boy. There were a few welding tools that my father used to make jewelry, and drawings of sailors in a Japanese bar standing with prostitutes in high heels. My father had sketched them when he was stationed at Yokohama, Japan. I could take what I liked, Uncle Al said. I looked through it, but had no interest in keeping anything inside. It represented family, and family represented unwanted baggage.

During dinner, they asked questions and listened attentively. Aunt Charlotte studied me with soft blue eyes. Uncle Al beamed at me, with what seemed to be pride. I wasn't sure why or what to make of them. I mentioned that Doren was involved with an upcoming visit of the Dalai Lama and that I was going to videotape the event at the Shrine Auditorium. Uncle Al said he would love to go. I had spare tickets. "You can have them," I said. It was a way to return their kindness.

Uncle Al held on to the suitcase, knowing what I didn't at the time. There would be a point in my life, he knew, when the past would matter to me.

❀

I was feeling increasingly old and out of place at the high school. Seventeen, going on eighteen, I was in class with kids who were a few years younger. They goofed off and talked during class, which annoyed me because I couldn't hear the teachers. After three semesters at La Habra, I left and enrolled in Fullerton, a local junior college that accepted students who had not graduated from high school.

My dream then was to become a doctor. I was fascinated by how the body works. I'd sit for hours watching live surgeries on the Discovery Channel. What doctors could do seemed nothing short of miraculous. At bookstores, I paged through anatomy books, studying pictures of muscles and nerves. I took chemistry and began copying my chemistry book, word for word, including formulas and ball-like drawings of molecules bonding together, into my notebook. I thought it would help me understand. But I was lost.

About that time, my mother called. I told her I was struggling. She had been to Boston and thought I should go there because it had good schools and she had friends there. Besides, she didn't like Whittier. It was too low-class, she thought. The California kids seemed spoiled and rude to her.

A month after I turned nineteen, I packed the same blue Samsonite suitcase that carried everything I owned from Italy to the United States. This time I had more clothes and music. I made sure to bring my English grammar and chemistry books, figuring I would need them for college. A relative gave me a copy of the article from *People* magazine that I had thrown away eight years earlier. I tucked that inside my backpack. I grabbed my sleeping bag and headed off to the Los Angeles train station. I didn't want to fly. In no hurry, I wanted to see the countryside.

My maternal great-grandmother, Bernardine Szold Fritz, whose interest in Eastern religion greatly shaped my own mother's life and ultimately mine

The willowy Rosemary Meston, my maternal grandmother, who lost a battle with depression and drinking

My mother as a young girl standing next to her father, John Meston, who gained fame for writing *Gunsmoke*

Dressed as a cowgirl, my mother shares a quiet moment with her mother

My father, Larry, trying on his big brother's Air Force cap after Uncle Al got out of the service.

My father standing with his older sister Rhoda, who was eleven years older and like a mother to him

My hippie parents in their tie-dyed outfits at their wedding reception (Beverly Hills, 1969)

My first few days of life, looking up at my mother (Geneva, Switzerland, 1970)

Me standing
somewhere
in Corfu,
a mophead
two year old

Surrounded by the strong arms of my father before his fragile mind snapped

My parents wearing traditional
Tibetan outfits shortly after they
arrived in Dharamsala, India (1972)

Me as a young boy (1974) standing
with Jampa Trinley, the stern man I
long believed was my father

I looked different from the other Trinley children, but I was never sure why

Happy and proud to be ordained a monk at the age of six and given the new name Thubten Wangchuk

My mother and me, in our robes, stand outside the monastery

Kitchen chores included rolling bread in the monastery kitchen

Memorizing scripture in the morning sun at Kopan Monastery

My white skin stands out in a group photo with the other monks at Kopan

My father and me sitting awkwardly at a small restaurant in Santa Monica one of the first times we met after I had moved to the United States (1988)

Me, Apa, and Phuni

Phuni and Feather on a boat in Mexico, a mariachi band behind them

Receiving my diploma from Brandeis (1996) and still feeling like I didn't deserve it

Uncle Al, Aunt Charlotte, Phuni, and me at my graduation

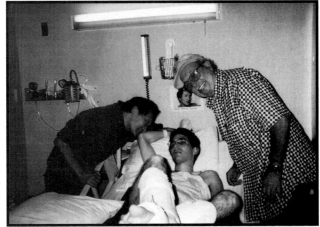

Recuperating in a Boston hospital after my jump to escape Chinese authorities, with Apa and Uncle Al at my side

My mother meeting Phuni for the first time, in 1992

My father, Phuni, and me, years later

Me in Tibet, with the Kunlun Mountains in the background

Chapter Seven

Phuni

Over the next three days, I tried to absorb and commit to memory as much of the American landscape as possible through the window of an Amtrak train. The Rockies gave way to the purple haze of the Painted Desert. Rivers sliced through chiseled orange canyons. Tall ponderosa pines pierced a cloudless blue sky.

I woke early to see the way the sun peeped over hilltops and watched as its setting pinkened the sky. Cities rose before me and then fell behind. Along the way, the train paused at city stations dwarfed by tall buildings and sped past smaller stations on the outskirts of sleepy towns. Looking out at tiny squares of illuminated windows, I imagined what people were doing inside.

Sitting around a dinner table, passing steaming bowls of potatoes from one person to the next. Studying at a desk in the glow
of a small tabletop lamp. Flipping off the light switches and
climbing into bed.

When my legs stiffened, I wandered up and down the aisle
of the train. Dozens of seats were empty. People kept to themselves. Unlike the crowded, dimly light, and noisy trains in
India, this was one quiet, bright, and clean. I talked to no one
other than the person selling pastries in the morning, plastic-
wrapped sandwiches at noon, and pizza at night in the snack car
at the far end of the train.

I arrived at South Station in downtown Boston on Halloween night, 1989. A monk in a plum-colored robe was waiting for me. My mother had arranged for me to stay with
Buddhist monks living in the area. She seemed intent on keeping me in the Buddhist fold whether I wanted that or not. We
took the Green Line subway to his third-floor apartment in
Brighton. Outside in the dark, children wearing plastic masks
dashed between houses, ringing doorbells and waiting, their
outstretched arms holding bags to be filled with candy.

Within days of arriving, it dawned on me that even though
I was in a new city and on a new adventure, in some ways I
hadn't gone anywhere. Local Buddhists gathered at the small
apartment for prayer services. I was asked to translate the Tibetan Buddhist's teachings to small groups of Western students.
Unfortunately for the students, I couldn't understand most of
the Tibetan teacher's big words and concepts. On top of that, I
didn't know enough English to offer a suitable translation. I sat
awkwardly, fumbling for something to say that made sense and
sounded wise. Students stared at me. I wasn't sure whether they
thought I was a fool or brilliant. Once again, I found myself sitting through rituals I thought I had escaped.

I took respite in long walks through the narrow streets of
downtown Boston. It was my first winter. A downy, two-inch

layer of snow rested on bony branches and iron railings. Foot-
prints from boots and Reeboks dimpled the sidewalk. Brighton
is wedged between Boston College and Boston University,
which makes it popular among students who don't want to live
on campus. Walking among them, I felt as if I was in slow motion. They moved with purpose morning, noon, and night, destined for someplace. I was going nowhere other than up and
down the same streets. My mother said there were good schools
out here, but now what? How was I supposed to get into them?

I wrote to her and told her I was having a hard time. I wanted
to go to college, needed advice, and didn't know who could help
me. My mother thought her Buddhists friends in Boston would
help me and was disappointed they didn't. But as she explained,
there was little she could do from India. "You're so far away, but
that's where you want to be. You've chosen to leave me, to leave
the East . . . and I have nothing to do in America." I couldn't help
but notice some bitterness. Knowing that she thought an American education was a waste, I shouldn't have been surprised that
she didn't want to help me get one.

A few months after I arrived, the telephone rang at the
monks' apartment. A woman named Sandy Kaplan was on the
phone. Sandy lived nearby in Newton. Apparently Aline, my
great-grandmother's sister, whom I had met in California, contacted her, telling her about my situation. At the time, I didn't
know that Aline and my mother had exchanged letters while I
was a young monk. In them, Aline questioned my mother's decision to send me to the monastery and my mother defended it.
I can only imagine Aline's conversation with Sandy. "He's a nice
young man, quiet, and well mannered. The poor boy spent
most of his childhood in a monastery in Nepal. . . . Wants desperately to go to college, but is woefully unprepared. . . . Only
two years of formal education. . . . No idea where to start. Right
now, he's stuck living with a couple of Buddhist monks. His
parents aren't any help. His father is mentally ill. His mother is

in Hong Kong or somewhere doing Buddhist retreats. We're the only family he has."

I didn't know Sandy was related, or how. She never mentioned it. Just that Aline called her. Aline, like my great-grandmother, was strong-willed and good at getting people to do things for her.

Sandy was a professional psychologist, who worked both out of her split-level home and at Wellesley College. She picked me up in her jeep and said I could stay in her son's room while he was at Brown University.

If she envisioned an engaging houseguest, I'm sure she was disappointed. Naturally shy, by this time I had developed a strong mistrust of people. I don't think I was even aware of it or could explain why. The seeds of that wariness were probably sown before my memory was even formed, when my parents, who were the center of my life as only they could be to a baby, became remote when I was two. After that—and these are things I do remember—came the Tibetan family. I came to believe they were my real parents and brothers and sisters, only to find out they weren't. Then there was my phantom mother, floating in and out of my life, giving me hope of togetherness one day and dashing it the next. As much as I wanted to count on her, I couldn't. During my trip to the States as a ten-year-old, I thought I finally had found a home and family, only to be taken back to a place I didn't belong.

People seemed interested in me only because I was different. I was a curiosity, like something you pick up off the shelf, examine, admire, put back down, and walk away from. The times I did get close to people, like the Redheads, they were gone before I knew it.

As a result, I had learned as a child not to depend on others to make me feel loved and to love. I had only myself. Buddhist teachings that attachments can lead to suffering only strengthened my resolve to rely only on myself. I didn't realize that was a

distorted view of Buddhism and a convenient rationale for closing myself off to others. I didn't need anyone else, and built a
sturdy wall around myself. I didn't know that relationships
could enhance rather than diminish life. I didn't know life without others was empty.

Sandy let me stay unconditionally and I was grateful for
that. But I also knew I couldn't ask her to take care of me indef-
initely. I was no longer a child. She had her own life and career.
Her son, Jeremy, would be returning and need his room with its
drum set and posters of rock bands taped to the wall.

Another distant relative, David Toby, came forward at Aline's request. David lived in New York City in an elegant apartment
overlooking Central Park West. He called Sandy's house and invited me to spend several days with him. I wasn't aware of the
family connection. He was simply another person parachuting
into my life. I was thrilled. My friends in Italy talked about the
amazing New York and skyscrapers. At one point I thought
New York and the United States were the same, the two names
used interchangeably by my Italian friends in describing the
West. When I landed in Los Angeles two years before, I assumed I was in New York.

The apartment was the most elegant place I had ever seen,
exclusive and private. I felt like I was in another world. Beautiful wood and leather sofas circled large glass-topped tables. Oil
paintings hung on the wall. The floor was black-and-white tile.
Sharp, futuristic stainless steel appliances glistened in the
kitchen. A man in a black suit wearing white gloves had opened
the front door of the building for me. Another man dressed the
same had opened the elevator door for me. He asked what floor
I wanted and pressed the button. Dustin Hoffman lived a few
floors above David. By then I had been to enough movies to

know the names and faces of the popular American actors and actresses. I secretly hoped to meet Hoffman or at least catch a glimpse of him walking in and out of the building.

David had white hair and a deep laugh. He was also an attentive tour guide. He took me to the observatory at the World Trade Center and pointed out Manhattan, the Brooklyn Bridge, and the Statue of Liberty. I took pictures. After, we went to see the aircraft carrier *Intrepid*. I didn't know it, but David had known about me for years. He traveled to the Far East on business and Aline had contacted him when I was still at the monastery in Nepal. Aline wanted his advice on how to bring me back to the States and was behind the missionary-woman incident years earlier.

David had attended Harvard and suggested I apply there. Before I left, he gave me the name and telephone number of Jeffrey Schnitzer, who had an office in Harvard Square. Call him when you get back to Boston, he said.

Within days, I was sitting on a couch in a library in the home of Jeffrey Schnitzer. It was a rich, masculine room with mahogany-colored bookcases and a polished dark wood floor. A small black-and-white cat slipped in and out of the room. Other than the cat, the large house seemed empty.

I was not entirely sure why I was there or what to expect. Schnitzer, a meticulous man in a freshly starched white dress shirt, asked me dozens of questions. He jotted notes in his legal pad, glancing up to study me through his plastic-framed glasses. I appeared to him as slightly reserved but friendly and earnest. He noted that I was tall, right-handed, good-looking. I had clear eyes and skin. I preferred short answers because I had difficulty finding the right word in English to explain myself. At times I would get frustrated when I couldn't express myself, but always persevered. I didn't seem anxious, and if I was, I masked it well. All of this I learned years later, after seeing the report he had compiled.

When he was done, he put down his pen and said I would need to take several tests. Over the course of a cold January and February, I returned for six long sessions, looking at scrambled pictures, trying to solve math problems, and reading passages. No one told me he was trying to figure out whether I was ready for college.

I took the tests in a room adjoining the dining room. Before each test, he offered me a cup of herbal tea. He would sit directly across from me at the table, always in his white shirt. He explained the directions, looked at his watch, and told me to begin. One day I was given a series of disassembled puzzles. I had never put a puzzle together. "When you're young, you play with these here. Not in Nepal. No puzzles," I explained to him. Under his watchful eye, I bent my head down and painstakingly tried to put them together. I managed to complete them all, but lost points for being slow and deliberate. At times I talked out loud, verbally rehearsing what I was about to do. When reading, I used my pencil or finger to follow the words, for fear of missing one. In between tests, I doodled, writing the Buddhist mantra OM— ॐ —over and over again on a scrap of paper. As in high school, math was the hardest. But some basic language tests baffled me, too. "S-ay" and "h-e" were printed on a piece of paper. I was supposed to pronounce them. I couldn't figure them out.

"How many weeks are in a year?" he asked.

"I think something like four times twelve, which is sixty-eight," I responded.

I thought a violin was a guitar and that people used bows to play guitars. Another time, he put out a series of pictures showing a fisherman trying to catch a fish. I couldn't figure out which went first—the fisherman with the fish, or the fisherman without the fish. I finished on a fifth-grade level in some tests and tenth-grade on others. He felt I was very bright. I repeated seven digits forward and five backward without error and could define complex words. But I couldn't fathom a syllable.

After all those sessions, I remained a mystery. He wasn't sure whether I had a diagnosable learning disability or was just socially and culturally challenged. His standardized tests couldn't answer that. "There are no tests designed especially for quasi-educated Americans who have been raised as Buddhist monks in Nepal," he noted in his evaluation. I was, in his words, "a group of one."

I had been that way in the monastery. And it appeared I was destined to be the same in the United States. I myself didn't know where I belonged. I was a citizen but also an immigrant. Intelligent but uneducated.

Being nineteen years old, I was too old to go back to high school to get my diploma. With Sandy's help, I signed up for courses at the adult education center at Brookline High to study for the GED test. On the first day, the instructor gave us a sample test. The next session, when he had the results, he told me I should take the GED test without taking the classes. I took it at Newton North. To my great surprise I got my GED.

In the meantime, I worked briefly packing and shipping books at Wisdom Publications, a Buddhist bookshop and small publishing house run by a former monk who was my mother's friend. The bookshop was tucked away in an older brick building on the corner of Massachusetts Avenue and Newbury Street, a bustling commercial intersection. A trendy clothing store and fancy pub occupied the first floor. Artists painted in lofts and galleries on the second floor. Wisdom occupied the third floor. Much of the space consisted of rows of cubicles where U.S.-born Buddhist monks and nuns wrote and edited books on the teachings of the Dalai Lama. Spines of books were color coded, indicating whether they were for beginner, intermediate, or advanced Buddhists. Those books, along with postcards of sacred temples, were sold in the small bookshop near the front window overlooking Newbury Street.

That winter, a group of monks and their lama from south India came to the States and stopped at Wisdom Publications for a special prayer service. At that point, my entire circle of acquaintances in Boston consisted of Buddhists. I went because everyone I knew was going and I didn't have anything else to do.

The cramped bookshop was crowded with monks, American Buddhists, and members of the small local Tibetan community. A carved wooden throne for the visiting lama rested beneath the window at the far end of the shop. The midafternoon sun cast it in a golden glow. Puffy, round, yellow and orange meditation cushions dotted the floor. The lama made his way through the crowd and took his place on the throne. Conversations stopped. People began assembling in front of the lama, sitting on the floor. Just before the service began, I slipped out. A few monks were standing idly in the hallway. They had heard of me. Apparently, people in the local Buddhist community talked about "this white man who could speak Tibetan." We chatted. I listened for the chants inside to reach a certain point, which signaled that the service was ending, and slipped back inside.

I was standing by myself when a short, round woman with a broad face came up to me. Although she looked half American Indian and half Mayan, I knew she was Tibetan because she wore the brightly colored traditional Tibetan apron. Her name was Sonam, she said. Was I the American who spoke Tibetan? Yes, I was. My name is Wangchuk, I said, giving my Tibetan name. She was here with her sister Phuntsok. Have you met my sister? No, I said. I told her it was nice meeting her and excused myself.

I milled around the bookstore, stepping lightly over the meditation cushions, and walked back out. The touring monks had set up a small table in the hallway to sell incense, holy pictures, scarves, and sweatshirts that said "Peace" in Tibetan. A tiny, delicate woman with a heart-shaped face and long, straight black hair stood behind the table, flanked by two monks. She was animated, helping explain the items to the curious. She wore a beautiful Tibetan chuba with the rainbow-colored apron.

I thought she was stunning. I had to pass the table to leave and paused to talk to the monks. I said hello to the woman. She knew who I was. Her sister, apparently the small, round woman I had met earlier, had pointed me out. She was Phuntsok.

"Where are you staying?" she asked.

"In Newton," I told her. I felt awkward. I was never good at small talk in general and even worse with women. People were trying to maneuver in the narrow hallway around me. Feeling in the way, I started to leave, but she stopped me and asked for my phone number. I wrote it down on a piece of scrap paper, handed it to her, and left.

A few days later, I went to a cookout in Chestnut Hill held in honor of the traveling band of monks. Phuntsok was there. We sat at a picnic table, our feet playfully tapping each other's. I felt comfortable talking with her and used her nickname, Phuni. She was about my age. We were both immigrants and grew up in the same part of the world. Her parents escaped Tibet after the invasion by China in 1959 and settled in a refugee camp in southern India. She was born in a tent. Her mother had died. Her father and the rest of her siblings, aside from her sister Sonam, still lived in the camp. Like me, she had come to the States for schooling. She was living with a local Unitarian minister, who sponsored her trip, and his wife and family.

The week after the picnic, she called and invited me to a house in Concord, where her sister Sonam worked as a live-in babysitter. A few days later, I took her to a Thai restaurant and left my entire dinner untouched. I was so dazzled by her beauty that I forgot to eat. After, we walked to the closest movie theater. I didn't care what was showing. I just wanted to be with her. It happened to be *Glory*, a Civil War movie about a regiment of black soldiers. Black men in blue uniforms carrying rifled muskets, galloping horses, and unfurled flags flashed on the screen. Phuni and I sat in the back, kissing. We became inseparable.

One day she called me on the phone and gave me an abrupt ultimatum: Marry me or we can't see each other. "I'm not interested in just dating," she said.

I was shocked. I was only nineteen and didn't want to get married. I didn't want to lose her either. What's the rush? I asked her. Neither of us had our own place. I wanted to go to college. I didn't have a job. But Phuni was insistent. Marry me or never see me again.

I had no idea whether this was normal. I mentioned the conversation to Sandy. "Think about it carefully," she said.

The only other person I wanted to talk to was my mother. I wanted her advice, but I also wanted to share the excitement of meeting someone I cared about. On an impulse, I decided to surprise her and travel to India. I didn't tell her I was coming because I didn't want to explain why over the phone. Instead, I showed up on her doorstep in Dharamsala. I didn't know what to expect or how she would react to news about my first love. I was nervous. In her mind, girls were temptation and trouble. I knew she was bothered when people teased me about finding a girlfriend. Still, I wanted her blessing.

I told her I had a girlfriend. "I'm thinking of getting married," I said.

Her eyes widened and she looked panicked. "You're way too young. You're only nineteen, Wangchuk," she almost shouted. Leaving the monastery, she felt, was a mistake. Getting married would be a bigger one. "You just got to the States. The whole point was to get an education." I listened quietly and nodded my head. She was right. She made me promise I wouldn't do anything foolish like get married. I promised.

I was actually relieved. In my heart, I didn't want to get married. Not that I didn't love Phuni. It was the concept of marriage itself and my view of it. I had no idea what marriage was about. I grew up with monks. I never saw my own parents as a couple, let alone a happy and loving one. Having lived in a monastery for such a long time and renounced the lay world, its temptations and entanglements, I had a heightened wariness of what others accepted as normal and desirable, including marriage. The cause of all suffering is attachment, be it to things or individuals, I had learned. Marriage is the ultimate attachment. I wanted to live simply, not complicate my life. On the flight back to Boston, I thought of what I would say to Phuni. I'd reason with her, explain that we shouldn't rush into anything. We're happy the way things are. Let's keep it that way, I'd tell her.

After I got back to Boston, I vomited for two weeks and ended up in a hospital emergency room. Doctors suspected I picked up dysentery in India. Phuni was at my side, giving me cool compresses, feeding me ice chips and sips of water. She continued talking about getting married. I offered my arguments against it. We were in a deadlock.

That fall, I enrolled at Becker College, a junior college in Worcester, Massachusetts, that accepted me as an incoming freshman, and moved into a dormitory room with three seniors. Phuni came with me and helped unpack my clothes and make my bed. When she walked out the door, I panicked. That night, I called her five times to reassure myself that she was still there and didn't disappear from my life.

I tried to get along with my roommates and made a fool of myself. One guy was from New York and spoke very fast. He asked where I was from. I started to answer, trying to talk as fast as he did with a New York accent. My words tripped over one another. Hearing the garble coming out of my mouth, I thought, This guy must think I'm an idiot. From then on, I tried to keep my responses to a good-natured "Yeah" and a nod of the head. Every time he laughed, I laughed even though I didn't understand what was so funny. I'm sure he thought I was strange. Interacting with people always felt forced. If I had to choose between spending a day alone in a field or attending a party, I would choose solitude in the field.

My third night at Becker, about ten people came into our room with bottles of vodka and cases of beer. It was close to midnight. I was at my desk, writing. I turned, said "Hello," and went back to my work. I had a test the next day and an 8:30 A.M. class. They sat down on the beds and chairs and started drinking. Cigarette smoke swirled around me. Someone turned up the volume on the radio. As much as I tried to concentrate, all I could think of was, I wonder what they think of me. I wished they would just leave.

I felt like the misfit again. In the dining hall, I sat by myself. I didn't have the guts to start conversations. My accent was foreign. After four years here, I still had a hard time coming up with the right words. Each day, I missed Phuni more. On the phone, she pressed me harder to get married.

Finally, I gave in. It wasn't that we had a breakthrough discussion or that I resolved my internal conflicts. I simply didn't have the energy to fight anymore. I was overwhelmed with school. Plus, I didn't want to lose her.

The day after my twentieth birthday, I found myself reluctantly standing at her side at the minister's house where Phuni was living. I felt trapped. Why couldn't I have refused? Was I afraid that being disagreeable meant I wasn't good? Or would hurt someone's feelings? Did I think being agreeable would make me more lovable? Throughout my life, I had avoided conflict, trying to be as invisible as possible.

I had accepted vows twice before in my life and regretted them. Here I was, vowing my life away again. The Unitarian minister performed the ceremony. Four people came—Phuni's sister Sonam and her friends, an African-American man, his Indian wife, and their child. I didn't know them. That was it. The day lacked celebration. We did nothing to distinguish it or make it memorable, which was fine with me because I didn't want to be there anyway. There was no party, no wedding cake, no bridesmaids or groomsmen. We didn't break a wineglass as in the Jewish tradition. We didn't drink rice wine and wear white scarves as in the Tibetan tradition. No one took pictures to preserve the moment. I moved into the minister's house.

I dreaded the phone call to my mother. She answered and asked how I was doing and how school was going. Good, I said. A long pause followed. I got married, I told her.

Nearly hysterical, she began yelling and sobbing, telling me I had broken my promise to her. I had made a big mistake, she said, and didn't know what I was getting myself into.

Shortly after, I received a long letter from my mother. In it, she begged me to reconsider and annul the marriage. If I didn't, she would cut me off financially. I was on my own.

I felt terrible that I had hurt her. I wrote back and apologized for upsetting her. I tried to explain why I broke my promise. "There is no one around here who is there for me when I am in desperate need. Almost everybody around here seems to be just for themselves and doesn't care about others whatsoever. I did not intend to hurt you or betray your trust in any way. . . . You are the only mother I will ever have in this life. And I will always remember your kindness, no matter what."

Phuni insisted we travel to India so I could meet her family and so she could meet my mother. She booked two rooms at the Sikkim Guest House in New Delhi, in northern India. One was for us. The other was for her father, two brothers, and their wives, who were coming via bus and train from their remote refugee camp in southern India. The trip took them two days. Her father, Apa, was a small, compact man with a thin mustache and a large black birthmark just below his left eye. His skin was very dark and he was thin from working in the fields and biking every day to buy meat at a nearby village. His dark, gentle eyes followed Phuni as she bustled about the room, posing for pictures. He beamed at seeing Phuni look happy.

Her brothers, their wives, and Apa were polite. They referred to me as *makpa,* using a special respectful Tibetan term for a son-in-law. Every time they used the word, my insides cringed. I felt pigeonholed, forced into a role that I was not willing to play. That made me tense. So did the money we were spending. Phuni paid for their trip, their hotel and meals. At the restaurant, she ordered for everyone, sensing they might hold back from getting what they really wanted because of the cost. I knew they couldn't afford it, but neither could we. We were already in debt.

I called my mother, inviting her to join us. She was at her home in Dharamsala, a day's travel. She refused to come. Distance wasn't an issue. She didn't want anything to do with Phuni or her family. Meeting them, she said, would condone the marriage, which she wasn't willing to do under any circumstances.

Soon after Phuni and I got married, I transferred to one of Becker's campuses that was closer to the white wooden farmhouse where we lived with the Unitarian minister. It was in the small rural town in Northborough. A charismatic man, he had met Phuni and her family in their refugee camp in southern India. He offered to bring her back to the States and pay for her education. He showed them school brochures, showing young girls riding bikes. Phuni's parents never went to school. They couldn't even write their own names. With an education, she could escape the refugee life. The minister promised to treat Phuni like his own daughter.

She was sixteen when she arrived in Boston, with a few pieces of clothing and $20. Dressed in Tibetan clothes, she spoke only a few words of English. He took her back to his house and introduced her to his wife and stepdaughter. Phuni lived on the front porch on the first floor.

The house stood by itself on a hill, surrounded by tall, dark trees. It was isolated. We stayed there for several months. The minister's wife and stepdaughter had moved out a few years earlier. I went to classes and helped around the house. Phuni washed the minister's clothes, ironed all his shirts, and cooked his meals. She polished the wood floors to a perfect shine and then fretted that they weren't clean enough. Her chores didn't end there.

The minister watched TV in his overstuffed chair, his feet stretched out in front of him on a footstool. Phuni rubbed cream on his feet and massaged them for hours. I watched a little uncomfortably, but dismissed it as a condition for living there. I noticed she was clingier than before we got married, holding on to my arm as we moved from room to room and climbed the steps. She wrapped her arms around my waist when we stood still. After a while, two of Phuni's cousins from India moved into the minister's house. He was sponsoring their education, too. Word spread that we needed a place to stay to make room for the cousins. Georgia Duquet, a slim older woman with glasses and a greyhound, said she had room in the basement of her condominium in Grafton, a small town just outside of Worcester. She was a member of the minister's congregation. The basement had white walls and concrete floors. It was cold and damp except when the dryer ran.

Phuni started babysitting for a local family. I continued my classes at Becker. My English teacher told us to write an essay about ourselves. "I have changed so much and gone through so many different experiences in so little time that I feel like an old man. These last two years in the U.S. have shocked me and challenged my values more than anything that has happened in my life."

Little did I know the challenges ahead.

❉

Phuni began acting strangely. She grew irritable. She wore a tense frown. Small things set her off. She was obsessed about cleaning, vacuuming, and mopping the already clean floors of a sterile basement. Bedsheets and towels were washed almost daily. Trash cans were emptied before they were even close to full. If I left a piece of paper on a table she had just cleaned, she snapped at me.

We argued about money. Already in debt, she wanted me to take out more loans to send money back to her family via Western Union. Every time she heard someone in the local Tibetan community was going to southern India, she went out and bought clothes and shoes. She packed them in a suitcase and asked the traveler to give it to her father. The arguments grew more tense and frightening. She would start pulling her finger across her forehead. "It is written on my forehead that I should suffer all my life," she yelled. "You can never understand me. I was meant to suffer."

It was eerie. I didn't know what to make of it. She grew violent. In the middle of an argument, she would begin pulling her long dark hair and beating her head with her fists. I tried to hold her hands down, but she thrashed about. She hit her head against the wall and then fell in a heap on the floor. Her eyes were open, but she didn't seem to see anything, as if she were in a trance. I was terrified. I didn't know what was wrong with her. I consciously restrained myself from hitting her to make her stop. Instead, I desperately began hitting myself and banging my head against the wall. By turning my anger and frustration on myself, I hoped she would get concerned and stop whatever she was doing to herself.

Sometimes it worked. Other times, it escalated the tension to the point where each of us grabbed knives, threatening to kill ourselves. I never knew what she might do, whether she would stab herself or run out into the street in front of a car. I wrapped my arms tightly around her. She kicked and screamed. I held on to her until she became exhausted from fighting and collapsed into sobs.

Sleep offered no relief. Nightmares woke her. Someone was after her. "He's chasing me," she cried.

"It's just a bad dream," I told her, holding her heaving body. "Nothing is going to happen to you now."

It was as if she was haunted by some unspeakable demon. I was twenty years old, raised by pacifists. I had never seen anyone out of control and had no idea how to help her or anyone to ask for help. What would I say anyway? My wife is trying to kill herself? Plus I felt responsible. I must have caused her suffering, but I didn't know how. Being unable to console her left me feeling inadequate. I regretted getting married more than ever.

One evening we were driving back to Georgia's house from Phuni's babysitting job. Phuni looked out the window at the passing lights.

"I'm worried about my cousins," she said, quietly and tentatively. I knew she was talking about the ones who came from India and were living with the minister.

"Why?" I asked. She didn't answer directly.

"We have to get them out of there," she said. "He's going to make them suffer, too."

"What are you talking about?" I pressed her.

"We just have to get them out of there."

Once we got home, Phuni went downstairs to the basement. I stayed upstairs. Georgia was there. I mentioned Phuni's concern about her cousins to Georgia. She looked grave and concerned. Instinctively, she seemed to pick up on something. It made me worry. She asked if Phuni would talk to her. I walked down the steps, feeling increasingly anxious. Upstairs, Georgia was on the phone calling a few parishioners.

Before I knew it, a handful of people were at Georgia's house. Phuni was in tears. The parishioners talked among themselves and to us. In order to protect the cousins, we had to go to the police, they said. Phuni and I agreed, not knowing what to expect.

The police station was a blur. People talking to Phuni. Phuni crying. Me at her side, trying to understand what was going on, hearing terms I had never heard before—rape, assault,

battery. Before we left, charges of rape, unnatural rape, and indecent assault and battery were filed against the minister. I
didn't know what they meant or what Phuni had actually en-
dured. The only thing I understood was that this man was bad,
that Phuni had suffered, and that we had to get the cousins out.

Phuni couldn't bring herself to tell me details. Not only was
it too painful to reconstruct, but she was ashamed and afraid
that I would turn against her or think less of her. All she would
say was that he made her suffer.

I didn't want to press her further because she was so fragile.
She woke in tears and cried throughout the day. We referred to
what happened only as "suffering." I never used his name, referring only to "him" or "the monster." Couching it in vague terms
somehow helped create a distance with what happened. I
wouldn't know the full extent of her suffering and its impact on
her until years later.

Phuni had been the minister's slave. He made her cook and
clean for him and massage his feet. Then he raped her. For five
years, she felt invisible and helpless. Alone and secluded in a
wooded area, she was unable to speak English and eleven thousand miles from her home. He threatened her. Mention this to
anyone, the minister told her, and her family in India would go
to jail and she would go to prison. She didn't know she could
call the police or that he was lying about prison. She didn't
know about the world. Up until that time, she had never been
away from her refugee camp. Besides, no one would believe her,
he told her. She was a nobody. He was a respected local minister
with two white steeple-topped churches. He had been a local
town official. Parishioners and members of the community
thought he was a kind soul helping a poor refugee girl.

The day I met Phuni, she latched on to me. She saw me as
her savior, the ticket out of that house. Only then did I understand her adamancy about getting married.

The following months were a nightmare. The case divided

the congregation. No one wanted to believe that something so ugly could go undetected for so long. Some parishioners believed the minister and supported him, saying Phuni was lying. Some in the local Tibetan community turned against us. We shouldn't have gone to the police, they said. We were giving Tibetans a bad name. No one would want to sponsor young Tibetans in the United States anymore. Phuni should be grateful the minister brought her here.

I called my mother. She wrote back, saying she consulted her lama and that we shouldn't prosecute the minister. Doing so probably wouldn't stop him anyway. Plus, sending him to jail would create bad karma for us. The Buddhist approach, she said, would be to talk to him and try to help him see how his actions are harmful to himself and others. The case was proof to her that I never should have married.

As I read her letter, I was both hurt and angry. I know the Dalai Lama teaches us to cultivate compassion for all humans. But I was her son. My wife had suffered for years. If we didn't stop that man, he would abuse others. I turned to her for support and she offered none. No consoling words. No emotional response. No practical help. Any respect I had for her judgments withered.

People who supported Phuni and me but barely knew us helped us find an attorney. One sympathetic couple invited Phuni and me to live in their Boston apartment on the wharf. We were both consumed with anxiety. The nightmares continued. Each morning I woke in dread of the day. I was incapable of being everything Phuni needed. I had taken a semester off from Becker and was working at Venus Seafood on the wharf, making salads. I was trying to understand the legal process, make some money, deal with my own feelings about what happened, and be supportive to my wife. I couldn't do it all.

We called her father in India, saying vaguely that we were having a hard time and needed him to come. He did, gladly, and in doing so lifted some of the burden from me. My wife had her beloved father to depend on. Apa stayed with us in the apartment. Since he had no money to offer the couple who sheltered us, he began carving special prayer stones with a hammer and a chisel to give as a gift. I knew it was painful for him. He had severe arthritis in his right wrist from carving hundreds of those stones as special offerings after his wife died of cancer. He wanted to contribute something, anything, for his room and board. After he arrived, we explained to him in Tibetan that the minister who brought Phuni to the States was a monster and that he had lied to the family about wanting to bring her back for an education. We had to go to a courtroom, we told Apa, to prevent the minister from hurting others.

The three-day trial followed at Worcester Superior Court. It's an imposing building with huge, fluted pillars out front. For most of the trial, I sat on a wooden bench just outside the courtroom doors because I was a witness. I was allowed in only when they needed me to testify and for sentencing. Newspaper reporters from the *Boston Globe* and the *Telegram & Gazette* slipped in and out of the courtroom. Stories appeared in local newspapers. "Woman says minister abused her for years." While I sat outside, Phuni described how the minister came into her room and covered her mouth so she couldn't be heard. Other times, he tied her arms to a bedpost. She lay in bed, terrified, dreading the sound of his footsteps on the creaking wooden steps.

Every day, Apa sat in the courtroom, not understanding what his daughter and others were saying. He was there because his daughter needed him close to her. The simple act of being present registered deep within me. I would pull out those images and memories later, and examine them. I saw how important his presence and tender support were. The selfless act of sitting there, day after day, for no other reason than his daughter wanting him at her side, was what being a parent was all about.

If Apa was privately worried or distraught at his daughter's suffering, he never showed it. He was the father. She needed him to be strong and he took that responsibility seriously. He held her hand. He told her he loved her and that he would be there for her. He urged us to be strong, whispering in Tibetan, "Grow a bone in your heart," meaning, "Be tough." He was a nomad, having been exiled from his homeland and forced to survive by his wits. In the refugee camp in India, he delivered his children in their tent. He rummaged through the Dumpsters of the Indian army to find enough food for the family to live on. The only other way he could provide for his family was to resell buffalo meat. Rising at 4 A.M., he rode his bicycle for two miles to a nearby village, where he bought meat. He lugged it back on his bike and sold it to neighbors.

His presence in Boston gave Phuni strength. She insisted we maintain our dignity. I didn't care how I looked, whether my clothes were ironed or not. She did. One morning I didn't shave. She insisted we stop at a drugstore near the courthouse to buy a disposable razor. I argued with her, saying it didn't matter. She was adamant that neither of us would sacrifice the dignity the minister had tried to strip from her for five years. I didn't recognize her resilience and character then. Here she was, having to testify and relive the nightmares, endure the taunts and vicious stares of people who didn't believe her. Yet she wanted to make sure I was clean-shaven so we didn't look defeated.

When the verdict was reached, I was allowed in the courtroom. I sat next to Apa and glanced over at the jury of seven men and five women sitting under stately portraits of judges and governors. The minister was found guilty on two counts of rape, two counts of unnatural rape, and two counts of indecent assault and battery. I wasn't happy or joyful. I was relieved it was over.

He received a ten-to-twenty-year jail sentence and served four years in prison. His passport was taken away for ten years, while he was on probation. Apa returned to India.

Chapter Eight

Brandeis

*O*ur first home, where we paid rent and weren't guests in someone else's house, was a room on the second floor of a large brick building in a leafy section of Newton. A sign made of wood and painted red with the words "Walker Center" in gold was planted in the little garden of white flowers out front, establishing our building as part of a collection, including a 140-year-old mansion, named after a missionary woman whose last name was Walker. A century earlier, she turned her family estate into a home for children. Over the years, missionaries retired there, gathering on benches in the shade of trees. Theology students from around the world made it their temporary home while going to school.

It was a pleasant space, small and square, with tiny flowered wallpaper and a green carpet. Our single window looked out onto the parking lot, where I parked our bright red Plymouth Sundance. It had belonged to Dena's sister Aline. After she died, her granddaughter offered it to us. We flew out to Los Angeles and drove it back, stopping to see the sights I didn't see on the train, like the Grand Canyon and the Petrified Forest.

I set up my desk and lamp on one side of the window. On the other, a color TV dwarfed a small table we found in the basement of the building where students left what they didn't want to take with them. A tower of portable kitchen appliances, consisting of a waist-high refrigerator topped by a boxy microwave and crowned with a toaster oven, stood in the corner. We stored two pots, plates, and spoons in a cabinet in the hallway. If we needed a stove, we used the communal kitchen on the first floor, where simmering soups, curries, and stir fries from the Far East, Africa, and Europe blended into one aromatic ethnic stew. Lacking a table and chairs, we ate our meals sitting cross-legged on the floor. A bed took up most of the other wall. We shared a bathroom with the person living on the other side of the bathroom. It wasn't much, but it was the first time we weren't boarders.

A framed photograph of Apa, Phuni, and me hung above our bed. We had it taken at Woolworth's in downtown Boston when Apa came to stay with us for the court case. The family portrait was Phuni's idea. I resisted. The monk in me preferred to live simply without a lot of material things. I gave in. With all the turmoil she was going through, Phuni needed to celebrate and honor what was important in her life—her tiny family circle of her father and me—but I did not understand that at the time. By now, I had learned that when Phuni set her mind to something, there was no changing it. Her tiny, five-foot-tall, ninety-five-pound frame, engaging smile, and dimples belied a fierce determination. I butted up against it many times over the years. Her resolve frustrated me at first, but I came to admire it. Without it, I'm not sure either of us would have gotten through the trial and its aftermath.

She picked outfits and insisted we wear them for the picture. A blue-and-white button-down shirt for Apa. A green shirt, tie, and blue suit jacket for me. A flowered dress with red trim for herself. Apa wore a brown fedora, pulled down to the middle of his forehead. Whenever there is a special event, Apa wears a hat. Hats lend dignity to the occasion. To him, it's the proper thing to do. I've often thought that exiled nomads like Apa, who had their very homeland taken from them, uphold what can't be snatched away, like pride and dignity. In the picture, he is grinning so wide that his tiny cheeks puff out like those of a cartoon mouse.

Though we shared a tiny physical space and were trying to make a life together, I found myself often withdrawing into my own separate world, struggling privately with doubts about what to do with my life. The court case left us drained and joyless and me resentful. I never wanted to get married in the first place. Privately, I blamed the whole ordeal on being married and Phuni. Phuni was still traumatized, and often distraught and tearful. Neither of us slept well. Nightmares woke her. In turn, she woke me because she was frightened. I didn't want to hear about her dreams because I didn't know what to say. I just wanted to sleep. Apa stayed for only a month and had to return to the refugee camp. He was no longer there to deflect and absorb tension and offer a calming, peaceful presence. We were in debt and lived on credit cards. I had taken out loans to pay the $12,000 yearly tuition for Becker. Phuni continued to send her family money, insisting we had more than they did. Rent was $450 a month. Relations with my mother deteriorated. She didn't like Phuni and said I had grown distant, angry, and uncommunicative. Her letters and phone calls left me so despondent at times I wished she wouldn't bother staying in touch.

Phuni desperately wanted to have a baby, thinking it would help put the past behind us and provide some normalcy to our lives. Family was the most important thing to her. Tibetan women married and had children. Knowing no other role, she expected she would do the same. Relatives hounded us, asking why we didn't have children. Deep down, she worried that maybe she couldn't conceive because of the abuse. When she saw a beautiful baby in a stroller, or met a friend on the street with small children at her side, she would say, "Aren't they beautiful?" or, "You would be such a great father."

On this issue, I wouldn't budge. I refused. This was the one area I was more adamant about than she. I wanted to go back to school. We didn't have money, a house, or stable jobs. I was mowing lawns, trimming hedges, and raking leaves with a landscaping company. It was noisy, dirty work. The lifeless drone of blowers and mowers rang in my ears for eight hours. Pieces of dried-up leaves and grass clung to my hair and clothes. A thin layer of dirt coated my face and neck. I kept to myself, wondering why I was wasting my time doing something I didn't like, madly rushing to cram in as many yards as we could while the day still had sunlight, yet frustrated because I didn't know what else I could be doing. At lunch break, in between bites of white bread sandwiches, the other guys in the crew talked about women, drinking, baseball, and football. I'd arrive home. Phuni would be at the window searching for my car to pull into the parking lot. Dinner was waiting. Rather than feel grateful and loved, I felt suffocated. She was afraid to leave our apartment for months, leaving a reluctant me her only companion. Eventually, she ventured out and got a job down the street at Bruegger's Bagels, making coffee and smearing cream cheese on bagels for eight hours a day. Ones that were too old to sell, she brought home for us.

Those reasons against having children were all true. But I was also afraid. Nearly every memory of my mother and father

was braided with pain, longing, and confusion. I was emotionally unavailable to everyone around me. My wife. My mother.
The few relatives I met. I didn't know if I was capable of being
available to anyone, even my own child. The walls I had built
around myself were formidable. Being distant and withdrawn,
how could I give a child the confidence, love, and comfort that
I longed for myself growing up? I didn't want my child to go
through life unsure of my affection and questioning his worth.
Doing so would continue the legacy of hurt that had been
handed down from one generation to the next.

Growing up as a monk, I looked at family and children as
obstacles to a spiritual life. They sap you and meddle and make
you unhappy. With them, you can't possibly live a simple, soli-
tary life. Attachments only cause suffering. Phuni and I couldn't
have been at greater odds. We came from irreconcilable views.
She came from a strongly knit, tightly bonded family.

I couldn't imagine myself as a father.

Looking out the window of an MBTA commuter train, I saw
wide green bushes trimmed in the shape of letters, spelling out
B-R-A-N-D-E-I-S. Students in shorts and T-shirts played soccer
in a green field. The campus rose and dipped over manicured
hills traversed by tree-lined paths. I didn't see Budweiser beer
cans strewn about as I did at Becker. An admiring spectator, I
saw it as a place for others. At some point, I told myself, I need
to get back to school. The immigrant in me believed firmly in
the power and worth of a college degree.

Brandeis was a ten-minute drive away. I probably wouldn't
have gone over there if it weren't for Phuni. Besides being insistent, she had this unwavering faith in my abilities. Where I saw
only obstacles, she saw opportunity. Whenever I asked, "Why
bother?" she said, "Why not? You have nothing to lose." I envied

that confidence. Once I asked her where or how she got it, especially having grown up with nothing. Her nomadic family had no home or belongings. No one in her family had distinguished themselves. Her parents never learned to read or write. She couldn't give me a specific milestone or event that gave her confidence and doesn't remember them sitting her down to teach her things. Instead, she learned by example, the way they lived their daily lives.

Their life was harsh, the demands unrelenting. There was no room for error, no extravagance, and no day off. When the sun rose, they had to find food for that day. Nothing went to waste. Pieces of worn clothing were used to make tents. Hardened animal dung was heated to keep them warm. Her parents befriended others, offering to share their own meager resources because it was the right thing to do and they might need a new friend's help someday. In that way, though fiercely independent, they recognized their interdependence. Phuni is like that, too. Whenever she could help, she would. You don't squirrel away for the future.

Growing up as she did with little but the clothes on her back and a few animals, family became her universe. As she talked about a brother giving her the coat off his back if she was cold, her father delivering his children in their tent, her mother nursing their wounds, she painted a gossamer picture of warmth and security. Despite being forced from their homeland, her parents weren't defeated by their lives or circumstances. Song, dance, and celebration were as much a part of the rhythm of the day as scrounging for food. She never remembers them being bitter about what they didn't have, only grateful for what they did. Their example of strength and confidence seeped by osmosis into Phuni. As significant as that example was, more important was the sense of security they instilled by being there for her when she came in from playing, woke in the morning, and went to bed at night.

Phuni suggested we drive over to Brandeis University one afternoon. The driveway leading up to the admissions office passed a stone castle that had been converted into dormitory space. Its thick stone walls and turrets made the university seem all the more unavailable. Students with backpacks crossed the campus. I was twenty-three but felt much older. "If they can do it, so can you," Phuni said, looking out the window at them. The admissions office was in Kutz, a nondescript, practical brick building. It wasn't imposing but it wasn't inviting either. We walked up a set of steps and opened the door to an unexpected smell of fresh-baked cookies. I looked at tabletops, expecting to see a plateful, but never did.

On the wall of the admissions office hung a painting (called a *thangka*) of a Buddhist deity surrounded by lotus flowers. We had one in our room at the Walker Center. I saw it the minute we walked in. So did Phuni. We looked at each other. You don't often see *thangkas* in Boston unless you are in a Tibetan home. Jampa Trinley had several. So did the monastery. Seeing one unexpectedly in the admissions office of a liberal arts college in the white, working-class, old mill town of Waltham, Massachusetts, seemed like a good omen and made the place a little less alien.

A pleasant and pudgy brunette receptionist greeted us and asked if she could help. Too embarrassed to say anything, I let Phuni do the talking and went straight to the back of the office, where brochures were displayed. Glancing through them, I picked up one or two. I could hear Phuni ask the receptionist about the wall hanging. The university's Rose Art Museum had an entire collection of Tibetan art in the basement.

On the way back home, Phuni said I should apply right away. The Tibetan art was a good sign. It's a waste of time, I told her. We were already in debt from Becker. There was no way we could afford it. I'd never get in.

"You have nothing to lose," she pushed. She was right, of course.

Friends from Boston helped me fill out the application and pick a major. I had already dismissed the idea of studying medicine. A few chemistry classes had made that obvious. International relations sounded like a good fit. Since I didn't have much in the way of awards or achievements or school records, they suggested I send a copy of the *People* magazine article with the application. I shrugged. It had never interested me and I couldn't understand why it might interest anyone at Brandeis. I included it anyway, figuring they knew more than I did. Two friends wrote letters of recommendation. Reading them, and seeing words like "superb," "self-reliant," and "articulate," made me uncomfortable because I didn't see myself as anything close to that. Sheepishly, I folded them up and mailed them off.

I had a 10 A.M. appointment with Cliff Hauptman, who was working in the admissions department. Phuni had to work. Be strong, she told me before leaving that morning. And dress nicely. I wore my only suit, the dark one I wore in the Woolworth family portrait two years earlier and had not worn since.

Walking up the steps toward the admissions office, I felt foolish. Why bother wasting his time trying to convince him I'm Brandeis material when I'm not? Classes had ended for the school year. The building seemed deserted. My footsteps echoed through the narrow, linoleum-floored hallway. Hearing me come through the door, the receptionist looked up from the paperwork covering her desk. She asked me to have a seat. I waited in a chair outside the admissions office, smelling phantom cookies again.

I was either nervous, hot from the suit, or both, and began sweating. Perspiration beaded on my forehead and my upper lip. I couldn't take off my jacket because I thought that would be inappropriate. This was my first formal interview and I didn't know what to expect. At Venus Seafood, I filled out applications and that was it. Becker College didn't require a formal interview.

A bearded man came out of the office and introduced himself. "I'm Cliff Hauptman," he said. He extended his hand. I shook it. He wasn't wearing a suit jacket. Feeling overdressed, I became more self-conscious. He invited me to take a seat in his bright office with large glass windows.

Cliff had evidently read the *People* article because he knew that my mother was a nun and that I had been a Buddhist monk. He knew my grandfather was the creator and producer of *Gunsmoke* and that my great-grandmother was one of the first Paris correspondents for the *New Yorker* and that she knew Scott and Zelda Fitzgerald and Ernest Hemingway. He knew that my grandmother was a *Vogue* model and actress and my stepgrandmother was one of the first female matadors. He also knew that a distant relative was Henrietta Szold, who founded Hadassah, the Women's Zionist Organization of America, and helped establish schools and hospitals in Israel that took care of both Israelis and Palestinians.

Wanting to make sure the facts weren't fabricated or overblown, he held up the magazine and asked if everything was true. I had paged through the article several times but never really read it closely, I confessed. It was just something I filed away with important papers. The little boy in the article was me and I was a monk. I knew that for sure.

"What do other monks do once they leave the monastery?" he asked.

"Most get into some kind of business helping their families earn a living," I answered tentatively and softly, choosing my words deliberately.

As if sensing my discomfort, he smiled often. "Is it normal for an ex-monk to go to college?" he asked.

"No," I answered.

"So, you're blazing a new trail," he said.

I didn't know what to say because I had never heard that expression and wasn't sure what I was doing. My answers probably weren't very reassuring. Here he was, trying to figure out whether I would be able to make the transition to Brandeis, and

I was telling him there were really no precedents. People with my background don't go to college.

We reviewed my schooling thus far. It didn't take long. At twenty-three, I had less than five years of formal education. Being well-read seemed important to him.

"What do you read?" he asked.

"The *New York Times* occasionally," I said. In California I read *Of Mice and Men* and *The Old Man and the Sea*. That was about it.

"What about writing?"

"I kept a short journal at Becker for one class and wrote a couple of papers."

Frankly, he said, he was concerned about how I might do academically at Brandeis. The courses were hard, even for students who had twelve years of school and taken honors classes.

"I know Brandeis is going to be difficult. That's why I want to come here. I'm willing to struggle and work hard," I told him. Looking back, it's a good thing I didn't know how rigorous Brandeis was. I never would have applied. As unprepared academically as I was, I'm surprised I was even granted an interview. My application must have seemed ludicrous.

We never discussed cost. I didn't bring it up because I felt like the whole process was simply a nice gesture granted to all applicants. I assumed the morning would end with a handshake. I would thank him for the courtesy of talking with me, walk out the door, down the steps, and probably never see him again. As I was about to leave, he handed me a few pages of Henrietta Szold's biography with a small black-and-white picture of her on the front. She was a severe-looking woman with short, tight curls around her head. I didn't realize that Brandeis was the only nonsectarian Jewish-sponsored college or university in the country. Henrietta Szold would be well known to people there. Later that evening, I put it away without reading it. By this point, I had developed a habit of collecting documents and papers even if I did not know their significance.

I went directly to work at Cornucopia Restaurant, where I made salad, without any hopes of getting into Brandeis.

Several weeks later, Phuni called me at work. An envelope from Brandeis had arrived in the mail. She put it unopened under our pillow, saying a prayer as she did. That evening, when I got home, I opened the letter quickly. I wasn't excited or nervous like Phuni. I just wanted to get the rejection over with and dismiss the idea from her head. I read it silently. Phuni looked over my shoulder. When I was done, I read it again out loud to make sure I was reading it correctly.

"The Committee on Admissions is pleased to notify you that you have been accepted to Brandeis University as a transfer student for September 1993. This action represents our confidence in your continuing promise as a student." The letter was signed, "Sincerely, David Gould, Dean of Admissions."

I didn't know it at the time, but after I left the interview, Cliff went to the dean of admissions and lobbied on my behalf. Relating my life story, he said that while I may not have had a formal education, I had an education of another sort that was enriching in other ways. In his mind, having come as far as I had in life, I was a fast learner and adaptable. Just because I lacked some formal classes didn't mean I should be passed by, he said. Lucky for me, Brandeis was a relatively young university, founded in 1948. It prided itself on being a maverick, willing to take risks on students that tradition-bound, inflexible, hundred-year-old institutions might dismiss. Looking back, being distantly related to Henrietta Szold probably didn't hurt.

Tears rolled down Phuni's cheeks as she read the letter again. I was subdued. I felt unworthy of being accepted and worried I would fail. The next day at work, I was on break in the kitchen with one of the other prep cooks at Cornucopia. He asked me what I was going to be doing in the fall. I told him that I had been accepted at Brandeis. I was lucky, he said. It's a good school. He looked at me differently after that. He seemed to respect me more. With the school's help, I cobbled together student loans, financial aid, and grants to help pay for tuition.

That summer, a thick hardcover book with a picture of the earth taken from space arrived in the mail. It was called *Beyond the Limits: Confronting Global Collapse, Envisioning a Sustainable Future.* A letter said it was to be read before classes started in September. I paged through it and blanched. Graphs charted industrial output, population growth, and food consumption from the year 1900. I grabbed the dictionary and flipped through the pages to find out what "industrial" and "output" meant. I took the book with me to work, reading it on the train. During breaks, I found a quiet corner in the kitchen or went outside and pored over chapters on solar energy. I was certain I would be tested the first day of school. I didn't know Brandeis sent the book to all new students, simply to have a theme for orientation. All I knew was that I had not started classes yet and had to figure out whether the globe was going to collapse.

I took the minimum three classes, selecting the most rudimentary ones offered—basic composition, freshman writing seminar, and one art class. Those three seemed doable. None of them had long reading lists or involved projects. What made me nervous was that two of the three involved writing. Haunted by the lecture in the monastery years before about the sacredness of the written word, I had this notion that only wise adults, which I wasn't, could write. At Becker, I had to keep a journal, but it wasn't formal or graded.

The most intimidating aspect of writing was having to come up with my own ideas. I carried a lot of personal and culture baggage that I'm not sure I understood but that effectively muted me and convinced me I had nothing worthwhile to say. Humility was so drummed into me as a monk that I believed that voicing opinions and impressions was vain and self-indulgent. Being raised in a Tibetan culture reinforced that. Among Tibetans, stoicism and politeness trump honest expression. Personal feelings like hurt and sadness aren't considered important, let alone fodder for conversation.

Assigned my first paper, I sat down at my desk. A circle of light from my lamp formed a halo around my computer keyboard. For the next hour, I stared blankly at the tiny Apple Color Classic screen, waiting for the words to come. My fingers felt leaden, unable to type a single letter. I panicked. I had this notion that words come to people off the tops of their heads. Once they are seated, their fingers glide across the computer keyboard unleashed by some cosmic energy that I seemed to lack. Whatever they typed was golden. They printed out their paper and handed it in. At that point, I didn't know that writing involved a process of organizing notes, putting down ideas, and constant revision. Words don't normally burst forth. It's OK to write something and change it or start all over.

All I knew was that I had to deliver a paper, so I forced myself. The grueling process took me half the night.

My first paper came back with red marks all over it. All I could think of was red ants. A bunch of red ants had camped out on my paper. Little red curves appeared in the place of forgotten commas. Verbs were crossed out in red, having failed to agree with the subject. Nouns were generously inserted when I wrote sentences without them. I forgot little words like "in" and wrote "fallow," which I thought was how you spelled "follow." The lack of a single English grammar course in my formal education thus far was painfully apparent.

On one occasion, I surprised myself by having a strong opinion. The subject was culture shock, which was a new term to me. I looked it up in the dictionary. "Sense of confusion and uncertainty sometimes with feelings of anxiety that may affect people exposed to an alien culture or environment without adequate preparation," it read. It occurred to me that I was a culture shock expert. My life was a string of landings in alien cultures. Everywhere I lived, I was out of sync. Until I read the book, I didn't know my anxiety had a formal name. With some confidence, I wrote that being a child, alone, without parents to validate me, and being a different color exacerbated the anxiety of culture shock. My teacher wrote comments in the margins. "Ineffably sad and interesting. . . . I have never heard a richer story. . . . Every one of these statements is a volume . . . brilliant." On the last page, she gave me a check plus, the highest grade, and said she was keeping a copy of it. I was euphoric that day. Yet I felt it was a one-shot victory.

As the work became progressively harder, the possibility that I had miscalculated frightened me terribly. What if I was not up to my dream of college? What would I do then? A few weeks into my second semester, I dropped Renaissance Europe. I knew I was in trouble when the professor mentioned the French Revolution almost in passing as if everyone had heard of it. No one looked puzzled but me. Before I could even begin to think about the French Revolution, I had to do research to find out what "revolution" meant. At those times, I felt like I had to make up grade school and high school overnight. The first day of my lecture class, I frantically tried to write every word the professor said and realized it was impossible. The next day, I brought a tape recorder, for fear of missing something. Looking around the huge hall, I realized I was the only one taping the lecture. I sat in the back and tried to obscure it behind papers. Transcribing it took half the night. After classes, I would sprint past my classmates, who lingered outside the doors of the building, hurrying down the hill to my car parked in the lot behind the circular, three-story Springhold Theater. I sped out, anxious to get home and start homework. Looking in the rearview mirror at students strolling down the walk, I realized how different I was from them. Clustered in small groups, they talked and laughed, looking relaxed and comfortable. You'd never know they had homework. Most had gone to private schools or taken an accelerated high school course, so the thought of a ten-page paper didn't seem to unnerve them. In the course of twelve years of formal schooling, they had learned how to take notes and do research. They knew roughly how long it would take them to study for a test and complete a paper. With houndlike instinct, they went directly to the one shelf in the library or one computer file that contained the appropriate references. They knew shortcuts, like CliffsNotes, and organized study groups to help prepare for tests. Asked to join one, I declined because I was afraid they would discover how little I knew. As my classes became more consuming, Phuni and I grew increasingly frustrated with each other. She had changed jobs and managed a local bakery, leaving early in the morning and coming home after six, tired and hungry. I would be in the kitchen, chopping onions, tomatoes, garlic, and ginger, adding garam masala and turmeric to make Indian curry. I carried the two pots, one for rice and one for vegetables, upstairs. We set the plates on the floor and ate.

After dinner, I washed the dishes in the kitchen and came back up to study. For the next few hours, Phuni watched *Melrose Place* and the soap operas I taped for her earlier in the day. TV provided a needed escape for her, but it was an irritating distraction to me. Holding my hands on either side of my head, like a horse wearing blinders, I tried to block out the TV. I still couldn't concentrate. Finally, at 9 P.M., Phuni was ready for bed. I climbed into bed and began reading. The ceiling light glowed above our bed. After a few minutes, Phuni turned toward me.

"Turn off the light," she said.

"I have to study," I replied.

"I have to sleep," she shot back.

Night after night we argued about turning off the light, our priorities colliding, my need to study butting up against her need for sleep. Finally, I bought a small light that people wore around their heads in coal mines. I strapped it on and glanced in the mirror. I looked silly, but if it meant peace, it was worth it. We were both trying to survive. She was consumed with getting through each day, working and dealing with the painful memories of abuse. I was consumed with the anxiety of feeling hopelessly behind everyone else. She supported us, working eight hours a day, dealing with rude customers. She told me I was smart and would succeed. While nice, the words weren't reassuring. I didn't feel any of that within me.

Thankfully, our friend John Emery began living at the Walker Center at the start of my second year. I had met John about four years earlier at a Tibetan gathering. We were both white boys who spoke Tibetan, though he was much fairer than I, with light blond hair and pale skin. His father had been in the Peace Corps, stationed in Kathmandu, when John was born. Knowing that he had graduated from Oberlin College, in Ohio, but wasn't working, I suggested he move into the Walker Center. His room was on our floor. We shared a bathroom and a storage closet.

I cooked dinner for the three of us. He helped me with homework. Every evening, he joined Phuni and me in our room. We sat on our floor eating curry. After, we went into his room. I showed him my assignments. Step by step, he took me through them, going over the instructions. We went outside into the cold night, looking for the North Star and tracking the movement of stars across the sky for my astronomy class. When I had papers to write, he had me write as much as I could on my own. With my rough draft in hand, he suggested how to flesh out ideas and passages. Sometime around 1 or 2 A.M., I left his room. Climbing into bed, I felt relieved but also fragile. I could never do this on my own.

By my second year, I had changed majors from international relations to sociology, mainly because I liked the sociology professor, Gordon Fellman. He was approachable, letting students call him Gordie rather than Professor Fellman. One of his classes was an intense seminar class called "Sociology of Em-powerment." Chairs were arranged in a circle. Circles bothered me. In my other classes, I gravitated toward corners or back walls. I couldn't hide in this class. Everyone could see my face. Gordie would go around the circle and have each student talk about personal experiences. Part of the objective was to help people talk about deep issues in a safe environment.

During one class, we were asked to share experiences that were disempowering. Immediately, my mind returned to one af-ternoon in the monastery. I was probably about eight or nine years old. I had stolen something. I can't even remember what it was, but the monk police found out and came looking for me. I was in the kitchen, surrounded by fellow monks. The monk po-lice grabbed hold of my ear and led me away. A dozen shorn heads turned to stare at me as I passed, their whispers following me out the door. Desperate for leniency, I pulled one of my loose teeth to make my gum bleed. The sight of blood, I hoped, would make them sympathetic and overlook my offense. It didn't work. A lama was waiting in the courtyard for me. He had heard about what I'd done and took me out to the hills to lecture me. It was a small monastery. Word that I had stolen something and was caught traveled fast. For weeks, people talked about it. Knowing that I had done a terrible thing and that the entire monastery community knew about it made me feel like dirt. I don't think I ever felt lonelier or more worthless in my life than at that point.

Yet when it came to my turn to talk about my most disem-powering moment, I talked instead about the nicknames other monks gave me, like White Eye and Yellow Hair. I explained how in Nepal people had darker skin and that I stood out be-cause I was white. I smiled when I talked, like it wasn't all that hurtful. The tooth episode was too embarrassing and painful. I didn't want others to feel bad for me.

I rarely talked to anyone, except Phuni, about how I felt.

Often, I kept her at a distance, too. Gradually, my Apple computer became my trusted confidant and refuge. Alone in my room, the curtain drawn, music playing low, I typed nonstop, never pausing to think about grammar or structure. I'd explore my doubts and feelings and not worry about appearing self-indulgent. I could be angry without apology and admit that I missed my parents without being concerned about appearing weak. I'd ask myself questions that I would never utter out loud. Once they were on the screen, I could examine and explore them. "Why am I so unhappy? What is causing this within myself? Why am I complaining all the time? I have Phuni, school. I guess what I am looking for is a close family of my own. A group of people who care about me and would stand beside me in any situation. Someone like a close mother or father. What did I do wrong that leaves me with no close family of my own?" I wrote.

Lately, it seemed, I had been struck by little scenes I saw throughout the day. Parents were lined up in cars outside brick elementary schools to pick up their children. A mother at the grocery store was pushing a cart with a toddler seated in the front, facing her. A child, maybe four or five, and his mother were walking down the sidewalk. He was about waist high. His mitten-covered right hand was extended up and wrapped in his mother's glove. Walking several yards behind them, I couldn't keep my eyes off their clasped hands. I tried to put myself in that child's head and body, holding his mother's hand, and imagining what that felt like. Was it warm, soft, or sweaty?

I came home, sat at my desk, and turned on my computer. A clean faded-blue panel appeared on the computer screen. I began typing, posing questions to my mother. "Do you think about me at all? I think about you all the time, at least once every day I wonder what you are doing and wish that I were with you talking about life and opportunities. How much do you think about me? What do I mean to you? Am I this person who does not ever go away from your life, this parasite that cannot be gotten rid of? Do you wish I was never born? I wish you loved me and never wanted to leave me. When I see others with their mothers caring for one another so tenderly, I wonder how you would treat me."

My mother called me and said she was coming to Boston to visit. It would be the first time she met Phuni and I anticipated the worst. I knew my mother resented Phuni for taking away her son and dashing any lingering hope she harbored of me coming back to the monastery. In her eyes, I had become distant and uncommunicative since I got married.

Phuni didn't care for my mother, either. Phuni believed a mother should put her child first and that my mother failed to do so. What's more, as far as Phuni was concerned, my mother failed to appreciate me the way she did. "Why wouldn't your mother love you as much as I do?" she would ask me. It didn't help that my mother snubbed Phuni and her family, refusing to come to India to meet them. Before my mother arrived, I told Phuni to keep the conversation light.

We were meeting at a friend's house for dinner. I introduced my mother to everyone. Conversation was cordial. My mother was smiling. So was Phuni. I was too, but stiffly. We sat at the table. I was next to Phuni. My mother sat across from us, talking about her teachings and what she was doing in the United States. Truly passionate about it, she never had any trouble talking about Buddhism. As she went on about herself, I glanced over at Phuni. She wasn't eating. Her body grew rigid. I can't remember what prompted it—I often tuned my mother out when she was talking about her lamas—but suddenly Phuni lashed out at my mother.

"You don't do anything for him. You say you love him but you don't help him," she said to her. "I bet you didn't even want to have him."

Stunned, I looked across the table at my mother. "You can't tell me I don't love my son," she yelled back.

They went on back and forth, their angry words flung across abandoned, half-eaten meals. Phuni accused her of being selfish. My mother accused her of turning me against her. I sat in silence, totally outmatched by these two strong, angry women and not knowing what to say. My mother began crying. I had never seen her in tears. She was under siege. Everyone around the table was against her, myself included, because I offered nothing in her defense. She got up from the table and went outside on the fire escape. I followed her into the cool evening air. I felt torn. Everything Phuni said was true. But my mother was my mother. Seeing her battered and crying left a pit in my stomach.

She left a day later to open a Tibetan Buddhist center in Chicago and teach Buddhist philosophy and meditation. Several months later, she returned to Boston to visit us and other friends. I ended up acting as her chauffeur, driving her around the city. In the car, I realized nothing had changed. She talked about her center and what was happening with her lamas back at the monastery in Nepal. She wasn't interested in what was happening in my life.

"You don't love me," I told her.

"How do you know how I feel about you? I love you so much and am so worried about you," she said. We began arguing about everything. Education, money, marriage. Me leaving the monastery. Her leaving me with the Trinleys and then in the monastery. Her not acting like a mother. Me not acting like a son.

Enough, I thought. I looked over at her and realized we simply could not relate to each other. No common ground existed between us. It made no sense to talk to her. She was so caught up in her Buddhist world. I didn't understand how to relate to her, accept her approach to life. She had no sense of what I was going through, or didn't seem to care.

"I cannot change the fact that you are my mother, but that's it. You are my biological mother. End of sentence. We have nothing more. Period." I proposed an annulment in our relationship. We caused each other nothing but hurt.

I changed my phone number and refused to talk to her for months. She continued writing me letters, ending with "XOXOX," as in love and kisses. There was nothing behind them. Just a bunch of capitalized letters on a piece of paper. A blithe sign-off. The same as "Sincerely yours" but shorter. It grated on me.

At the same time, I couldn't put her out of my mind. Looking at families driving by in cars, walking in the park, eating dinner at restaurants, sitting in lighted windows of homes all reminded me of her and what we never had together. She was getting older. Her hips were bothering her. At different times of the day, I wondered where she was at that moment and what she was doing.

In the end, it was Phuni who got us back together. Life is too short, she told me. She is your one and only mother. Call her.

I did.

❖

In the summer of 1995, my sociology professor, Gordie, went to Israel to look over the possibility of making a documentary film, and said I would be welcome to join him. Knowing I had Jewish roots, I was interested in seeing the country. Phuni encouraged me to go. My uncle Al and his wife, my aunt Charlotte, offered to pay.

The evening before my flight, my mother called from Chicago. Five minutes into the call, she told me she was no longer a nun. She was married to a man from California. She and my father had never officially divorced, but no one seemed to raise that point. Her new husband had a troubled past but was now a devoted Buddhist. At first, I thought she must be joking. This is too weird and so out of the blue that it can't possibly be true. I was so dumbfounded I couldn't even form the questions racing through my mind, like "Are you crazy?" I scrambled for my tape recorder.

It was a strange habit, but I had begun taping our phone conversations. As time passed and our discussions became more involved, I understood her less rather than more. We might be on the phone for hours, my mother responding to my questions about why she didn't help me more, or support my education and marriage, by leading me on long intellectual discussions of Buddhism, karma, and reincarnation. I was so tangled at the end, I had to listen to her again to try to trace her logic. What she said to me mattered. I wasn't interested in other people's opinions and endorsements. I wanted my mother's. I'd replay the conversations, analyzing them, wondering whether I was too cold to her on the phone and whether she was trying to make amends or was happy with me. Sometimes, she said she loved me. Starting and stopping the tape, I'd try to discern her tone and whether she meant it. In a way, too, I wanted to be able to hear her voice anytime. It was reassuring. She was such a phantom. This was the only way I could think of to capture her and not have her slip away.

"This is your new father," she told me. I was struck by that. She had never introduced someone to me like that. "Your father." The unspoken message was that she was my mother. Up until then, she didn't refer to herself as my mother. She put him on the phone. Just as he started to play the guitar and sing a song, Phuni came home from work. I turned on the speakerphone so Phuni could hear. We just stared at each other, our eyes wide.

They were in Chicago but leaving to trek across Europe, just as she had done more than twenty years earlier with my father. My mother asked if I could come to Norway and meet him.

No, I was leaving for Israel and couldn't change my plans, I told her.

I hung up. Confused and worried about her, I didn't know what else to do but cry. I'm not sure she realized that what she did had an impact on me, that I would care enough about her to worry.

If I couldn't understand her before, now I was totally lost. I wanted to bang my head against the wall. All my life, she had been elusive. Appearing, fading, and reappearing, but always as the same person, the Buddhist nun in robes with a shaved head. The woman who gave me up as a little boy because she wanted so desperately to become a nun and was told she had to "let go of the attachment to your child and live like a nun." Now she gives that all up for a man I had never heard of.

All this was going through my head while in Israel. Gordie took me everywhere, introducing me to his friends and describing how I had just learned I was Jewish. I still wasn't sure what being Jewish meant or why people embraced me as their own. As we walked the streets of Jerusalem, he described the significance of various buildings, and talked about religion, culture, politics, and the issues relating to the Palestinian conflict. I listened and absorbed as much as I could, but it was almost overwhelmingly complicated. Still, I knew somewhere in the back of my mind that I had some connection to this place and faith.

As I grappled with this, I couldn't help but return to thoughts about my mother and her new husband. Postcards from my mother arrived while I was still in Israel, inviting me to join them. She recounted how she and her husband had climbed up to the Acropolis and that Athens was crowded and polluted. "I'm fine, happy . . . and my new life is interesting, and good for me, for my happiness, and growth. I was a little stuck. I love and miss you—a lot! Your mum." Letters from London told of their picnic in the park. In Dharamsala, her husband got to see His Holiness the Dalai Lama. She sent photos of them together, my mother in shorts and a sleeveless shirt, and this tall, heavy man with dark hair past his shoulders and a mustache, who looked like a hippie biker. In her letter, she writes that she prays that I will accept their marriage because he is a nice man and she loves him. Basically, she said, she was lonely as a nun. It never occurred to her that I was lonely as a boy.

❄

I was beginning to feel more comfortable at Brandeis.

For the first two years, the small class size intimidated me. I couldn't hide in the back. Teachers expected every student to participate. Fortunately, they rarely called on students, but expected us to volunteer to speak. Most students were quite eager to offer comments and I was happy they did. Even if I felt something, or understood a new connection, I was too afraid. Besides, I could not imagine I had anything of value to offer.

The turning point came when I took classes such as one called "Democracy and Civil Disobedience." We read Gandhi, Martin Luther King, and Henry Thoreau and discussed the tensions and the negotiations that take place between government and the people in a democracy. These people and their causes came alive to me as I read personal letters, including Martin Luther King's "Letter from a Birmingham Prison." Themes of civil rights, human rights, civil disobedience, and nonviolent movements echoed many Buddhist teachings and struck a personal chord with me. I wrote papers entitled "The Virtues of Democracy" and "Obligations of a Citizen."

About the same time, Gordie was organizing a Peace and Conflict Studies conference titled "A Culture in Exile," which was designed to explore the connections between Buddhism and Judaism. He felt I should be a part of the conference, having both a Buddhist and a Jewish background. Privately, I felt inadequate and that I would have nothing to offer. But I agreed to help in any way I could. Soon I was contacting and scheduling speakers and organizing an appearance of the dance team from the local Tibetan community. I called newspapers to advertise the event and made sure there were plenty of microphones and podiums. In the process of handling small details, I felt like I could play a helpful role in something beyond my small world. I was beginning to understand the concept of society, social constructs, and institutions. More important, I realized those were all built by people and could be changed and improved.

❈

Phuni wanted her father to come back and live with us. I was reluctant. We didn't have space for him in our small room. I wasn't sure whether having him around would mean more anxiety or less. She was resolute, though.

It was during this time that Phuni went through an important transformation. She always seemed to have a deep reserve of confidence and courage. I don't know if she was born with it or whether she developed it to survive as a child nomad, who was then separated from her family and subjected to years of sexual and psychological abuse. All I know is that she became even more confident as a person and a woman, and felt compelled to fight social injustices and speak out on behalf of other women. In the summer of 1995, she decided to attend the Fourth World Conference on Women in Beijing. It was a bold move. The Chinese government had said Tibetan exiles wouldn't be permitted to attend. Phuni and eight other Tibetan women decided to go anyway. To avoid attention, Phuni used her Western name, Kim Meston, and her American passport.

Before she left, she told me to get all of Apa's papers in order for him to move to the United States. All my assumptions about him complicating our lives were unfounded. It was only after he arrived, in the middle of my last year at Brandeis, that Phuni and I felt a degree of stability. Although I was beginning to feel more confident, I was still overwhelmed trying to keep up with my courses.

Once again, Apa took a burden from me. Before, he helped with the emotional burden. Now it was both emotional and physical. He cooked dinners, washed dishes, did the laundry, and shopped at the local Indian grocery store so I could study. He shopped, buying rice in economical twenty-five-pound bags to save money. To help pay for his room down the hall from us, he searched through Dumpsters and garbage cans looking for redeemable cans. For several hours a week, he babysat two little boys. They called him Baba. Although they spoke different languages, Apa had a way of connecting with children. Delighting in making them smile, he kept his pocket full of candy. He continued to carve prayer stones out of limestone. I painted them white, green, yellow, blue, and black. When the wind blows across them, they carry blessings to others.

I tried to teach Apa what I was learning. Taking flashlights, oranges, and apples, I tried to create my own mini solar system, showing him how the sun set and how the eclipse worked.

In the weeks leading up to graduation, I went through all the motions of preparation. I wrapped up final papers, ordered a cap and gown, and picked up graduation announcements. Phuni suggested I invite my uncle Al and aunt Charlotte in California, and my mom's cousin Lisa, who gave us Aline's car and came to Disneyland with me when I was ten. I wanted John Emery there. Without him I wouldn't have made it. I sent an invitation to Joe and Bridget Collins, too. The Collinses had let Phuni, Apa, and me live in their apartment during the trial and helped me fill out my college application.

I called my mother in Dharamsala, asking her to come. Before I had a chance to ask, she said had a leg problem and was having difficulty walking. My mother had problems with her hips. Each year, it seemed to have gotten worse. When I mentioned that I was calling to see whether she was coming to my graduation, she asked me what I was going to do after I graduated. I don't know, I told her. I'm just concentrating on finishing up right now. Graduation is May 19, I told her. I made sure she had my phone number and asked her to call me and let me know whether she could make it. I finished the conversation asking her to take care of herself and her leg.

She had always thought college was a waste of time. "I can't think of one useful thing I learned in college, other than maybe reading some nice literature," she once told me. Her one psychology class was stupid once the professor started talking about Freud. The philosophy professor ended up committing suicide. "I took one science class that I had to and had no idea what they were talking about. Probably got a D. Learned a tiny bit about art in the history of art maybe, but I learned much more when I had visited museums in Paris, alone. And grad school was even more of a waste of time . . . I finally dropped out. They weren't teaching anything practical about being a social worker . . . but things like 'the history of social work.'"

Two weeks before graduation, I received a letter from my mother. In it, she wrote that she wasn't coming because of her leg. She would have called, but couldn't because the office with the phone closes at 4 P.M., she wrote. It's too bad that she's halfway around the world and not in Chicago teaching as she had been. She wants to be here so much, she wrote, and will be with me at the graduation 100 percent in spirit.

I folded up the letter and put it away. My mother didn't bother going to her own graduation ceremony. She thought formal ceremonies were silly. She assumed I would feel the same. It really had nothing to do with the ceremony. I didn't like formal events either, all the uncomfortable clothes, the posed pictures, the handshakes. I just wanted her there. Her presence mattered. Having her there, applauding when I went up to receive my diploma, would make me proud and happy. It would mean she thought I had done a good job and supported me in all of my endeavors. She just didn't get it. In her mind, no one could possibly need her because she had little of value to offer. We both lack self-esteem, I realized. But I wonder, too, whether saying you have nothing to offer frees you from making the effort.

❁

The night before graduation, John Emery and I stayed up late in his room, drinking gin and tonic and smoking fat cigars. I inhaled. The thick smoke burned my throat. I coughed, and puffed again. By the end of the night, the soggy end of the cigar felt bloated in my mouth. My throat ached and my head felt thick and cottony. I climbed into bed next to Phuni. Tomorrow I would be graduating. I had made it. Three years before, I was staring blankly at a computer screen, my fingers immobile, sprinting to my car for fear of wasting time and never being able to finish what I had to do, arguing with Phuni over the night-light, looking for Venus in the cold winter night. It was over. I was graduating from one of the top universities in the country with honors. But I didn't feel accomplished.

I woke to a picture-perfect day with clear blue skies. Sunlight poured through the window into our room. Phuni was up, getting ready. The day before, she had gone to the beauty parlor and had her hair done. She bought a new Tibetan outfit with a bright yellow, red, and orange skirt. Apa wore his fedora. I wore a hot green wool jacket I found in a box of donated clothes in the basement.

Joining the class of 1996 in my black cap and gown, I marched into the Gosman gym through the underground entrance usually used by athletes and took my place on a metal folding chair. Scanning the hundreds of people in the bleachers, I spotted my family and friends. I was struck by what an eclectic group it was. Apa, a tiny Tibetan man in a big hat. Phuni in her

Tibetan outfit, her petite frame and gentle smile masking a tortured past and steely determination. The retired tire salesman,
Uncle Al, a big, gregarious man in his goatee, and slim Aunt Charlotte, his best friend and wife. Cousin Lisa, a tall blond in a pink
suit, from Laguna Beach. John, a pudgy blond from New England
born in Nepal. The Collinses, Joe, a former marine and a Harvard
graduate, who imported Italian shoes, dabbled in real estate, and
sold rigging for sailboats, and his wife, Bridget, a French socialite.
She once introduced Phuni and me to Julia Child.

I tried to concentrate on the speeches. Madeleine Albright
spoke eloquently about how we graduates can affect the world,
a speech meant to inspire action and good works. Wynton
Marsalis walked up and received an honorary degree. One
thought ran through my head: I don't belong here.

After the main speeches, the graduating class of 1996 broke
into smaller groups according to majors and assembled in desig-
nated parts of the campus to hear more speeches and receive our
diplomas. My group was on the land outside the Goldfarb Library. Each student was called by name. When my name was
called, I felt embarrassed. I graduated with honors, cum laude.
Phuni had told me that morning to make sure I stood up straight.
The year before, I had been called onstage to be recognized for
helping organize a conference. Without even realizing I was doing
it, I hunched my shoulders and bent over. Phuni watched from
the audience, wanting to shout, "Stand up straight."

Once the ceremony was over, people lingered, hugging and
posing for pictures. With my wool jacket and black gown,
standing in the sun, I felt dehydrated and dizzy. I wanted to
shed the gown. Phuni said no. She wanted to savor the momen-
tousness of the occasion. Like her father, she was proud and dig-
nified. As she watched me squinting in the sunlight, my
diploma in hand, her eyes flickered with pride.

A huge chasm existed between me and the celebration
around me. I was there physically, but mentally and emotionally

I was somewhere else, in a group of one—watching others pat one another on the back and talk about what they were doing after college—like a little planet that went astray, orbiting solo just beyond the galaxy. Some of the significance of the day was wasted on me. I was too caught up in feeling like an interloper. I tried to chase that away and enjoy the moment and pride in Phuni's face. But I kept coming back to the thought that I wouldn't have made it but for the help of friends. The diploma in my hand felt fraudulent. A certificate of knowledge, when I was convinced only of the degree of my ignorance.

After the ceremony, we went to the Collinses' condominium. Phuni arranged to have her Indian friend who owned restaurants in the Boston area deliver food. Over a dinner of chicken tika marsala, black lentils, rice, somosa, a spinach dish called sagg panier, and some Indian dessert, my relatives and friends toasted me.

I bought a sticker that read "Brandeis University Alumnus" and stuck it on the rear window of my car. After two days, I took it off.

It took me a long time to realize that Brandeis, more than anything else, opened my mind to learning. While in classes, I was so wrapped up in trying to catch up with the other students, and writing papers and taking tests, that I didn't have a chance to really think beyond the classroom. Part of that was my own doing. I was so focused on meeting deadlines and grades that I didn't allow myself to consider anything besides homework and to even enjoy learning.

It was only several years after I graduated that I began taking literature and memoir classes. For the first time in my life, I began to read books with joy.

Chapter Nine
Yak & Yeti

Years earlier, when I had arrived in California, a local newspaper heard about me, the seventeen-year-old ex–Buddhist monk attending a local high school. Apparently, someone at the newspaper thought I would make a nice offbeat feature story. At one point, the reporter asked what I wanted to do, and quoted my reply. "The most important thing in my life is helping other people. And if I cannot help, next most important is not to harm anyone." Nine years had passed since then and many events had dulled some of my youthful idealism. But the mandate to help people remained unshaken. Now that I had my degree, I had no excuses. It was time to prove to myself that I was capable of offering something worthy to the world. How and where stumped me. Mornings I woke feeling like Estragon or Vladimir, the two tramps in Samuel Beckett's *Waiting for Godot,* waking to spend the day by the roadside waiting for the never-arriving Godot. Godot for me was the perfect job.

I was a little less sanguine than the Godot characters, though. Several times a week, I stopped in at two different career centers. Following the advice of a career counselor there, I took a personality test, answering questions designed to help me find a job. There was a long list of them, all general. What do I dislike most? *(A)* People not caring about other people's feelings. Or *(B)* People not understanding how things work. I chose *A.* The test concluded I was flexible, had a spontaneous approach to life, and preferred to keep my options open. At first, I thought it was marvelously intuitive. Reading it again, I thought, this could apply to anyone, and didn't understand how that would help me find a job.

Scanning job openings at the center, I grew depressed. Looking down the list, I realized I wasn't suited for any of the interesting ones. They all required "strong writing and verbal skills." I did land a weeklong job at a nearby camp at the edge of a large lake, called Rolling Ridge. I had never been to a camp before. The buildings were drafty, old, and cold. All the kids were high-achieving teenagers, enrolled in a leadership training program. It was a perfect mismatch. My main duty was leading discussion groups. I was someone who rarely spoke in class and only in low decibels. Painfully shy, I couldn't get out of my own shell, let alone encourage teenagers to get out of theirs.

When I wasn't at career centers, I was at my computer, clicking through thousands of postings on Monster.com. The more I navigated through, the more rudderless and panicked I became. There were just too many possibilities and none of them right. Human resources sounded good until I realized they wanted recruiters for the pharmaceutical industry. One listing caught my eye. Flight attendant. At least I could travel. Sitting through a one-day seminar at Logan Airport, listening to instructors talk about uniform requirements, proper use of oxygen masks, and unruly passengers, I didn't bother filling in the application.

Two other leads that sounded promising fizzled. Facing History and Ourselves, an organization that works with teachers and students to explore ways to battle racism, prejudice, and anti-Semitism, was hiring. I went in for an interview, but nothing came of it. The organization wanted someone dynamic. The State Department needed an assistant in the Tibetan affairs office. I applied and never heard back. Other applicants had master's degrees.

As weeks passed, I realized I couldn't wait around for meaningful work. I needed a paycheck. One Wednesday morning, I saw an ad in the weekly newspaper, the *Newton TAB:* "Warehouse Help." Boston International, a wholesaler of paper napkins and plates, had openings at a distribution center in our neighborhood of Newton, next to the Massachusetts Turnpike. Davis Edwards, a tall, scruffy man with a goatee, interviewed me with a cup of coffee in one hand and a lit cigarette in the other. He hired me on the spot.

The next morning, I packed a Tupperware container filled with leftover rice, vegetables, and curry and drove to the warehouse, a huge building with concrete floors and stacks of brown cardboard boxes on metal racks and wooden pallets. Fancy paper napkins and matching plates neatly portioned in clear plastic packages of 25, 50 or 100 filled the boxes. I had never seen so many sizes, colors, and patterns. Flowered ones were named Magnolia, Lily of the Valley, and Hydrangea, depending on the blossom. Lively little orange and green vegetables marked the Carrots and Peas line. Wild Thing had leopard spots. My job was to stick address labels on boxes and tape them shut. If one order had several boxes, say four, I wrote "1 of 4" on the box, letting the customer know that three other boxes were coming. The napkins ended up at cocktail and dinner parties all over the country. The foreman was an African-American with dreadlocks and a Jamaican accent. His main job was getting orders out the door. "Come ooon, let's gooooo, let's goooo," he'd say. "Rack 'em, pack 'em, and stack 'em."

The work was boring. I wondered how people could do the same chore every day. One woman in accounts payable and receivable had been doing the same work for forty years. Her job and her pets were her life. Our conversations were limited to her latest car trouble, television sitcoms, aggravating customers, and precocious animals.

The two men who owned the business, along with the office workers, kept to their air-conditioned cubicles in the front of the warehouse. Eventually, I joined them. I was assigned a cubicle with a desk, chair, computer, and phone. The head of accounting, a very large woman, needed an assistant to make dunning calls. Each day I received a stack of sheets listing names, phones numbers, and overdue payments. I dialed the number. "Hello. This is Daja Meston from Boston International. I am calling about a payment that is overdue by three months." Dutifully, I took the name of the person I talked to and what was promised in terms of paying the bill. After hanging up, I went to the next delinquent napkin customer.

Apa needed a job. I approached the warehouse manager to see if Apa could work there. "He doesn't speak a word of English," I said, "but he's an incredibly hard worker."

"If you can train him, OK," he said.

The first day, I taught Apa how to use the tape gun. The next day, I explained in Tibetan how to mark boxes with a big black felt pen—"1 of 4," "2 of 4," "3 of 4," "4 of 4." Since he barely knew how to write, that night he practiced, with me at his side, trying to perfect four numbers. Whenever possible, the boss had Apa running the large paper shredder so he didn't have to write. Apa stood vigilant by the boxy machine, faithfully feeding it old newspapers and creating mounds of thinly sliced paper that we used to cushion the starchy-looking napkins and plates in boxes.

I learned much about Apa on our early-morning and late-afternoon drives to and from work. Apa told me stories about how he used to take care of his sheep and yaks in the open fields of western Tibet. He recognized individual sheep out of the hundreds. He knew which ones were pregnant, when they were about to deliver, and which ones were sick and needed extra attention. To protect newborns against wolves and the cold, he cradled them against his bare skin in his sheepskin chuba, keeping them warm through the night until the sun came up. He told me how nomads gathered sheep droppings and heated them on a stone over the fire. Once the droppings were hot, they packed them in the bottom of the sheep's wool that swaddled their own babies. His own baby daughter died of chickenpox. He had to take her tiny body, clean it, and carry it on his back to the side of a cliff, where he left it. Every time he passed the site, he grieved. Time and the birth of Phuni a year later helped take away some of the pain. In loving detail, he talked about how a newborn baby can console an injured spirit. The money that he earned paid for rent and food. Any that was left over, he sent back to his sons, brothers, and sisters in the refugee camp.

When Apa wasn't at the warehouse, he collected recyclable cans and bottles. Saturday and Sunday mornings, he set off on his bicycle with three or four empty trash bags. Hours later, he returned wobbly on his bike, two bulging bags dangling from each handlebar. At first, he went to every house on trash day, until he figured out which ones had the most dependable collection of cans and bottles. He began his rounds earlier after he found another Asian man patrolling the same neighborhood with a car. Once he peered into a Dumpster behind Lasell College and discovered a bounty in one place. From that point on, he quit going house to house, leaving those cans to the Asian with the car. Armed with a stick and pair of gloves to protect his hands from broken glass and germs, he climbed into the Dumpster. One by one, he methodically opened each trash bag, poked through it with his stick, pulled out every can and bottle. All day, he would sit in the hot metal Dumpster. Phuni and I would tell him it wasn't necessary, but he insisted. After he got his recyclables home, he washed them out in the sink and carried them down into the dark basement of the Walker Center. There he separated them into glass, plastic, and aluminum, and counted them out. Fifty glass bottles in a bag. I drove him and his bags to the redemption center, which was staffed by a group of Vietnamese men and women. Apa was exacting in his count, never shortchanging the center or himself. After a while, they didn't bother making him count out the cans and bottles.

Over time, he befriended the Lasell College janitor, Jim. Jim told Apa what days were better for beer bottles and set off to one side the trash bags that seemed to have more cans. One day, during a heavy downpour, he lent Apa his heavy blue work jacket, with "Jim" written just below the right shoulder. Apa didn't speak English, but he managed to touch people. I think they recognized his humble spirit. People went out of their way to be kind to him. Students began giving him a few dollars. Families cleaned out their cans for him so he didn't have to. In an average week Apa collected up to two thousand cans, earning $100 or more. He picked up every can he came across at the train station or lying in the grass or in the parking lot outside a building. "That's two rupees in India," he'd say. Many people in India earn less then thirty rupees in a day. He had to pick up only fifteen cans to match that.

It wasn't just cans and bottles he gathered. The Dumpsters and curb fronts of select houses contained remarkable finds. Vacuum cleaners, shoes, pens, glasses, watches, toys, clothes, cassette players, video cameras, alarm clocks, snow boots, VCRs, and small and large TVs in working condition with remotes thoughtfully taped on the top by the owner. Sometimes he wasn't quite sure what he found, but brought it home because it looked valuable. One day he came smiling into our room carrying a laptop computer that worked. Another day, he burst through the door clutching an electric razor. The watch that looked like a Rolex turned out to be a fake, but kept time. "Why would they throw such things away?" Apa asked. What we didn't need, we gave away to people at the Walker Center or sent to his village in India.

If he found something too big to carry home, the two of us would fetch it in the car. To make sure no one took off with his prize before we arrived, he hid it behind trees and bushes. When he couldn't hide an entire dresser, he took out the drawers and scattered them, knowing that most people wouldn't take a drawerless dresser. Same approach for couches. He took the cushions off and tucked them under bushes and shrubs. Before he left for work, he packed his duffel bag with unopened packages of cookies, crackers, or candy or whole pieces of fruit that he found in the Lasell College Dumpster. He distributed them to women prisoners who arrived every morning in a van as part of a work release program. One day he asked me to buy medicine to relieve a toothache. I asked if his tooth hurt. No, he said. It was for one of the prisoners. She had asked Apa to buy the medicine, which she used during the day. She returned it to Apa for safekeeping for the evening because she wasn't allowed to bring anything back to her cell.

❀

While working at the warehouse job in the summer of 1996 and wishing I was doing something else, I received a voice mail from John Ackerly, president of the International Campaign for Tibet. I had become more politically active on the issue of Ti-

betan rights while at Brandeis. My last year, I helped organize a
Peace and Conflict Studies forum, assembling Boston-area Chinese and Tibetan students to discuss China's occupation of
Tibet. I wrote an article for the *Boston Globe,* urging dialogue
between Beijing and the Dalai Lama, Tibet's exiled spiritual
leader. I attended rallies and protests. Along the way, I met
John. He seemed particularly impressed that I could speak Tibetan like a native. If I could ever be of help, I told him, let me
know. In the voice message, he said the *Philadelphia Inquirer*
was looking for an American who could speak Tibetan to help a
reporter. He left the name and number of an editor at the paper.
The next day, I was on the phone with Jonathan Newman, an
editor at the *Philadelphia Inquirer.* One of his reporters, Loretta
Tofani, was planning to investigate the plight of Tibetans under
Chinese occupation and needed someone to go with her and
her photographer who could speak the language.

I jumped at the opportunity. Here was my chance to travel,
which I missed, and actually see Tibet. Although I was married
to a Tibetan, involved in Tibetan politics, spoke Tibetan, and
was raised by a Tibetan family and Tibetan monks, I had never
gone to Tibet. Only Nepal and India. The idea of working with
an investigative reporter and seeing firsthand what I had only
heard seemed like my Godot. This was what the whole Tibetan
movement was about. Conferences and symposiums were important, but they also left me feeling a bit helpless, like there
was nothing I could do. Getting a case of Carrots and Peas napkins to the right address mattered to the guys who ran the warehouse, but not to me.

I expected adventure and the trip lived up to that. Our
moves were monitored by the Chinese police. We were locked in
our hotel room at night. Chinese security guards set up road-
blocks, so we walked during the night, over mountains and
along the river, sleeping in ditches during the day, traveling along
with fourteen Tibetan Buddhist nuns, monks, and political dis-

senters who had been imprisoned, tortured, and raped, as they escaped through the Himalayas to Nepal. I kept names written on small pieces of paper hidden under the sole of my boot. The reporter broke her leg. I had to carry her down a mountain in the dark of night. The four-part series, "Inside Tibet: Country Tortured," focused on Chinese imprisonment, torture, and murder of Tibetan Buddhists and was a finalist for the Pulitzer Prize. Although I wasn't writing the story, I felt that I helped make it happen. My reputation as a Tibetan interpreter spread within the Tibetan community and among human rights groups.

The following summer, I went back to Tibet with U.S. representative Frank Wolf of Virginia, who was investigating human rights issues and the persecution of Tibetan Buddhists by the Chinese. The pressure was greater this time. His success and the impact of his trip depended on me getting him to the right places and to the right people. We drove by a series of prison complexes in Lhasa, the capital of Tibet. Chinese soldiers watched us from guard towers as the cab driver slowed down so we could take pictures. I wanted to get out of there before they got our license plate number, and I worried that the Tibetan driver would be arrested.

After three nights in Lhasa, Representative Wolf and his aide left. I stayed behind to gather information about religious persecution for the International Campaign for Tibet. I was terrified because I didn't have any diplomatic or journalist credentials to protect me. Without them, I could be captured, beaten, and left in a ditch to die, I thought. Authorities could lie, saying I had been attacked by thieves, and no one would know the truth. I was afraid to leave my hotel room or even look out the window. When I finally left and landed at the Kathmandu airport, it was as if a hundred-pound weight had been lifted. Never before had the distinction between a free country and China's regime registered so strongly on me.

Back in Washington, after our trip, Representative Wolf,

who said he was only the second House member to visit the remote Himalayan region since Chinese occupation began in the
1950s, told a news conference he was appalled at the human
rights situation there. "There is no freedom in Tibet, period,"
he said. "In Tibet human progress is not even inching along and
repressed people live under unspeakably brutal conditions in the
dim shadow of international awareness." Chinese reaction was
fierce, calling his report an outrageous lie. "Wolf Bares Fangs
with Distorted Facts on Tibet," read one headline in the *Beijing
Review.* The hotel we stayed in during our stay was shut down
for months, as apparent punishment for housing us. New travelers were banned and Tibetan homes searched. Chinese authorities identified me as the American leading Wolf and his aide.
My name, friends told me, was on an official blacklist of unwanted visitors. The trip buoyed my confidence. I had proven
myself as a capable and reliable interpreter and felt as if I had
done something worthwhile.

❀

During the trip with the reporter, I had a layover in Kathmandu, returning to the childhood home I had left a decade
earlier. The Trinley family had moved from the old pink stucco
house and opened a hotel. One of the boys offered to give me a
ride on the back of his motorbike to the monastery. Even from a
distance I could see that it had changed. It looked less green and
spacious. Mangoes, bamboo, and shrubs had been cleared out
to make room for a row of new dormitories. Scaffolding made
out of bamboo crisscrossed a big concrete structure where the
old temple once stood. Inside the dining room, the walls looked
brighter than I remembered. The benches and tables were new.
As we walked the grounds, I looked for familiar hiding spots
where I had slept and studied. Most were gone. Stung by unexpected feelings of melancholy, I wanted to leave—partly because

things had changed so much and nothing looked familiar, and partly because the painful memories of being lonely, sad, and afraid returned uninvited.

Before I could leave, I wanted to see my old teacher, Lama Lhundrup. Knocking on his door, I heard his deep voice inviting me in. I offered him a white scarf, the traditional greeting for a lama, and sat down. We talked. He was as gentle and supportive as he had always been, asking me about Phuni and my schooling. He complimented me on the goatee I had grown. I told him I was going to be in the city for two weeks. He suggested a two-week Green Tara retreat. Having nothing better to do, I agreed to come back the next day.

I had never done a retreat before. When I was a monk, I was too young to spend two weeks in solitude. He led me to a small room with a bed, an altar with the seven offering bowls, and a few statues, and left me with a book of prayers and scripture. The one window looked out on a thick wall of bamboo. I sat down and dutifully recited the prayers. I meditated. I filled the offering bowls with water each morning, the whole time feeling uncomfortable, as if I was an impostor. Even as my eyes followed scripture text, my mind was elsewhere: back in the States, wondering what Phuni was doing, wondering about getting a new job, about going back to school. I worried about my mother. She was still married.

Mostly I thought about how glad I was not to be a monk. It became clear that one reason I returned to the monastery was to make sure I had made the right decision. In the decade since I left, my mother had told me many times that I made a mistake leaving the monastery, that I would have been better off and happier in the monastery. Sometimes, when I was depressed and struggling, I wondered privately if she was right. Now I could honestly say she wasn't. Once I discovered that, I ended the retreat.

As fate would have it, as I was leaving the monastery one of the older monks who knew my mother mentioned that she was in Kathmandu. She had come to Nepal to attend a Buddhist meditation course. We had not seen each other in several years. I invited her to lunch at the Yak & Yeti, a five-star hotel in Kathmandu, with antique fountains, gilded temples, and an emerald garden. The only reason I could afford it was that the newspaper was paying for it.

Sitting at a table covered with white linen tablecloths and a centerpiece of fresh flowers, I looked up and spotted my mother making her way toward me among a flock of waiters in maroon suit jackets and little round hats. It was the first time I saw her not wearing robes. She looked wonderful. Tiny golden hoops dangled from her ears. Her hair, dyed a reddish brown, was parted in the middle and swooped in soft waves to her neck. Blue looks good on her, I thought, admiring her pants and printed shirt. Around her neck, she wore a necklace. The minute I saw her, my heart soared. I got up and hugged her. As strange as it sounds, being in regular street clothes transformed her in my mind. Whenever she was in robes, she was a spiritual ambassador, updating me on the latest news about the monastery, the monks, the lamas, her teachings, a world that I left behind. Many times in the past, she had argued that her vows and commitment as a nun prevented her from close contact with me. Gazing at my mother across the table, I thought we weren't so different now. Maybe now that she looked like an American, she would return home, come to Boston, and live with Phuni, Apa, and me. I could take care of her there. Looking back, it probably seemed naive, expecting her to suddenly leave what had been her home and world for more than two decades and move to Boston. But it didn't seem impossible then. She had done unexpected things in the past.

After lunch we went up to my room. Sitting by her side on the double bed, I told her how much she meant to me, and that I worried about her. Her legs were bothering her. I thought her husband was taking advantage of her compassion. I had seen this before. Over the years, a string of male monks had befriended my mother and convinced her to give them money. Most of all, I wanted her home with me. "I've missed you so much," I said. As I uttered those words, I began sobbing uncontrollably. It was as if the dam had burst. I cried out of frustration, struggling to come up with the right words and feeling that all were inadequate to convey what I was feeling. I cried, too, from relief at finally seeing my mother and being able to talk to her in person.

Quietly, she listened. Her deep blue eyes softened. For the first time in my life, I felt as if she understood how I felt. She could be my mother and I could be her son. We could take care of each other.

"Please, come home with me," I begged.

"I'll think about it," she told me. "I'll see what I can do."

The next morning, we met again in my room. She said she was going back to India to her husband. I was crushed but hoped that since she was no longer a nun, it was only a matter of time before she came back to the States.

We saw each other again at the airport. My mother was there, waiting for her flight to New Delhi. I went over and sat in a vinyl chair next to her. Our bodies were rigid. We didn't know what to say. I asked a person in the waiting area to take our picture. It seemed like a fitting thing to do. She leaned toward me and clutched my arm. I kept my hands in my lap, but smiled. My flight was first. We gave each other an uncomfortable hug. As I walked away to the gate, I felt a strong tug on my heart, my throat tightened. I kept walking toward the Cathay Pacific gate to catch my flight to Hong Kong. I looked back. She waved.

❀

I was planning to visit Uncle Al and Aunt Charlotte on my way back since the plane stopped at LAX. Phuni arranged a week off work and met me there. She was eager, almost insistent, about meeting my father. I suspect she and Uncle Al talked about it while I was in Tibet. Each of them was keenly aware of the gap between my father and me. The last time I had seen him was sixteen years earlier, and then for only about ten minutes. We didn't go see my father immediately. My uncle Al waited a day and then made a suggestion. "We could go and take Larry out to lunch tomorrow," he said. Phuni and Charlotte jumped at the offer. I was outnumbered.

"What should I say?" I asked Phuni when we were alone. "He's your father," she told me. "Ask him questions. Tell him about yourself. Give him a hug."

Before we went, my uncle explained what he knew about my father's illness, which wasn't much. He was a paranoid schizophrenic. No one knows what triggers it. His conversation consisted of yes or no answers. He didn't smile, or frown. His face and his eyes were blank. My father lived at Brentwood Manor, a two-story rose-colored stucco house for older people with mental illness. Only in his fifties, his thick hair still mostly black, he was the youngest resident. It was a depressing place, doused in disinfectant. Walking in, I glanced to my right. A dozen people sat in the living room, watching television and reading the paper. For having so many people in a little room, it seemed strangely quiet. People wedged together on one couch seemed unaware of one another. It was creepy. In a room across the front hallways, scattered wheelchairs and the people in them faced in different directions. I heard talking, but the conversations were one-way. Off to the side was a small office with a glass window. Inside, Oscar, a slightly overweight Latino with a goatee, greeted my uncle. "Will Larry Greeneye please come down to the front desk," Oscar said over the speaker system.

Moments later, my father, a big, burly man with a ragged beard, shuffled into the room. Uncle Al introduced my father to Phuni and reintroduced me. I hugged him tentatively, wrapping my arms loosely around his burly body. I wasn't sure whether I should pat him on the back or give him a squeeze, and did neither. I backed away quickly. His soiled clothes smelled like old cigarette smoke and sweat. A sudden image flashed into my head: A big man with a dark beard and plastic glasses playing peekaboo. His thick hands opening and closing over his eyes. His dark brown eyes lighting up. A smile on his face. We must have been in Greece or stopped somewhere on our way to Nepal. As quickly as the image appeared, it disappeared. In front of me stood a disheveled middle-aged man.

Heavily medicated, he strained to keep his eyes open. "Let's get lunch," Uncle Al said. My father nodded. On the way, my father sat in the backseat of the Ford Explorer between Phuni and me. He looked straight ahead. My uncle Al tried to crack jokes.

We went to a local diner nearby. Luckily, it was empty. I sat on a round stool at a small Formica table, across from my father. He folded his hands on the table. His brown checked hat, pulled down to his thick eyebrows, clashed with a chaotically patterned blue-and-white shirt open at the collar. Uncle Al took our picture. I held up my can of 7UP and said, "Cheers." I ordered a hamburger. My father had a pastrami sandwich that he gulped down in silence. After, he helped himself to the French fries on my plate. I would have been happy to take my father back to Brentwood, but Uncle Al drove us to the Promenade, a fancy outdoor shopping area, for a walk. A central street, blocked off to traffic and lined with expensive clothing boutiques and restaurants, pulsed with shoppers, tourists, panhandlers, and gawkers. Businessmen in sports jackets with determined strides glided past meandering sightseeing couples, the men in pressed linen pants and the women in clingy pastel skirts, with tanned legs.

We started out together, the five of us walking abreast. After a few minutes, Uncle Al, Aunt Charlotte, and Phuni slowed down, leaving my father and me alone. I knew they were doing it on purpose, trying to give my father and me the opportunity to connect. My father stopped, stooped over, and picked a cigarette butt off the concrete walk and shoved it into his pocket. Seeing a garbage can, he walked over to it and rummaged through. He pulled out a half-eaten doughnut and shoved it into his mouth. "Don't do that," I told him. "It's not good for you." I worried he might get sick, but mostly I just wanted him to stop because I was embarrassed. He didn't seem to hear me.

Not knowing what to talk about, I asked my father whether he had been to the Promenade before. "Yes," he answered. Then silence. A minute later, I asked if he liked it. "Yes." Silence followed. Do you come here often? "No." He stumbled, tripping over his feet. The medication subdued outbursts and relaxed his muscles to the point where they went limp at times. He mumbled something about telepathy. It was nonsense. His face and eyes were dull, drained of any expression or emotion. He could have been a mannequin, but even they have smiles painted on. People walking by looked straight ahead to avoid his glance, almost as if they were afraid he might approach them. I looked back at Uncle Al and Aunt Charlotte and Phuni, wishing they would catch up. Uncle Al wiped his eyes. He was crying.

My father tired easily, so we went back to the car. I couldn't wait to drop him back off at Brentwood.

❈

Uncle Al had heard little from my parents after they married and left for Europe. He knew I was born, but nothing else. A few years later, he received a phone call from a Pan American Airways employee, saying his younger brother, my father, was begging in the streets of India and acting strangely. The airline helped local governments get unwanted expatriates back home, if someone would pay for the ticket. Uncle Al sent money for a nonrefundable ticket to bring him home. He heard nothing for a long period, then received a call from someone at the Los Angeles airport saying, "I've got your brother here."

Uncle Al didn't recognize him at first. My father, barefoot and dirty, was mumbling. "He thought he was Jesus, Buddha, and Moses all wrapped up in one," Uncle Al said. He invited my father to live in their condo in Marina del Rey. It didn't work out. There were forty-three other tenants. My father would act strange at the pool and make people feel uncomfortable. Uncle Al worked with local social service agencies to find a residential treatment program for his brother. Occasionally my father would disappear for weeks. Uncle Al found him once, barely recognizable, with a group of homeless men on a nearby promenade. "At first I felt like a martyr. Now we're very close," he said.

We visited my father once again that week. Driving up, I saw him on the second-floor balcony, standing in the sun and smoking a cigarette. Upon seeing us pull into the parking lot, he took his last puff and dropped his cigarette butt in a trash can.

This time, we went up to his room. As we followed him through a narrow, pale blue corridor, residents turned their heads and tracked us with their eyes. Just before we got to his door, my father whispered for us to keep quiet because his roommate was sleeping and he didn't want to disturb him. He and his roommate, a heavy Lebanese man with short hair, were protective of each other. My father's bed was on the side of the room with the window. He had a cabinet for clothes. Nothing hung on the walls. No art. No photos. Uncle Al said my father was a talented artist at one point, but had not painted or sketched in years.

❁

When I returned to Boston, I sent my father pens, pencils, and sketchbooks and wrote that I would love to see his drawings.

Over time his art became our comfortable medium. "What is this?" I'd ask him during my trips to California, pointing to a small figure on a sketch pad.

At first, his answers consisted of one word. A bird, a face, a demon, with no further explanation. Gradually as my visits became more frequent, he added a few more words, elaborating to point out the wings, the beak. He sketched and painted seemingly nonstop, in his room and on the balcony, from morning through night, handing thick sheaves of finished work to Uncle Al or me. Every page of the spiral sketchbooks I sent him returned filled. His drawings spanned the entire white space, reaching into four corners, as if out of frugality, not wanting to waste space and having so much to convey. Faces and bodies were distorted, almost Picasso-like. A nose sits under an eye. A neck grows out of an ear. On some pages, he fills the background with grassy hills and flowers. Many drawings are in plain black ink. Others combine ink and watercolors and crayons. Sprinkled throughout are short sayings, most uplifting and inspirational.

"Practice makes a good day out of a lousy one."

"Be OK with all and be happy all you want. Be of good cheer and luck will follow until it catches you."

"Become the inner you, and the outer you will manifest."

There's no trace of bitterness or cynicism. At the end of one book, he flashed his humor, closing with "Sorry ran out of gas." His art opened a window to what rested just below his mental illness and allowed him to express what he couldn't verbalize. In his sketches and little one-line pearls, I saw a gentle person, polite and generous.

❀

The day of Princess Diana's funeral I received a call from my mother. News stations carried images of the somber procession of cars along London streets lined with thousands of mourners of the fabled princess who died in a car crash, along with earlier film footage of her laughing with her two handsome sons, Princes William and Harry. They had their mother's doe eyes. Mother asked if I had been watching the funeral.

"It's sad," she said. I agreed. "Particularly for the children," she added. She sounded lonely. The Diana funeral might have stirred up some feelings about loss and mortality. I felt bad for her. I didn't ask the question running through my mind: Why do you feel such sympathy for Diana's sons, whom you never met, and have trouble conveying sympathy for me? Thinking back, I don't remember sympathy when I was lonely for her at the Trinleys'. Instead, she seemed to want to hurry away from me. When I was a teenager and immigrant, feeling completely lost in the United States, she didn't offer sympathy either. Instead, she said I chose to leave the monastery and was essentially on my own. Same for when I got married, and my wife and I felt completely alone and hated as we fought the abuse case against a popular minister. When I was trying to get through Brandeis and feeling incapable and frustrated, she questioned the value of a college education anyway, rather than sympathize. I didn't say any of that. She would get defensive and I didn't want to fight with her anymore.

"How do you feel about me?" I asked her. "Do you think of me?"

"I've told you so many times that I love you. Of course I love you. I don't know what you expect when you keep asking me those questions," she answered. I could hear the frustration in her voice.

I asked her whether she sees me differently than her beloved friends.

"I don't see any difference between you and any of my dharma friends," said my mother. "We are all connected." I was at a loss for words. It's true that we are connected. I can't argue with that. But a parent has to be responsible to provide for and protect her children. You can't expect the amorphous human race to provide the day's meals, shelter, and clothing, let alone the more consuming and critical intangibles of security and self-worth.

I pressed her. "Don't you think there is something sacred about the bond between the two of us?"

"No, I wouldn't call it sacred." Her refusal to acknowledge me as anything special hurt me deeply. Even if she didn't believe it, or couldn't use the term "sacred" because it is reserved for deities, she could have pretended and agreed if only to give me a simple joy of feeling special. Instead, she called me her cyber-son, referring to our e-mail contact. We have a virtual relationship. Ethereal mother-son.

I hung up, frustrated but trying not to be angry. Regardless of what she has or has not done for me, in the end she is my mother. We are all human, with weaknesses. I don't want to regret not having been good to her. She is already in her sixties, and not in good health. When she goes into town, she needs a walking stick. She tires easily. I do not think she has ever meant to harm me, although she didn't try very hard to make me happy or feel secure.

After conversations like that, I found myself pulling out my scrapbook of photos and letters that I had been gathering over the years. Unexpected packets would arrive every once in a while, when a relative was cleaning out drawers or attics.

In one small black-and-white picture, taken in a field somewhere in Greece, I'm a baby. My bearded father lifts me up in the air. Our faces are inches apart, our mouths open in laughter. My father is captured in a moment when he is whole, before his fragile mind fractured. He's a dad consumed by the gift of being a father and making his small child laugh. I am captured in glee. In another, I'm with my mother, my tiny body asleep and curled up in a cocoonlike cloth carrier she wears against her chest. Her hair, long and wild, is blowing in the wind. She's wearing a white peasant blouse and a long printed skirt. Smiling, her hands on her hips, she almost looks proud, maybe even content with having a baby son, his warm breath against her. I felt sympathy for that child in the pictures. He looks so innocent and unprotected. I grieved for the loss of the family that we were and for not having similar moments of affection throughout my childhood. Life might have been much easier for me if we had remained together. Maybe not, but I wished I could have turned to my parents over the years with confidence that they would be there for me.

Closing the book, I scolded myself for self-indulgent reveries. It's not healthy to dwell on the past. Let's move. Get going. As my mother has told me again and again, many people have unhappy childhoods.

❈

Phuni and I were watching a nature show on TV on venom and animals. Bark scorpions hid in the bark of trees waiting for their prey. Jellyfish tentacles snapped at passing fish, rendering them limp. There is nothing grotesque about it or even surprising, except perhaps for the sheer speed in which some venom kills. It's all part of nature's cycle.

That night after Phuni went to bed, I thought about the impermanence of life and wrote my thoughts on my computer. "I am willing to accept death as part of nature and part of the cycle of existence. Taking life for granted is so easy. It is not until one is faced with the sure impermanence of life that things become scary. Impermanence is the surest thing. I am not afraid of death. I would rather live for another thousand years but the reality is, sooner or later, death is certain. Why be afraid of it? Why should I place more value on my life than on any other being? It is part of nature to die. There is no escaping it. I have several sincere requests. I do not want to be buried, do not want to be on extensive life support systems, and wish to be remembered as a curious and unique person."

Aunt Charlotte was not doing well. During one of my visits, Uncle Al and I took her to the UCLA Medical Center. Doctors said she was dying of cancer. Phuni urged me to stay with them. Having watched her own father nurse her mother for more than a year before she died of ovarian cancer, she knew how much work Uncle Al faced. "Tell them you really want to be there and help with anything you can," she told me over the phone. I stayed for two months. When Aunt Charlotte could not maneuver steps, we set up a bed downstairs. She watched Uncle Al and me play computer blackjack. We put on a show, yelling at the computer when it dealt us a bad hand because it made her laugh. I drove them to the doctors, cooked, and ran errands. Other days, I did nothing more than get her drinks and rub her back and arms with lotion. If Uncle Al was overcome with grief, I acted as an intermediary between him and the hospice nurse. I was grateful for the chance to help and be with them. They had done so much for me, coming to my graduation, paying for my trip to Israel, offering advice and help, and caring for my father.

Aunt Charlotte died at home. Uncle Al was distraught. I tried consoling him, talking about how life doesn't end but continues through reincarnation. Uncle Al turned to me. "Damn it, Daja. I don't want you to be logical with me. If I want to be emotional, let me be emotional."

❀

In between my trips, I worked at the warehouse. The job wore on me. Not the actual physical labor itself but the fact that I was still at it, three years after graduation. I felt guilty because I wasn't doing anything worthwhile. The trips to Tibet were personally gratifying, but they were one-shot deals. Now I was spending too much time watching TV. When I got bored with that, I turned on my computer and tried to write.

"I am not sure what direction I am moving in and what is going to happen to me," I wrote in the spring of 1999. "I know I can just get out there and get a job, but under what context? I feel like nothing is going in the right direction. I know I am experiencing symptoms of depression. I also know that I have been experiencing a low level of depression for a long time and it might be getting a bit worse because I feel incapable of changing my circumstances. I am also incapable of expressing these feelings to other people because of my fear of embarrassment. I look at other people and think, Why can't I just do what they are doing? I look at my wife and think, I wish I was able to do what she does, the way she is able to work and get things done with seemingly little effort. She knows how to just get things done. What is blocking me so much? There is something that I can almost feel physically that is constricting my ability to operate. It is forbidding me from being able to function in this harsh world."

In July 1999 I received another voice mail from John Ackerly, with the International Campaign for Tibet. "We're looking for someone to go to Amdo. This has to do with the World Bank project and I think you would be perfect. Call me as soon as you can. Bye."

Amdo, the Tibetan birthplace of the Dalai Lama, had become the focus of a controversial project that was to be funded by the World Bank to build dams and transform barren desert lands into farmland. But in the process, thousands of Chinese would be transferred into lands historically claimed by Tibet, outside the so-called Tibetan Autonomous Region but inside what some referred to as "Greater Tibet." For centuries Tibetans had lived there and much of the time had ruled that area. Having the World Bank fund the project might legitimize Chinese expansion and marginalize Tibet. China gave assurances that the Tibetans were behind the project, but Tibetan rights groups, including the International Campaign for Tibet, weren't convinced. I had my own doubts. The two previous trips had opened my eyes to the harsh treatment of Tibetans. The International Campaign for Tibet had requested a formal investigation by the World Bank, and until the investigation was done, the project was on hold. Not wanting to jeopardize the loan, China's government had announced publicly that it welcomed visitors to see for themselves that Tibetans weren't being uprooted against their will. It organized tours of local monasteries and invited journalists.

I called John back. He wanted me to go to Amdo and report back to the World Bank panel. My gut said not to go. I didn't speak any Chinese. The local Amdo dialect was indecipherable. In recent months, I had watched tensions grow between the United States and China. U.S. planes had bombed the Chinese embassy in Belgrade. In response, Chinese demonstrators attacked American embassies. China was cracking down on religious groups opposed to the Communist Party. Tibet was another sore point, with the United States urging Beijing unsuccessfully to open a dialogue with the exiled Dalai Lama. During my earlier trips, at least I was with someone, a congressman with diplomatic immunity, a reporter with credentials. This time I would be solo.

"What if I'm arrested?" I asked John. Chances are slim, he said. China had too much to lose by arresting visitors. "But what if I was?" I pressed further. I was certain I had a huge bull's-eye on my back from the trip with the congressman who was openly critical of China. "You'd probably be put on a plane and sent back to the U.S.," John said. If someone like John, who helped found an organization loathed by the Chinese, could get in and out of Tibet without much trouble, then I'm being paranoid. The little alarm bells clanging inside me were silly, I told myself.

"OK, then. I'll go. But only if someone else comes with me," I said.

We came up with an academic, Gabriel Lafitte, an Australian Tibetan supporter. I had heard of him. He had a good reputation and had been through Tibet several times and was familiar with the project.

I spent the next two weeks poring over World Bank documents and newspaper articles. The more I read, the more the red flags waved. I didn't know anything about irrigation systems. Not knowing the language and having so few contacts weighed heavily on my mind. So, too, did the underlying significance to the Tibetan people. Halting the project was a once-in-a-lifetime opportunity to reverse or at least delay the incursion and make some small contribution to help preserve a nation and way of life. The pressure was huge.

When I confided my misgivings to Phuni, she responded with her trademark passion and conviction that I could do it and was the perfect person. The mission had greater personal significance to her. I knew that. If her family and thousands of other Tibetans had not been forced to leave Tibet following the Chinese invasion, they wouldn't have been displaced from their cultural and economic resources. Her family would not have been vulnerable to the minister's persuasion that he could offer her a better life.

The morning of my Northwest Airlines flight out of Boston, Apa woke up at his usual early hour. After making Tibetan tea, he came to our room and began burning juniper incense on the fire escape and strung colorful prayer flags. He told me that what I was doing was important. I did not know how to argue with that. With his prayers and blessing, I was off with my duffel bag to Logan Airport. Inside were the small Lonely Planet guidebook for Tibet, World Bank documents, and copies of editorials from the *Boston Globe* and the *New York Times* arguing against the World Bank project. Just before I boarded the flight from Detroit to Beijing, I dumped most of the heavy World Bank documents.

Four weeks later, I woke up at 4 A.M. in a Chinese hospital room, screaming in pain. Rubber tubes protruded from my stomach. An oxygen mask covered my face. Both feet were bound tightly in plaster casts that reached halfway up my calf. Each of my wrists was tied to the railings of the bed.

"My feet," I yelled, my head thrashing about on my pillow. A group of security men hovered over me, laughing. A doctor appeared at the door. A young Chinese girl who spoke English translated what I was saying to him. He cut open the casts, relieving the throbbing pain and pressure.

Glancing around, I tried to figure out where I was. The window of the hotel room flashed before me. I remembered stepping out and then nothing. It was a blank. How much time had lapsed, I didn't know. The faces of the guards peering down at me looked familiar. They were the same foreign ministry guards who had arrested me. That told me all I needed to know. I was still in custody in China and had to get out of there. "What you did was a terrible thing, you should not have done that," the Chinese girl scolded me. The only footsteps I heard led to and away from my room. I was alone in the ward.

Rather than be grateful to be alive, I was distraught. Once again, I had failed. I had failed to protect the Tibetan translator and Gabriel, who might be dead or in prison. I had failed in my mission of reporting back to the International Campaign for Tibet. I had failed the chance to preserve a part of the Tibetan homeland. I had failed Phuni and Apa. Now I had failed the chance to elude my captors and prison, by surviving the fall. The Chinese would use my leap to intended death against me. "See, he jumped because he knew he was guilty," they would say. I wished for an earthquake to destroy the hospital and all of us inside.

I had spent the last two days in intensive care. Shortly after I had arrived at the hospital, my blood pressure dropped, my heart began beating rapidly, and I went into shock. Doctors opened up my stomach and found heavy internal bleeding. My shattered feet were put in casts to immobilize them. A long fresh scar stretched across my stomach where doctors removed my spleen and repaired my lacerated liver.

Hours after my gaining consciousness, the interrogations resumed. A man in a suit sat at a desk at the foot of my bed. A man with a video camera recorded every statement I made. Another guard took pictures of my lacerated wrists. "Now you must tell the truth," the suited man said. "You must apologize to the Chinese people and confess your crimes."

I thought I had already done that. "I don't know what else to say, just tell me what to write and I will write it," I said with frustration. He wanted me to admit I had jumped out the window so the government wouldn't be responsible for my injuries. Fine. I jumped out the window. I'll write that statement down, I told them. One of the guards raised my hospital bed so I could be upright to write. I screamed in pain from my broken back. The guards laughed. Only after I had written more confession statements did they leave.

I was alone, unable to move. My body and spirit were broken. A white curtain surrounded my bed. Scenarios spun through my mind. I was certain that by now the Chinese knew of my previous trips and work on behalf of Tibetans. Once I was well enough, I'd be put on trial for spying or treason in a Chinese court and thrown into one of the dark, isolated prisons I had driven by and felt horrified for the people inside. Security guards came in and out, smoking and laughing, mocking me as they took the bedpan away. I was placed on a gurney, taken in and out of white rooms. No one ever explained what they were doing. I felt like an animal being processed.

Phuni couldn't know where I was, that I had been captured and was now guarded in a small hospital room. Uncle Al didn't know. All they knew was that I was somewhere in Tibet. By the time they found out, it would be too late. I would be in prison.

I had to find another way out. A guard sat on a squeaky wooden chair next to my bed. That afternoon, I noticed the guard doze off. I leaned my head toward my bound wrists and wrapped the clear rubber oxygen tubes around my neck, pulling as hard as I could to choke myself. I could feel a numbing, darkening sensation, but didn't panic. The feeling was strangely comfortable. The guard woke. I turned my head away from him and slipped off my oxygen mask. Suspicious, the guard got up and put it back on. Each time I moved, I throbbed with pain.

The next afternoon, a security guard came into my room. He talked to the interpreter. She turned to me and said I needed to get cleaned up. Someone from the U.S. consulate was coming to see me. My heart skipped a beat. For the first time since I was arrested, I realized I had not been forgotten. An older woman came in, carrying a washbasin of gray water, a dirty rag, and a dull razor to shave me. Unbeknownst to me, back in the States Phuni had called the embassy, the consulate, and the media because she had not heard from me. She was making plans to fly to Tibet and find me when she heard I was in Chinese custody. Though it was dangerous for a Tibetan woman to come, she immediately booked a flight to Beijing. "If I must move a mountain, I will," she told my uncle Al and her father. "I'm getting him." By this time, I was the subject of international news stories. Gabriel had been released and sent back to Australia, where he told reporters he had been subject to intense psychological pressure by Chinese authorities. He had been told by the Chinese authorities that he was lucky he was not an American. In the U.S. State Department, officials held news briefings on my condition.

An hour later, an American man with a pair of glasses appeared in the room. The man identified himself as Jim Heller, from the U.S. consulate. He stood several feet away from my bed until the Chinese authorities said he could approach me. I wanted to remove the oxygen mask and talk to him, but the guard stepped in and stopped me. I overheard the translator telling him that I had to keep the mask on for health reasons. Heller handed me a strange assortment of gifts, a broken Rubik's Cube, books, a tiny shortwave radio, fruit roll-ups, and small packages of corn flakes.

The authorities said he could stay for a half hour. He seemed to have three things on his mind. First was letting me know that coming to China was a mistake, especially for someone who had been involved politically in the Tibetan rights movement. "There are better ways of doing this," he said. The second, more pressing point for him was finding out whether I had jumped or was pushed. Before I could explain anything, he said the Chinese said I had jumped and that my injuries were consistent with a parachutist fall. I sensed I had caused trouble. "I'm sorry this happened," I told him. "I was afraid." My hospitalization was expensive, he said. Who could be contacted to ask for the money to reimburse the Chinese? I gave him three names. My mother, Uncle Al, and John Emery. He said he would try to come by and see me the next day.

Before he left, he handed me a faxed letter from Phuni and Uncle Al. "Everybody knows the situation, that you are kept in detention, and you are not alone. We are following this very closely and doing everything we can," Phuni wrote. Uncle Al joked about getting together to play computer blackjack and getting to work having a baby as soon as I got home.

A few days later, a miracle: Phuni appeared at the side of my bed. Her eyes were swollen and red from days of crying. I wanted to take the oxygen mask off to let her know I was OK, and to make sure she didn't say anything that would get us both into more trouble. I was certain our meeting was being recorded. I pulled my sheet up to my neck. I didn't want her to see my bruised stomach and fresh stitches, or my lacerated wrists. Phuni had been so confident that I would do something great for the Tibetans. Shame filled me. Had I overreacted? I felt guilty for making a commotion and was afraid that people thought I was a coward and had capitulated.

"Don't worry. I'm taking you home," she assured me. "Rest now."

The next day, the Chinese girl informed me that I was free as of eleven o'clock that morning and that I could tell the foreign ministry officials standing around my bed to leave. The two of us began talking politics. She seemed to sympathize with the Tibetans and said she would like to visit the States. I asked why she didn't. People like her can't leave China, she told me. I was suspicious and thought she might be taping our conversations, but was beyond fear at that point. A bright yellow stretcher with black nylon straps and plastic buckles appeared next to my bed. I was moved from the bed to the stretcher. Outside, an ambulance waited. With sirens flashing, it led a motorcade of police cars and U.S. consulate officials to the airport. Local officials stared at us.

On a medevac flight from Xining to Hong Kong, organized by the International Campaign for Tibet, I began choking. My heart raced. The nurse and doctor exchanged worried glances. My lungs were collapsing. The doctor took a needle and injected me with steroids. They watched the blips on the heart monitor. The nurse took my pulse. They strapped an oxygen mask over my face. Phuni cradled my head and kissed my forehead. I was dying and afraid. I had caused so much trouble. As if it mattered, I kept asking her what people were saying outside China. I was so unsure about what I had done. She assured me that everything was OK. Then she began talking about having a baby. We have to have a baby after we got home, she said. I promised her we would.

Once we landed, I was taken to the Baptist Hospital in Hong Kong.

Phuni stayed at my side. In the morning, she shaved me. Throughout the day, she helped me with the bedpan and urinal. She brought me oxtail soup and chocolate, which I wasn't supposed to have because of my abdominal surgery, but craved. The nurses, some of the most gentle, kind, and attentive people I have ever met, pretended not to notice. Intuitively, she seemed to know when I was uncomfortable and adjusted the bed.

My mother was in India. She had broken up with her husband and been reordained as a nun. Word of my arrest and hospitalization had spread through the Tibetan community and reached her in Dharamsala. She contacted the embassy and found out Phuni was already en route. She decided not to come to the hospital, figuring a Buddhist nun would be unwelcome in Xining and might cause problems for me. She talked to me on the phone when I was in the hospital, letting me know that the Dalai Lama and others were praying for me. People would come up to her and say, "Ah, you're his mother." All Tibetans and Tibetan supporters saw me as a hero to their cause.

Chapter Ten
Rebirth

Just past midnight, August 31, 1999, my wife and I arrived at Logan Airport in a Learjet. As we were pulling up on the tarmac, I looked out the window. Groups of friends including Apa waited, and reporters with cameras and microphones. The plane doors opened. Flashes illuminated the inside of the jet. I didn't talk to anyone. An ambulance took me to Brigham and Women's Hospital. The director of the hospital stood at the entrance and welcomed me. As I was taken through the hospital lobby on the stretcher, a large crowd of people held flowers and placards that said, "Welcome home, Wangchuk-la." Some of the children held white Tibetan scarves to wish me well. Tibetan women in their traditional colorful aprons cried. I was deeply humbled and mouthed "Hello" to them. Flowers filled my room. Signs in Tibetan and English were taped on the walls.

Once I was in my room, a young nurse removed the stitches from my belly and put fresh bandages on the incisions. Another nurse inserted an IV line into my right arm and gave me a cold can of ginger ale and water. I felt surprisingly healthy. My mind was calm. The next morning, I woke to see the orange morning sun hitting the windows of the adjacent buildings.

I spent the next month in the hospital, my chest full of fluids, fighting high fevers. I was vomiting and steadily losing weight. Nothing I ate stayed down. Doctors ran tests for dozens of infections and viruses and couldn't pinpoint the cause. Drawing from his days as a nomad, caring for sick families in tents and on mountain paths with no medication, Apa cooked a special lamb stew with Tibetan roasted barley flour at the Walker Center. He packed it in a Tupperware container and filled a thermos with Tibetan tea, boarded the subway, and brought it to the hospital. Standing at the side of my bed, he dipped a spoon into the stew and gently urged me to try it. He held lime wedges to my lips so I could suck on them. Feeding me took more than an hour. Whether it was the citrus or the barley or the combination, the stew was the only thing I ate that didn't make me sick. Gradually, I grew stronger. When I slept, he napped on the floor. If he wasn't there, Phuni was, each of them relieving the other so the other could go to work. In loving concert, they applied cold compresses, removed the bedpans, helped me in and out of my wheelchair, and changed my clothes.

Once the fevers were under control, doctors began the long, painstaking task of piecing together my shattered feet into a mosaic of bone piece and metal pins, screws, and plates. Physical therapists came to my room to stretch my muscles so they wouldn't atrophy. I wouldn't be able to walk until my feet heeled. Other surgeries would follow. Doctors said I might walk like a duck for the rest of my life. All things considered, that didn't seem too bad.

I was back in Boston, out of danger. My traveling companions were safe. The Australian had been deported within days of my jump. Our Tibetan interpreter had been taken to another location and questioned for an additional four days before he, too, was let go. He told me years later that if I had not jumped, he might never have been released.

People all over the world were praying for my well-being. Flowers and dozens of cards arrived daily. My old college professors visited. Reporters wrote stories about the incident. The office of the Dalai Lama sent me a letter. "We are inspired by your selfless efforts to bring to light the reality of the situation inside Tibet," it read. Students at Brandeis held a benefit concert with Run-D.M.C. and 10,000 Maniacs to help pay medical expenses. For months, people at supermarkets, gas stations, and barbershops came up to Phuni and Apa asking how I was. On the other side of the world, Tibetans and monks stopped my mother in the street and on retreats, inquiring about my health.

A month later I left the hospital in a wheelchair, my legs and feet propped up and encased in thick casts. We moved into a first-floor apartment at the Walker Center because of my wheelchair. I hung a sheet in between the living room and the bedroom for privacy. It was a depressing apartment. The rooms were dark, damp, and cold. Every time a toilet flushed in the building, water gurgled through the exposed sewer pipes that were painted beige and ran through our bedroom, against the wall and next to our bed. Since the kitchen was in another building, we kept a small refrigerator in our closet and an electric hot plate on top of our bureau. Hot plates weren't allowed because they kept blowing fuses. We used it sparingly. Apa slept in a small room on the third floor, with only a bed and a table. Before and after he went to work, he came to our living room with tea and meals that he prepared in the kitchen and carried over. Uncle Al bought us a six-month cable subscription so I could watch the Discovery Channel while recuperating.

Phuni wanted to quit working and take care of me. "No. I'm fine. Go," I told her. I told the same to Apa. A friend built a wooden ramp so I could wheel myself out our front door and onto a patch of grass. I sat there for hours, reading, dozing off, listening to the birds. After a while, I wheeled myself back inside and watched cable. Most of the day, I waited for Phuni and Apa to come home. Occasionally I wrote profiles for the International Campaign for Tibet of former Tibetan political prisoners—including a monk jailed for displaying a Tibetan flag—interviewing by phone and writing on my computer. Eventually I took a literature class.

Empty weeks stretched into empty months. My life revolved around visits to the doctor and physical therapists. As soon as I recovered from one surgery, another was scheduled. New screws and pins were inserted and bone spurs removed. After each, I spent days in the hospital hooked up to machines, attended by a team of nurses monitoring my temperature, oxygen level, heart rate, blood pressure, oxygen saturation, and pain level. Everyone was doing his or her best. but I doubted I would ever walk again. I gained weight from the medication and inactivity. My doctors encouraged me to go to the Brandeis gym and stretch my muscles, but I didn't go. I was damaged merchandise and had only myself to blame. Phuni tried to keep my spirits up. Apa told me that I had accomplished something worthy. If each person does one thing that is worthy of his life, he is lucky, he said. You have done that. Have a happy mind.

I couldn't. The events in China replayed themselves over and over in my head. As far as the rest of the world knew, I jumped to escape my captors. Technically that was true. No one had to know I didn't plan on surviving the fall. I told close friends, but said nothing to set the record straight to reporters.

People called what I did heroic. It made me uncomfortable, but I kept silent for political reasons. Left uncorrected, the scenario of jumping to escape my captors kept the pressure on the Chinese unabated. They were culpable for so much, the tormentors who somehow forced me out the window. Correcting that image might cause pressure to ease up and focus on my weakness, not their wrongness. I had admitted to taking the pictures. The area was not defined as restricted when I did so. I didn't do anything illegal. They were wrong. Keeping that front meant weighing my words carefully. I couldn't slip. Rather than say anything, I became withdrawn. When the media called, I referred reporters to others in the Tibetan movement. It wouldn't be unlike me to do that anyway.

The goal was achieved. A year after my visit, the Chinese government, under growing international pressure and lacking the necessary votes at the World Bank, withdrew its request for funding from the bank. Tibetans and their supporters worldwide, who rallied around this project, could claim a victory. That was the important thing. My personal struggles were irrelevant, and those struggles continued long after the project was halted. Painful and embarrassing questions circled through my head. Did I overreact? Was I irrational, too emotional, too cowardly, too frightened, and too impulsive? Was I practical, or naive? Did I make the right choice? I later talked to Tibetan scholars who assured me I was in an untenable situation and that by jumping out the window, I had ruined my captors' plans. I read books about Chinese methods of mental torture. What they described was hauntingly familiar.

The tougher, more troubling question for me, and one that I kept at a distance, was *why?* Why was I was so willing to die? Didn't I have anything to live for? My ambivalence went beyond not missing life because of my spiritual belief that another life would follow. I simply felt that I wasn't leaving much behind. I had grown so insular that I had failed to make any strong bonds that would have pulled me back from the ledge that August afternoon.

❀

One morning I received an e-mail. Planning to respond, I pushed the reply button. The empty blue-white screen waited. When I went to write simple words I had written countless times before—"dear," "doctor," "medicine"—I couldn't remember how to spell them. My mind went blank. The same thing happened the next day and the next. I couldn't remember what had happened minutes earlier. Simple decisions tormented me. I spent entire days trying to decide whether I should return a phone call or respond to a single e-mail. By nightfall, I still had not made up my mind and would go to bed mad at myself for not responding. The next morning, I'd wake up and do the same thing all over again. I began skipping my literature classes, which had been my one source of stimulation. I didn't want to study or think. I didn't want to do anything. Alone, the curtain and doors closed, I drank ginger ale and cheap gin and listened to Bob Marley sing, "Get up, stand up, stand up for your rights." No part of the day held relief. I dreaded early mornings, sunny afternoons, and quiet evenings equally.

Watching television, I saw a Zoloft ad. A little head bounced on the screen, talking about signs of depression. All of them described what I was feeling. Logging on the computer, I checked the Zoloft Web site. *Answer yes to the following symptoms and you may be suffering from depression. See your doctor.* Going through the list, I mentally checked them all off. Yes, I had a persistent sad, anxious, or "empty" mood. Yes, I had feelings of hopelessness, pessimism. Yes, I felt guilty, worthless, and helpless. I lost interest and pleasure in activities that I once enjoyed, like reading and classes. I had little energy, difficulty in concentration and making decisions. I slept too much, thought of death too much, and was irritable.

Though I seemed to fit every category, I didn't think I was depressed. What I was feeling was normal for me. I'm just in a funk. Everyone gets down once in a while. My problem was that I needed to work harder, and quit feeling sorry for myself. I needed to mentally will my mood and spirits upward. What I have is a character flaw, not a mental illness. Besides, the notion that a little pill could help seemed far-fetched. At the same time, even with all my denial and rationalizing, I knew something was wrong.

I called the Brigham and Women's outpatient psychiatry department. A woman answered. "What are you looking for?" she asked. All I really wanted was a pill, but I didn't think that would be a good answer. Nor did I want to tell her about my vague blahs. I needed a specific problem.

"I've had some surgeries. I'm about to have more and am having difficulty coping with that," I said. The woman gave me an appointment with Kimberly Fitch, a resident psychiatrist.

Her office was on the fourth floor in a complex of assorted medical buildings. Hobbling through the hallway on crutches, wearing a white protective boot on my left foot, I was glad that I blended in with the white lab coats and blue scrubs. As far as anyone knew, I could be going to any one of a dozen doctors' offices. No one could tell I was going to see a psychiatrist. On the elevator up, I thought of pushing the button for the first floor, returning to my car, and going back home. Accepting the fact that I might have a mental problem terrified me and embarrassed me. All I could think of was my father when I first met him. Dirty, smelly, and expressionless.

Several chairs in the waiting room were empty. I took the one tucked in the corner, rested my crutches on the floor next to it, and sat down. A pile of magazines rested on the nearby table. I picked one off the top and put it up in front of my face so no one could see me. A short time later, a tall blond woman appeared and introduced herself as Dr. Fitch. She showed me into her office.

It was a small and windowless space that felt more private than dark or clinical. Reproductions of famous paintings of landscapes and portraits hung on the cream-colored walls. Paperback and hardback books about the mind and relationships occupied the bookshelf. Her desk was pushed to the corner. She sat facing me, behind her desk. I leaned my crutches against the wall and hopped over to the comfortable fabric-covered office chair in front of her, and lowered myself down into it.

"So, why are you here?" she asked.

I hesitated, mentally reviewing what I wanted to say. Be careful and deliberate, I thought. You don't know her and you don't know what she will do with the information. Whether it was rational or not, I could imagine word that I was mentally ill somehow seeping out of this office and reaching friends and supporters worldwide, who thought of me as confident and mature. It was one thing for me to feel there was something inherently wrong with me. It was another for other people to know that. I didn't confide in friends who seemed to care about me. Why should I confide in her? Write me a prescription for Zoloft, I thought, and I'll go away. Quickly, I realized it didn't work that way. I was going to have to give before I could get.

Steering clear of emotional pain, I stuck to the safer physical problems.

"I've had several surgeries and have to have another. I'm worried about it," I told her.

"What are you worried about?" I had to stop and think. Not the physical pain, I realized, but rather that the surgeries would never end. I wake up in recovery rooms, surrounded by a team of nurses, watching new beds arrive and leave and family members huddle, and wonder whether this latest surgery might be the last one. It never was. All I did was go to the doctor, stay at home, and try to recover. Once I felt a little better, it was time for another operation. I wasn't sure I would ever walk again. I was out of shape and wanted to go to the gym, but couldn't, I told her.

"Why not?" she asked.

Again, I stopped to think. What was stopping me? I could drive with crutches and a special cast. So it wasn't transportation. As a Brandeis graduate, I could use the gym. So it wasn't a lack of a gym. I felt I didn't belong in a big room where everyone else looked like my high school gym teacher. I looked like a cripple. People would stare. I didn't want to be stared at again. I had enough of that as a young, white monk.

She scheduled me for another appointment the following week. Each week, I drove to her office and spent fifty minutes talking about my life Slowly, over the course of two years, I opened up. In the safety of her office, I tried to answer her one simple, often repeated question of "Why?" Why did I feel like something was inherently wrong with me? With her help, I took each feeling—fear, confusion, sadness, alienation, insecurity, anger, and unworthiness—and untangled it from the others. Once it was isolated, I could examine it, turn it over in my mind, and follow it to its source. I was surprised at how much it reminded me of the meditation of my youth. I had forgotten how I used to pay close attention to my mind, developing a third eye to objectively track my mind's wanderings. It was a time-consuming and at times painful process, unearthing the loneliness and fear that I felt as a child.

The one subject I wanted to avoid kept returning week after week. My mother. I had seen my mother only once since China. She was teaching in Mexico now and begged me to come and visit. I knew she didn't want Phuni to come, but I insisted. Relations had deteriorated so much that when my mother called from India, she put someone else on the phone in case Phuni answered. That person would tell Phuni that my mother wanted to talk to me.

My mother met us at the airport in Mexico. I spotted her robes immediately. She waved and started coming toward us. Her gait was slow and uneven. She leaned heavily on a cane. She could barely walk and could no longer tie her own shoes. She was terrified of falling and breaking her hip. Her face was lined with age. It was the first time my mother ever looked frail and weak. I hugged her gingerly. Those few days, we acted like tourists, going to an artist colony and on a boat ride with mariachi players. Around us, people sang and danced, drank beer and ate. One member of the band asked Phuni to dance. My mother and I sat off to the side. I tried to keep conversations free of emotions and hurt. We entered into a long debate about the value of education, feminism, and activism. On every fundamental topic, we disagreed. How could two people from the same gene pool be so totally at odds? Was there any part of our life where we weren't in conflict? The only thing we had in common, it seemed, was our damaged legs.

Each time I pulled a strand of my life to examine why I felt unworthy, or why I felt I didn't belong anywhere, the little figure of my mother in her nun robes emerged dangling from the end: taking me as child to a foreign land and culture where I stood out as strange, not being there to affirm that there was nothing wrong with me, appearing in my life and giving me hope we could be together and then disappearing, only to resurface in a new city, a new country. She reminded me of quicksand, something that looked grounded but gave way the minute you approached it, leaving you floundering. The more Dr. Fitch asked me about her, the more I realized how little I knew about her own life. We would see each other every few years. In between, we talked on the phone, exchanged letters and e-mails. I knew nothing of her childhood, her feelings, what made her happy or sad.

I began asking my mother questions. Why did you leave me? I wanted to know what would lead a mother to do that. I wanted to know about her own life, what shaped her. At first, she was defensive. Talking about the past, her family, and her childhood didn't interest her. The present, not the past, is what matters, she would argue. Let go of the past.

I pushed her further. Without knowing her history, I couldn't know or begin to try to understand the forces that shaped her and ultimately me. Clinging to the past sounds petty and weak. Putting it behind, without wanting to examine it or deal with it, can also be a convenient way to avoid taking responsibility for what happened.

Through a series of e-mails, long phone conversations, and letters, I learned much. The basic facts I knew. She adored her grandmother Dena. Her father, John, was famous. Her mother, Rosemary, was beautiful. Her parents were divorced. Her mother committed suicide. But I never considered how that affected her. I realized she never learned how to parent because her own parents weren't there for her. I didn't know how much she missed her father's attention, or that she felt the American lifestyle corrupted her family and that she wanted to take me away from all that. I found out she was afraid of living in America, surrounded by the same temptations that ruined her parents and becoming an alcoholic herself. I was floored to hear my mother—still a Buddhist nun, but in her sixties now—recently tell me that one main reason she became a nun was that she loved the smell, sight, and taste of beer, wine, and booze and thought the vows would keep her away from it.

"Some people don't like booze, drugs," she e-mailed me. "I like sex, drugs, and rock 'n' roll . . . totally. So, better to be a nun and be clear and no disasters." Those admissions revealed a vulnerable side to my mother that I never knew before. It made her more human to me. All her life, she had been struggling with her own baggage from the past.

She wrote me a letter in which she talked about her childhood, her parents, painful disappointments, and her grandmother. She confessed that she did not understand the needs of a child. "I'm sorry you felt separated from me and your extended family and your American roots, but I had found that had brought me nothing but pain, and I didn't want you to have to experience that. I realize now there were times you needed me that I wasn't there, that there are some things that I didn't provide for you emotionally, etc., and I am so sorry for that. I truly am. I didn't ever intend for you to suffer. I felt the life I was preparing for you would give you happiness . . . that's the only reason I did what I did . . . as a parent you wish for the best for your child. As a human, one makes mistakes. When I was 26, I didn't have all the knowledge in the world and couldn't predict the future. . . . I'd like for us to have an open relationship in which we enjoy talking to each other like people normally do and accept and forgive each other. I know you feel I've been a bad parent but if we ever hope to learn from each other we need to let go of the past and move on . . . especially before either of us dies and we lose the opportunity to connect."

I had spent too much of my life banging my head against the wall in terms of my mother. I expected her to offer comfort or understanding. Even if she didn't agree with me, or didn't support my marriage or my college degree, I wanted her to pretend that she did to make me feel good. It wouldn't have cost a cent and would have been priceless. Somewhere along the line, she inherited a stubborn streak and wouldn't budge. I thought I could anger or ignore her into the person I wanted her to be. That was unfair. All I can do and should do, I've learned, is understand and accept, and forgive her.

You can change the way you relate to a person and have a completely different relationship even if that person hasn't changed. It's a matter of perception. While my circumstances and experiences growing up were largely determined by my parents, I am not set in stone. Even if we miss out on something as children and lose that golden moment, we can make it up after.

Growing up without parents to affirm me, I became insecure and alienated. But that doesn't mean I have to spend my entire life that way. The walls I built around myself can fall. I realized I had blamed her more than I should have. I held her accountable when I felt sullen or unhappy and expected her to rescue me from all hardships. For a long time, I never bothered to, or couldn't, see that I was putting all the responsibility on her for my happiness and not accepting responsibility myself.

The strain that laced our conversations is gone. I no longer start with my question "Do you love me?" I realize she does in her own way. Recently, we conversed online. I was telling her how I felt when she came to visit me at the Trinleys'. In the past, the exchange would have been different. More angry and defensive.

"I remember wondering why you left without me. I couldn't understand. That was very painful. You all had to be ingenious to distract me."

"I'm so so sorry. How awful. I would do all that differently now. So sorry."

"I just couldn't make sense and began to think maybe something was very wrong with me that you did not take me with you."

"How awful."

"I missed you too much."

"I'm so sorry."

"You were my mama and nothing was going to change that."

"I know. But I still am."

Each time we talk, I learn more about her. She's funny and loves to laugh. I had forgotten how she howled when I imitated the hoity-toity walk of one of Dena's friends. I admire the way she makes me think, forcing me to look at questions or problems or issues from a different viewpoint. I might not agree, but her point of view expands my own. The fact that she chose a very specific path, and devoted her life to it, is admirable. The truth is, she could have lapsed into drinking and drugs and blamed her own unhappy childhood for doing so. But she didn't. Instead, she found a way to avoid that.

I doubt we will ever agree on the importance of family and the bond between mother and son. She still doesn't see any special connection. "Seeing your own child as so special or as a particular joy or whatever is totally coming from a mind of attachment, not compassion or wisdom. What is so special about this person or child as compared to another one? Each parent thinks their child is the most wonderful, handsome, bright, clever child on earth. I find this so strange and even silly. Each human being is special and deserving of happiness, care, love, etc. . . . each one. Each child."

My mother moved to the States. The damp weather and physically demanding life in India were too difficult for her. Her hip needed to be replaced. She is not here willingly. "To this day, I'd rather be living in any country other than this one, almost," she wrote to me. "This place is weird, uptight, aggressive, expensive, unspiritual in a deep way, warlike, and now it's becoming a right-wing, Christian-fundamentalist-republic, warring nation. What benefits are there to living here? Maybe faster communication, less lines to wait for this and that . . . easier shopping . . . and then?"

She is, in her heart, a good human being and means well. Her compassion for prisoners, writing them letters, and for the downtrodden is inspiring. I felt she simply didn't know how to be a mother.

After her hip surgery, I called her to see how she was doing. She cried over the phone, saying how much I must have hurt going through surgery after surgery. We debate Buddhism. She says I'm not a good Buddhist because I no longer practice many of the rituals.

I argue that Buddhism is a way of life. It's about empathy and concern for other living beings. It's a sense that we are all connected, if not directly in this life, certainly in past lives and again in future lives. Buddhism, for me, never was in the rituals or the studying. It's in my very being. I can't act without wondering how my actions affect others. I avoid conflicts. I can no more separate Buddhism from me than I can change my DNA. It's part of my mind and soul.

Once I asked her whether Buddhism meant avoiding attachments. It never made sense to me how she could use Buddhism to justify leaving me. She offers, now, a more nuanced explanation. Love, she explains, is what is needed. Not attachment. "Attachment is 'I need you for my happiness.' Love is wanting the other person to be happy unconditionally."

I visit my father and Uncle Al several times a year. Uncle Al kept my parents' suitcase that I said he could throw away because he knew people attach different values to things at different points in their lives. He knew I would change and might regret having casually thrown away a telling artifact. More than ever, I needed to revisit the things that belonged to my parents and family. Seeing what my parents chose to keep defines what they cherished.

Inside the suitcase was an article my mother's beloved Dena wrote about a party for virtuoso pianist Arthur Rubinstein and stories clipped from various society pages chronicling Dena's globe-trotting adventures and Rosemary's education in boarding schools. There was a picture of my mother as a little girl, wearing chaps, a vest, and a cowboy tie around her neck, idolizing her father's *Gunsmoke* world. A picture of *Gunsmoke* star James Arness, dressed as U.S. Marshal Matt Dillon and signed "To Feather, my very best wishes. Always, James Arness." I realize how much her father's inattention must have hurt. Only recently did I find out that he never left her anything in his will.

There was a soft portrait of my mother, snapped on a sidewalk in France, smiling, wearing a fashionable trench coat and leather gloves, her dimples deep and her hair short and curled. She's radiant. I told her recently how beautiful she was, which surprised her. She never saw herself as pretty.

Among my father's belongings was an eight-by-ten-inch black-and-white photo. In it, my father is a little boy, maybe three or four years old. He's trying on Uncle Al's military cap. Uncle Al took it shortly after he got back from the service. The little boy in that picture has no idea that he will be sent to an orphanage. It's hard to imagine my father, now gray and bearded, that young. His eyes have the same gentleness after all these years. I examined the tools my father used to make intricate metal jewelry. They belonged to the skilled craftsman my father was. His detailed black ink sketches are snapshots of a time when he was mentally whole. Reading the captions written on the backs of photos taken of me as a baby, I learned that my father had collected little pieces of driftwood and seashells to delight me and that my mother crocheted blankets and hats for me. The photos, letters, and drawings provide another dimension of my parents.

After going through the suitcase, we went to see my father at Brentwood. Oscar called my father over the speaker system. Within five minutes, my father appeared in the hallway, wearing a purple baseball cap and a pair of kid's sunglasses with fluorescent temples. My father had run away from Brentwood for five weeks and just returned. During that time, Uncle Al was frantic, making and distributing flyers reading, "Have You Seen My Brother?" and showing my father's picture. The flyers said my father might be disoriented and needed medication daily, and asked people to contact my uncle, the police, or Brentwood with any information regarding his whereabouts. He delivered them to restaurants and shops in the Santa Monica area to post in their windows.

Police eventually found my father sitting on a bench at the Promenade. When he returned, I called him. "Why did you run away?" I asked him. "I needed a break," he said.

Now, his pants looked baggy from all the weight he had lost while living on the street. I gave him a hug, my embrace firm, not tentative as at our first meeting. His arms tightened around me.

He pointed his finger toward his room. "Daja, I have some pictures I made for you," he said. He led Uncle Al and me to his room. New medicines have helped my father. He's neater, his beard less unruly. He's more communicative. My father realizes he has a condition and needs to live in a place like Brentwood, where he can get help. He is not angry or resentful. My graduation picture sits on his bureau. In his wallet, my father carries a picture of Phuni and me. His finished paintings were propped up at an angle against the cabinet. He took them out and handed them to me. Many are painted on scraps of paper he picked up off the street or found in garbage cans. He preferred that. "I can create something out of nothing," he told me.

We drove to a Chinese restaurant that offered $5 lunch specials.

"Hey, look at what you've created here," Uncle Al said to my father, nodding toward me. "Do you realize that you are responsible for creating this monster? One good thing you did in your life was to create him, you know that?"

"Yaaap," my father said, staring straight ahead through the windshield. Uncle Al continued, "Did you ever think you could come up with something like that?" Uncle Al rubbed his gray beard. "He is yours, you know?"

"Yaaap," said Larry.

At the restaurant, Uncle Al put his arms on the linoleum-topped table, looked at my father, and asked, "What did it feel like when you created him?" My father thought for a moment. "Well, it felt like a big explosion," he said and began laughing with deep heaves. When his wonton soup arrived, Uncle Al sifted out carrots and broccoli, leaving only the soft mushrooms for my father. My father no longer has any teeth. A dentist at UCLA pulled them all. It's not clear why, whether my father had a problem with his teeth or it was easier to just pull them out so no one had to worry about cleaning them or filling cavities.

That small gesture of removing the vegetables struck me as tender. Uncle Al discounted the effort. "He's my brother. Of course I take care of him." I'm grateful for my uncle's devotion to my father over the decades. It couldn't have been easy caring for someone who can act irrationally and is so needy, especially when you are twenty years older.

I call my father every week or so, mostly to touch base, to let him know I'm thinking of him, and to find out how he is. I worry about him. Often he makes me laugh. My father doesn't have his own phone. Oscar pages him. A few minutes later, he picks up the phone.

"Hello."

"It's Daja. What are you doing?"

"Listening to Mariah Carey."

"Do you like her?"

"I guess she is not too cool."

"How was the food today?"

"Kind of like skid row food."

I laughed. "I think a lot about you," I told him.

"I think about you, too. Not enough. I have other things to occupy my mind," he said.

"The most important thing is to stay happy inside regardless of what is happening or the surroundings," I said.

"Allen Ginsberg says that," he said.

I was surprised to hear that from him. "Did you know Ginsberg died?" I asked. He didn't.

"Do you read the newspaper?"

"No, newspapers have too much bad news," he replied.

Such flashes of lucidity and insight are both delightful and frustrating because I know I will never really know what my father is thinking or feeling. Once I asked my father about the people he lived with, whether he talked to them much. "No. Most are waiting to die," he said. "I'm not." Lately, I've been having dreams about my father. In them, I make him well.

I send him care packages of chocolate, soaps, pencils, books, and ballpoint pens. Apa put together a Ziploc bag filled with Indian and Tibetan music cassettes and paints and pens that he picked up from the garbage in Auburndale, thinking my father might want them. It struck me. Both my father and father-in-law rummaged through the garbage cans.

§

Apa was as strong as a horse. Even when he felt sick, or his knees and wrists bothered him from arthritis, he went to work. His lungs and heart were hale from biking all weekend in search of bottles. He ate well. Before he arrived in the States, his family was concerned that he was drinking too much. He still liked to drink beer, but it didn't seem to be a problem. I took him regularly to the doctor for checkups.

One day I went to see Apa in the basement where he had all of his cans, plastic bags, and other odds and ends from the Dumpsters carefully organized on the shelves. "When I die, you will see all this and laugh at how Apa had collected all these things," he said.

"You have at least another ten years in you," I said.

I was helping him get ready for a trip back to India. He had not been back to visit family and friends and was adamant about going. I didn't think it was a good idea. Lately, he had not been eating well. He would make himself a kind of *tsampa* soup in the morning and nibble Doritos in his bed in the evening. Something didn't feel right, he said, and touched the area around his stomach to show me where. I took him in for a checkup. Doctors said it was indigestion and gave him a prescription for acid reflux. I bought him liquid meal replacements like Ensure to make sure he was getting enough nutrients.

I helped him pack large duffel bags filled with the shoes, toys, clothes, and diapers that he bought to take back to family and friends in the refugee village, and drove him to the airport. At the gate, I found an Indian couple waiting for the same flight. I introduced myself and asked whether they could make sure Apa made the right connections. They agreed. Both Apa and I were relieved. He was anxious to see how everyone was at home. We hugged. He boarded the plane.

A month later, I went to pick him up at the airport. Flight attendants brought him out in a wheelchair. He looked like the emaciated Buddha in Kopan's temple, with hollow cheeks and eyes sunken in their sockets. He could barely hold his head up. In his hand he held a plastic container to hold his vomit. As the flight attendant wheeled him closer, I could hear him breathing heavily and see him sweating from fever.

Apa had liver cancer. Apparently, he had been in pain for months but never complained about it. While he was in India, he became very ill and weak. His family took him to the hospital, where doctors diagnosed the cancer. Phuni and I thought the doctors in India must be wrong. Apa had been to the doctors just before his trip. If there was anything seriously wrong, they would have found it.

I took Apa to Brigham and Women's Hospital. CAT scans showed that his cancerous liver was twice its normal size. Doctors came in to tell us what they found. They tried to let us know Apa was dying without saying those words. Apa knew already. I suspect that is why he was so insistent about going back to India. He wanted to say good-bye. He was also determined to make it back to Phuni and me. Apa thanked the doctors and said he wasn't worried at all. He had faith. He was more worried about the doctors' time and told them they needed to see other patients. Don't worry about me. Often, Apa would tell me over the years that when the time came, no doctor could stop death.

I brought him home. We had moved out of the Walker Center to a large home we were house-sitting. We didn't want any ambulances. Before climbing the steps, he looked around the yard and noticed some of the last remnants of snow. Once in bed, he wanted to be left alone. He told Phuni to go to work. I gave him liquid morphine for the pain and let him rest. The time I spent with Aunt Charlotte when she was dying prepared me for what to expect. The pain would be intense. He wouldn't be able to eat. He would become weak and constipated. He would vomit. He would go downhill quickly. I called my mother and talked to her, letting her know Apa was in bad shape. She knew Apa's devotion to the Dalai Lama. Make sure he has a picture of His Holiness the Dalai Lama, she said. In my room, I had a framed photo of the Dalai Lama taken when he came to visit Brandeis. I brought it to Apa's room. He was going in and out of consciousness. When I approached his bed, I told him I had a picture of His Holiness the Dalai Lama. Apa seemed to will himself to consciousness. His eyes opened. Seeing the photo, they widened. He lifted his head, put his hands together and prayed. Once he was done, he rested his head back on the pillow. I left the picture on the table next to him and went upstairs to my room.

Phuni's sister Sonam stayed with him. Ten minutes later, she came running to find me, screaming for me to come quick. Foam was coming from Apa's mouth. I grabbed the phone and called the palliative care people. He's dying, they said. I called Phuni and went to Apa and gave him morphine. He looked at me and gave me a thumbs-up sign. I rubbed his arms, legs, and chest, and stroked his head to clear away the drops of sweat. Once Phuni arrived, I told him everything was fine and that he didn't have to worry about anything. He could let go. Moments later, he took his last breath. His hands curled but his face relaxed. He looked serene. His lips bore a faint smile.

All my life, I had stubbornly avoided relationships and attachments. I claimed it was virtuous to be free from them. I denied the importance of family, rejecting it as unnecessary. Now I realize that family gives you a sense of identity and belonging and safety. Those are the relationships that we take to the grave.

That's why I'm grateful to have my parents in my life. I have more than forgiven my mother. I have come to accept and love her for who she is. Like many of us, she is a flawed human, trying her best to get through life. She has apologized for her mistakes; she has cried and accepted that she did not appreciate how much I needed her, and said that if she could do it again she would do it differently. I think she was honestly confused and torn about what to do with me. She thought America would be bad for me. She didn't know what I needed because she never had what she needed as a child herself.

As for my father, I accept him for who he is. More than that. I love and admire him for his gentle ways and artistic talents. His poetry, drawings, and humor delight me. I was never angry with him. I didn't know him until much later in my life and didn't have expectations as I did with my mother. If anything, I was more embarrassed about his appearance and the label "crazy." I'm the one to be forgiven for being ashamed, and I'm confident my father has forgiven me,

Reconnecting with my parents has been a gift to me. For this, I owe Phuni. She was the one who always saw value in family, who pushed me to talk and keep in touch with my mother and father, and Uncle Al. She never gave up, even when I pushed back and refused. Instead, she was motivated by a deep love for me, sensing that I needed these relationships for my own peace and healing. Without them, I couldn't move on.

We recently opened our own boutique, named Karma,

which means "star" in Tibetan and is also the name of Phuni's brother. She is the creative force behind it, filling it with beautiful jewelry, scarves, and fabrics from India. We spend our afternoons in the shop, talking with each other and our customers, and dreaming.

Our dream is nothing more or less than living a calm, simple life. We want to be active socially, fighting injustices such as human trafficking. We want to have a family. I never would have imagined myself a father. Now I want nothing more than to share the love given to me.

Acknowledgments

I am deeply grateful to all the people who prayed and supported me during my ordeal in Amdo, Tibet, in September 1999, especially the Tibetan community and its international supporters. It was your prayers that got me through those difficult months of recovery from all of the injuries. I also want to thank Representatives Frank Wolf and Barney Frank, and Senators Edward Kennedy and John Kerry, who advocated for my release, as well as John Ackerly of the International Campaign for Tibet and Robert Barnett, a Tibetan scholar at Columbia University.

I learned from the Tibetans I encountered during my visits to Tibet their unwavering hope and their devotion to His Holiness the Dalai Lama. Although the Tibetan people continue to suffer occupation, their resilience will ultimately prevail.

I am grateful to my uncle Albert Greenberg and his late wife, Charlotte, for giving me so much love and endless support that I never knew before. Most of all I am forever grateful for Uncle Al's immense love and devotion in taking care of my father, Larry. I am thankful to my cousin Ken Greenberg and his wife, Sara, for their wisdom and their care for my well-being.

This book would not be what it is without Clare Ansberry's patience, eye for details, empathy, and clear vision. Working with Clare has been a pure pleasure and an enriching experience. It was inspiring to watch Clare balance the birth of her son, Eli, and our project.

I would also like to thank the following people: Marjorie Lyon, for asking me every time I saw her if I was writing the book. Professor Ivan Gold, for taking me under his wing during my early introduction to Western literature. My mother, for her cooperation with this book. Cliff Hauptman, for taking a chance on me at Brandeis University.

I am also grateful to Dr. Joel Gorn, a friend who oversaw my medical treatment after my China trip; the staff at Brigham and Women's Hospital; John Emery, who helped me get through Brandeis; Professor Gordie Fellman, my mentor at Brandeis; Carl and Chris Williams, Amnesty International members who supported Phuni when she came to China to take me back home; Tsering Dorje, the Tibetan interpreter who risked his life to accompany me and Gabriel on our visit to Amdo; Kuncho and Yeshy Palsang's family, Tashi Lokyitsang, Acha Phurbu Tsomo, all members of the Boston Tibetan community who supported Phuni and me through the years; Rose Young and Surinder Singh, family friends; Risa Mednick, a human rights activist dedicated to fighting human trafficking; Nick Ribush, founder of Wisdom Publications; and finally, the love and support of Phuni's family.

About the Authors

Daja Wangchuk Meston was left by his hippie parents at a Tibetan monastery in Nepal in the early 1970s. He made his way back to America and eventually graduated from Brandeis University. He now lives in Boston with his wife, Phuni.

Clare Ansberry is the Pittsburgh bureau chief for the *Wall Street Journal* and is the author of *The Women of Troy Hill*. She lives in Pittsburgh with her husband, Matt Smith, and three children, Jessie, Peter, and Eli.